# Dedication

This book is dedicated to those Sons
of the British Empire, who answered the
clarion call, to fight her battles on land,
on sea and in the air in the world war ;
and to those who now and hereafter,
serve the Motherland and shall "make
Her mightier yet."

*A Foreword by*

# FIELD MARSHAL LORD METHUEN,

### G.C.B., G.C V.O., G C.M.G

Corsham Court,

Wiltshire.

I remember in 1911, when I was Commander-in-Chief in South Africa, Professor Rathenau, who held a high position in Germany during and after the War, and was murdered a few days after Field-Marshal Sir Henry Wilson, saying to me, " You may not learn as much in your Public Schools as we do; but I tell you what you do, you develop Character." This was shown in the late War, when so many old Public School Men were lost in defence of our country and freedom.

It is this character that showed itself in their leadership, and gained for them the confidence and love of those they commanded.

*Field-Marshal.*

7th October, 1927.

*A Foreword by*

## ADMIRAL EARL JELLICOE,

O.M., G.C.B., G.C.V.O., OF SCAPA.

80, Portland Place, W.1.

A book which treats of the War Memorials of our leading Public Schools cannot fail to be of deep interest, both to the present generation and to those who come after, for it is a record of magnificent Service for the Empire and of splendid self-sacrifice. Our Public Schools have ever in the past given Leaders to the Nation, and it is the character training which plays so important a part in the Public School life which develops leadership both in peace and war.

Were proof of this needed, the Great War supplies that proof, for the history of the War teems with examples of the fine leading of Public School trained men, and whilst it is pitiful to recall the loss of thousands of most valuable lives, yet the example thus set to future generations of boys cannot fail to act as an incentive to great deeds.

And the book written by Mr. Kernot will play a part in this great work, as will the War Memorials which are described in these pages.

*Admiral of the Fleet.*

20th September, 1927.

# PREFACE

*" Oh, my England, Oh, my England, we the offspring of thy sod,*
*Do we tread the strenuous pathway that our great forefathers trod,*
*Who have fought, and made and held thee, by the*
*Grace and Power of God? "*

My sincere thanks are given to the Headmasters, Bursars, Editors of School Magazines and Secretaries of Old Boys' Associations of the Public Schools, without whose willing and valuable assistance this work would have been impossible. I am especially indebted to those who lent illustrations of Memorials.

At some Schools the Memorial is not yet erected. I hope they will inform me on the completion, in the event of a new edition of this book being possible.

My thanks are also due to Mr. Kenneth H. Black and Mr. Henry C. T. Kernot, to my publishers, and to Mr. O. M. Haider, of the Arc Engraving Co., Ltd., who reproduced many of the illustrations.

It is well to remember that this war was indeed the Great War: greatest in its horror and scientific methods. We can appreciate the Great War when we realise that before it air raids were unknown, submarine warfare on merchant and hospital ships was inconceivable, poison gas was used for the first time (against the Canadians at St. Julien in 1915), hospital bases were attacked, and long-range guns of the calibre of " Big Bertha " and " Long Max " were used.

*" The cross was broken; blood-stained might*
*Moved like a tiger from its lair;*
*And all that Heaven had died to quell*
*Awoke, and mingled earth with hell."*

The cemeteries of France and Flanders, " tenderly and lovingly cared for," are a constant testimony to England's sacrifice. Our dead lie buried on the Mount of Olives, from Zeebrugge to Coronel, from Dunkirk to the wilderness of East Africa. They girdle the earth—a generation of manhood.

To the Public Schools of the Empire it means this: the average day's attendance is practically the number of those who were killed. But something was gained—a tradition of comradeship and endurance, of finer and nobler qualities which men honour.

Can a War Memorial have any meaning unless it is a living thought of those who died but are even yet our comrades? In this thought I see the foundation of a better and purer world, built upon the imitation of the life of Christ, the steadfast hope of the Resurrection and the Fellowship of the Saints in light.

> " *The one sure Light, the one sure way,*
> *The one firm base of Liberty;*
> *The one firm road, that men have trod*
> *Through chaos to the Throne of God.*"

There are some who desire to forget the War. Let not the horror and devastation of war overwhelm you, but think rather of those things which are greatest: England's honour was upheld, her faith was never shaken, right overcame might.

This book would be a stimulant against post-war apathy, a humble contribution to the history of our epoch, and a grateful and sincere tribute to the memory of those who, at the Call, answered, "We are ready."

I am convinced that the boys of this generation would be, if the necessity arose, even as their fathers in Loyalty, Devotion to Duty, and Self-Sacrifice.

I leave you with the words of Browning:—

" *That which I strove to be and was not, comforts me.*"
" *The shape and colour of a mind and life*
> *Lives for his children, ever at its best and fullest.*"

*C. F. Kernot.*

London, November 11th, 1927.

# INDEX

Blocks illustrating the memorials were kindly loaned by the schools indicated with an (*).

# BERKHAMSTED SCHOOL

*" Virtus laudata crescit."*

THE Memorial Library and Museum were opened on September 27th, 1924, by Sir Frederic Kenyon, K.C.B., Director of the British Museum.

The Buildings are of brick and stone; mullioned windows were inserted to be in keeping with the Old Hall and other surrounding School Buildings, which date back to 1545. There is a suitable inscription engraved over the entrance.

The Roll of Honour contains Two Hundred and Thirty One names.

The architects were Messrs. Forsyth & Maule, of London.

BERKHAMSTED SCHOOL MEMORIAL

9

# ALDENHAM SCHOOL

*" In God is our trust."*

HERE are two forms of Memorial at this School: one a pair of Marble Tablets on which are inscribed the names of the One Hundred and Sixty Old Boys who fell, and the words *" Moriorem hac dilectionem nemo habet, ut animam suam ponat quis pro amicis suis "*; the other is a Memorial Library Building with classrooms. Over the entrance doorway is the following inscription: *" In thankful memory of the sons of this School who gave their lives in the Great War "*; while on a chronogram over the inside of the door are the words: *" Ecce liber tuus lucerna pedibus meis."*

The style of the architecture is Georgian. The designs were made by Capt. M. Waterhouse, M.C.

ALDENHAM SCHOOL MEMORIAL.

The opening ceremony was held on May 14th, 1924.

The Very Rev. Paul O. Ashby, M.C. (O.A. 1879-85) conducted the first part, the Dean of Stamford reading the Founder's prayer. Then Lord Buckmaster (O.A. 1870-79) presented the Library to the Chairman of the Governors, saying: "Time moves so fast and memories grow so dim, that the war is rapidly becoming mere history. This new Building should serve as a reminder of what the Aldenhamians did when the call of Duty came. Courage, truth, honour, fidelity make a man's character, which all the School should strive to achieve."

The key of the building was presented by Capt. M. Waterhouse.

The Memorial Library harmonises with the new parts of the Head-master's House, while the inside is divided with numerous bay recesses for attentive study. The building stands in the south-east angle of the School Yard, overlooking the Playing Fields. Further new buildings are to be placed to the east, thus in time forming a fine Georgian Quadrangle.

ALDENHAM SCHOOL. MEMORIAL LIBRARY

AMPLEFORTH COLLEGE MEMORIAL

AMPLEFORTH COLLEGE MEMORIAL SHRINE

# AMPLEFORTH COLLEGE

*"Dieu le ward."*

HE Memorial takes the form of a Chantry Chapel in Early English Gothic style, forming part of the New Abbey Church. The Reredos is of richly carved and gilded oak, in the fifteenth century style; in the centre panel is a pietà, and the side panels portray the Dolours of Our Lady.

A Shrine was also constructed. Incorporated in the design are twining vines, and the figure of Christ Crucified. In the shrine is an illuminated book with the names of the Sixty Two gallant sons of the School who gave their lives in the Great War. On one page of the book is written: *"Liber nostrorum inscriptus nomina in bello mortuorum. MCMXIV—MCMXVIII."*

The Memorial was designed by Sir Giles Gilbert Scott, R.A., and was unveiled on September 15th, 1926. The Right Rev. W. Pearson, O.S.B., Bishop of Lancaster; the Right Rev. Joseph Thorman, Bishop of Newcastle, and Edmund Matthews, O.S.B., Abbot of Ampleforth, all assisted in the unveiling ceremonies.

---

# BOOTHAM SCHOOL, YORK

*"Membra sumus corporis magni."*

HE Memorial Tablet is of repoussé bronze with translucent and opaque enamels, very beautifully coloured. It is the work of E. Spencer, of the Artificers' Guild. The centre figure at the top represents Light, the Light that is referred to in the inscription below. The Roses of England and York are on either side, and on the scroll work are the dates "1914" and "1919." Then the following inscription: *"In memory of all Old Bootham Boys who have faithfully striven to follow the Light, and especially these our fallen comrades."* In two columns are the names of the Fifty Six comrades, and below are Greek characters, of which the following is a translation: *"He shall not walk in darkness but shall have the Light of Life."* Below this Greek inscription are the

emblems of the Pelican in her piety, and on either side attendant angels. The space between is occupied with leaves of Victory.

At the top of the decorative border around the names are two little golden crosses, one on either side.

On January 27th, 1920, the School met in the " John Bright Library " to receive the Memorial Tablet from the School Committee. Members of the Committee and representatives of the Mount School were present. The Headmaster, Arnold S. Rowntree, B.A., presided, and, the assembly standing, read the names of the fallen Comrades.

The Tablet was unveiled by Mr. F. L. P. Sturge, the Warden of Wildbrooke. He said: " One of the greatest of our poets and seers had tried to teach us that those who gladly answer to the voice of duty when she calls shall know something of the grace and benignity of her smile, a reflection of the very presence of God Himself."

The Head Reeve, Owen B. Lean, replied on behalf of the School, saying: " This bronze reminded us of the strength needed to carry out our work with the one aim in view—service—which each one is due to render to his fellow-men." The Headmaster said: " From time to time we shall hear them calling to us ' Why faintest thou? ' The light we sought is shining still."

About 289 Old Bootham Boys were in the King's Forces.

# ARDINGLY COLLEGE

THE School of St. Saviours War Memorial was dedicated on behalf of the Corporation of SS. Mary and Nicolas. The new wing contains 14 new classrooms, choir vestry, art-room, gymnasium, offices and dressing rooms, forming a fine Quadrangle. It adjoins the north side of the Chapel.

The ceremony started with a service in the Chapel. The Order of Service was as follows: Hymn, " Blessed are the pure in heart "; Prayers led by Rev. T. E. Wilson (Headmaster); Anthem, " O how amiable are Thy dwellings." Bishop H. K. Southwell, D.D., delivered the dedicatory prayers and address, in which he referred to the Foundation of the Society of St. Nicolas by the Rev. Nathanial Woodard, a London curate. There are now sixteen schools of this Foundation. The service ended with the " Blessing " by the Provost, after the rendering of " O Worship the Lord." Mr. G. T. Francis, F.R.C.O., was at the Organ and as the procession left the Chapel, Bach's Toccata and Fugue in D Minor were played.

ARDINGLY COLLEGE MEMORIAL

Sir Henry Cautley, K.C., M.P., J.P., opened the building, and said that the college possessed an ideal educational standpoint overlooking what he termed "the Valley of Views." The Senior Prefect was A. E. Cameron, the leading Crucifer, Prefect H. W. Roberts, and the Bishop's staff was borne by Prefect M. Gregory. The Guard of Honour of O.T.C., in charge of Capt. H. S. Crawford, paraded on the Terrace and was inspected by Sir Edward Boyle, the High Sheriff of Sussex. There were also present Archdeacon Hordern of Lewes, Rev. Canon R. J. Lea (Rural Dean of Hurst), and the Headmasters of Cranleigh (Rev. H. A. Rhodes), Lancing (Mr. C. H. Blakiston), the Provost of Lancing and the Rev. Marchant Pearson (formerly of Ardingly), and the following from the Corporation of SS. Mary and Nicolas: Senior Fellow (Mr. Martin Gibbs), Major J. B. Warren, M.C., Mr. S. Witherington, Mr. J. M. Sing (Bursar).

The foundation stone of this Wing was laid by Earl Winterton in June, 1926; the opening took place on Saturday, May 7th, 1927. Mr. W. E. Tower was the Architect.

---

# BURY GRAMMAR SCHOOL

*"Sanctas clavis fores aperit."*

A LARGE amount of the money raised for the War Memorial Fund was used to assist the education of sons of Old Boys who had fallen in the War. A certain amount was set aside for extra playing fields and the balance was used to erect a Memorial Tablet in the School Hall. J. L. Norton, M.A. (Oxon), the Senior Master at the School, unveiled the tablet on Monday, May 5th, 1924.

The Roll of Honour contains Ninety Seven names. Eight families lost two sons each.

The dedicatory prayer was said by the Bishop of Hulme (Dr. J. C. Hill, Rector of Bury). Mr. Norton read out the names of the Fallen, and in an address of great impressiveness he referred to the families which had endured a double sacrifice and anguish. "All this in order that you and I—let us never forget that—might live the lives of free men. Can we forget those whose graves lie in many foreign lands? Surely not." Then, turning to the Memorial, he said: "Heroic souls, who laid down your lives for us! This day we salute you with gratitude and affection." He ended with the words of the great French writer: "Let their tomb be strewn with the choicest flowers; the glory of their death has repaid us for their loss."

The hymn "Jerusalem" was sung, accompanied by Dr. Walter Williams.

The Memorial is the design of Mr. Fred Murgatroyd, of Bury, an Old Boy of the School, and was executed by Messrs. T. Lenegan, of Manchester. It is erected over the north entrance of the School Hall and is of solid bronze, oblong in shape. The central name portion is surmounted by the School Arms and Motto. The side ornaments are also bronze, the surrounding frame being in Shelliston alabastar. Above the names is the inscription: "*To the honour and memory of the Old Boys of this School who gave their lives in the Great War*, 1914-1919," and beneath are the words: "*Their names liveth for evermore.*"

The Service Roll has 640 names upon it, and the following distinctions were gained: 1 C.M.G., 2 D.S.O., 15 M.C., 2 D.C.M., 9 M.M., 1 C.B.E., 2 Croix de Guerre, 1 Legion of Honour (Belgian), 20 mentioned in despatches, 1 Serbian Order.

BURY GRAMMAR SCHOOL MEMORIAL

# BIRKENHEAD COLLEGE, LIVERPOOL

*" Beati mundo corde."*

AS a Memorial to the Fallen, Oak Panelling was placed round the interior of the School Chapel. It was unveiled in September, 1921, by the Right Rev. C. West-Watson, Bishop of Barrow-in-Furness, an old Boy of the School.

The Roll of Honour contains Ninety Six names.

The Panelling was the work of Messrs. Grayson & Barnish.

BIRKENHEAD COLLEGE MEMORIAL

BEAUMONT COLLEGE MEMORIAL

# BEAUMONT COLLEGE

*" Æterna non caduca."*

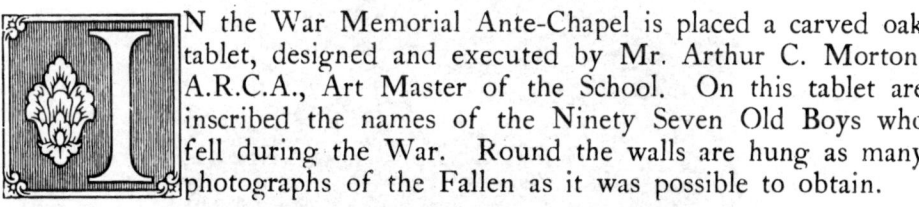HE Memorial takes the form of a large Greek Cenotaph, embodying a calvary with a life-size bronze figure, and a large Sarcophagus at the foot of the cross, on which is inscribed the names of the One Hundred and Thirty Three who gave their lives for King and Country.

Above the Christ Crucified appears the inscription: *" Æterna non caduca."* Under the Sarcophagus are the words: *" To the glorious memory of the Boys of Beaumont who gave their lives for their Country in the Great War, MCMXIV—MCMXVIII."* Along the foot of the Memorial appears: *" MCMXIV. Requiem æternam dona eis domine. MCMXVIII."*

The Memorial is the work of Sir Giles Gilbert Scott and Major A. Gilbert Scott. It was unveiled by Lieutenant-General Sir G. M. Macdonough K.C.B., K.C.M.G., on November 13th, 1921.

---

# WORKSOP COLLEGE

*" Semper ad coelestia."*

IN the War Memorial Ante-Chapel is placed a carved oak tablet, designed and executed by Mr. Arthur C. Morton, A.R.C.A., Art Master of the School. On this tablet are inscribed the names of the Ninety Seven Old Boys who fell during the War. Round the walls are hung as many photographs of the Fallen as it was possible to obtain.

The tablet was unveiled on Whit-Monday, 1926, by Sir F. Milner, Bart., and dedicated by the Bishop of Southwell.

There is also a closed exhibition of the annual value of £50 to St. Catherine's College, Cambridge, tenable by sons of Old Boys of the School.

# BLUNDELL'S SCHOOL

*" Pro patria populoque."*

 HE Memorial is a Cross, designed by Mr. Wykeham-Chancellor, of Chelmsford, and carved from Peebles granite. It is situated in the School grounds among trees and beautiful surroundings, and was unveiled by the Bishop of Crediton on November 2nd, 1920. The Two Hundred names of the Fallen are inscribed on tablets let into the outer wall of the " Big School " opposite the Memorial Cross.

In addition, Memorial Bursaries were founded for the education of sons of Old Blundellians.

BLUNDELL'S SCHOOL MEMORIAL.

# BISHOP'S STORTFORD COLLEGE

*" Soli Deo gloria."*

THE Assembly Hall, designed by Mr. William Ellis, architect, and built in Italian Renaissance style, is the War memorial.

This building serves the purpose of a Chapel and Lecture Hall. The main porch is reached by eight steps and is flanked by two Doric Pillars. The main double door leading into the Hall is dedicated to Mr. E. A. Knight, with a stone tablet on either side bearing the names of those who gave their lives.

The Hall was opened on May 5th, 1922, by Sir A. T. Quiller-Couch.

The Roll of Honour bears the names of the 480 who served; Fifty Seven were killed; One Master and One Employee.

BISHOP'S STORTFORD COLLEGE MEMORIAL

23

# BEDFORD GRAMMAR SCHOOL

*" Floreat schola Bedfordiensis."*

THE Old Bedfordians' Club erected a Memorial Hall to the honour of Four Hundred and Fifty Four Old Boys who were killed in the Great War. The building, which is placed to the west of the main School Building, contains a Hall, Library, Storerooms and Cloakrooms. It was opened by H.R.H. Prince Henry on July 26th, 1926. In the unavoidable absence of the Bishop of St. Albans, the Memorial was dedicated by the Lord Archbishop of Dublin, Dr. J. A. F. Gregg, an Old Bedfordian. The architect, O. P. Milne, Esq., F.R.I.B.A., the head of the firm of Messrs. S. F. Foster (the builders), and the general foreman, Mr. R. Robinson, were presented to His Royal Highness.

The Library occupies the lower floor of the building. Placed around the Hall, which is on the first floor immediately facing the staircase, is panelling on which is written the names of the Fallen. The panels are in blue with gold lettering; five are situated on each side of the central panel, on which is the following inscription: *" In memory of Old Bedfordians who gave their lives in the War*, 1914-1918." On either side of this inscription are the names of Countries and Battlefields in a scroll design.

This entailed a blank wall in the upper part of the North Gable, and here, outside, is a niche for a statue of St. George; under this niche are two Doric columns resting on a base stone with the dates " 1914-1918 " upon it. The alcove has a shell pattern canopy of fine design; the South Gable carries the School Arms, while over the inside of the Memorial Hall doors, in letters of gold, is the one word *" Remember."*

Two thousand three hundred and fifty Old Members of the School served in the Great War.

---

# BRIGHTON COLLEGE

THE existing Chapel, which only accommodated about 300 Scholars, was enlarged to a capacity of 500 to 600. This extension was very necessary, as in former times the Chapel was too small for all the Scholars to attend the same service.

The whole East Wall, under a very beautiful window, was panelled in oak and the names of the One Hundred and Fifty who fell in the War inscribed thereon. The additions to the Chapel were dedicated by the Bishop of Chichester in June, 1923.

The architect for the additions was the late Sir Thomas Graham Jackson, Bart., who was an Old Boy of the School. The extended Chapel now measures 110 feet by 70 feet.

BRIGHTON COLLEGE MEMORIAL.

REMEMBER

BRADFORD GRAMMAR SCHOOL MEMORIAL

# BRADFORD GRAMMAR SCHOOL

*" Hoc age."*

THIS Memorial consists of a handsome Mural Tablet, which is situated in the Assembly Hall of the School opposite to the entrance.

It takes the form suggestive of the Cenotaph, surmounted by a Crown. It was unveiled by the President of the Bradford Grammar School Old Boys' Association on April 28th, 1922, and Mr. J. D. Moore, a Governor of the School, received the Memorial on behalf of the School. The Roll of Honour contains Two Hundred and Fifteen names.

The Tablet was designed and executed by Messrs. T. H. & J. Healey; the bronze work was by Mr. E. Sickel; the stone work by Messrs. W. Farnish & Sons.

All the above names are those of Old Boys of the School.

---

# WORCESTER GRAMMAR SCHOOL

THE Memorial is a two-manual Organ with side panels, on which are inscribed the names of the Ninety One Old Boys who fell. It is situated in the alcove at the farthest end of the Perrins Hall. There are six stops on the Swell, seven on the Great, and two on the Pedal organ, allowing for future enlargements. It is blown by an electric motor in the basement of the building. The Organ, which is in daily use for Morning Prayers, was built by Conacher, Sheffield & Co., of Birmingham. The case is in light oak, and was designed by Mr. Alfred Parker.

This Memorial was dedicated on December 15th, 1923, by the Bishop of Worcester and unveiled by Lieutenant-General Sir Francis Davies, who had previously inspected the O.T.C. Sir Francis, in his address, said : " Schools of this kind are a peculiarly British institution. Nothing like them exists except under the British Flag. Boys learn to play the game, to obey, to command, and loyalty to their Old School—a very beautiful thing."

A speech by the Headmaster concluded with the words :—
"These laid the world away; poured out the red
Sweet wine of youth; gave up the years to be
Of work and joy, and that unhoped serene,
That men call age; and those who would have been,
Their sons, they gave, their immortality."

The " Last Post " was sounded. The centre panel of the Organ, bearing the inscription " *This Organ is given by the Old Boys of this School in memory of those who died in the Great War*, 1914-1918," was unveiled. The " Reveille " and the Hymn " O Valiant Hearts " followed. Sir Ivor Atkins accompanied on the Organ.

WORCESTER GRAMMAR SCHOOL MEMORIAL

# KING'S CATHEDRAL SCHOOL, WORCESTER

*" Regia schola vigorniensis."*

THE Memorial Fund had four objects, namely :—
1. To erect a Roll of Honour in the College Hall.
2. A Memorial Window in the Cathedral Cloisters.
3. A Scholarship, to the value of £50 per annum, for the sons of Old Boys who fell in the War.
4. To erect a Cricket Pavilion and Fives Courts.

All the objects were accomplished, and the Memorial Window was unveiled by the Dean of Worcester on Sunday, June 19th, 1921. On the Window is the inscription: *" Erected in memory of members of the King's School who gave their lives in the Great War, 1914-1918."* At the unveiling ceremony Canon W. H. Chappel (Sub-Dean of Coventry

KING'S SCHOOL MEMORIAL

and a former Headmaster) preached on the text James i, verses 22 and 24, and the lessons were read by the Headmaster, Rev. C. Creighton and the Archdeacon James.

The buglers of the School O.T.C. sounded the " Last Post " and the " Reveille."

The Cricket Pavilion was the gift of Mr. T. E. Rammell, Senior Master, and it was opened by Canon W. H. Chappel on June 19th, 1921. The following words are inscribed in the Pavilion: " *This Pavilion, the gift of T. E. Rammell, was erected in memory of those who, having learnt in this place to play the game for their School, played it also for their Country during the years 1914-1919.*" " *Hæc olim meminisse juvabit.*" The architect for the Pavilion was Mr. A. V. Rose, of Worcester.

The Roll of Honour in the School Hall contains Eighty Two names, and these names are recorded on the Memorial Window in the Cathedral.

―――――――――

# CHRIST'S HOSPITAL, WEST HORSHAM
## " *Love the Brotherhood.*"

THIS War Memorial is a series of tablets bearing the names of the Three Hundred and Seventy Eight fallen. The tablets are placed outside the dining hall, on each side of the Foundation Stone of the School. Upon them are figures of a Scholar (" Blue Coat Boy ") and a soldier in Khaki. The central inscription is: " *Sons of this House who gave their lives for their Country, 1914-1918.*" The architect was Sir Aston Webb, and the Lord Mayor of London accepted the Memorial from Mr. F. A. White, Treasurer of the Memorial Fund.

The Tablets were unveiled by H.R.H. The Duke of Connaught on Founders' Day, October 23rd, 1920. The Order of the Dedication Service commenced with the words: " The Religious, Royal and Ancient

Foundation of Christ's Hospital. May those prosper who love it, and may God increase their number." Then followed the Hymn: "Praise the Lord for our Foundation," and sentences from John xi, 25 and 26; Job xix, 25-27; I Timothy vi, 7, and Job i, 21. Part of the Psalm xxiii was sung by the choir. The lesson was from I Corinthians xv, 20-23 and 35-38. Then the words "We commemorate here those Old Blues who gave their lives for their Country" were pronounced, with quotations from Ecclesiasticus xliv, 14. Dr. Pearce, Bishop of Worcester, himself an Old Blue, dedicated the Memorial and pronounced the Benediction. The "Dead March" was played, and the Hymn "O God our Help in ages past" was sung.

There are 2,136 names upon the "Service Roll," and the following distinctions were awarded: 2 Posthumous Victoria Crosses, 1 Air Force Cross, 158 Military Crosses, 22 Military Medals, 32 Distinguished Service Orders and 53 Foreign Orders.

CHRIST'S HOSPITAL MEMORIAL

# GIGGLESWICK SCHOOL

*" Aut scribenda facere, aut legenda scribere."*

THE War Memorial takes the form of a Library. It is a two-storey building, chiefly of local stones, roofed with Westmorland Slate. The ground floor contains the Bursar's Office, a Book Store and an Athletic Shop. The Library occupies the first floor.

On either side of the fine arched open fireplace is an ingle seat, over which are oak banners supported by lions. The banners have inscribed on them the names of the One Hundred and Twenty Two who were killed, and the dates " 1914 " and " 1918."

The building was opened by Sir Alexander Godley, General at Gallipoli during the War, and dedicated by Dr. Henn, the Lord Bishop of Burnley, on June 26th, 1926—Speech Day at the School.

The architect was Mr. Isaac Taylor, an Old Boy.

An inscription in Greek appears on the Memorial :

GIGGLESWICK SCHOOL MEMORIAL LIBRARY

GIGGLESWICK SCHOOL MEMORIAL LIBRARY : OPENING CEREMONY

GIGGLESWICK SCHOOL MEMORIAL LIBRARY : INTERIOR

33

# CHELTENHAM COLLEGE

*" Labor omnia vincit."*

HIS School War Memorial consists of a Cloister in late Perpendicular Style connecting the College and the Chapel. The Vaulting is decorated with fan tracery. The Cloister was built in the same style as the Chapel, erected in 1896 by Mr. E. A. Prothero. The architect was Mr. L. Barnard, F.R.I.B.A.

The Roll of Honour contains Six Hundred and Seventy Five names, which are inscribed on brass tablets inside the Chapel.

The Foundation Stone of the new Cloister was laid by Lord Lee of Fareham, a former Cheltonian, on July 4th, 1919. The Dean of Hereford, Dr. R. Waterfield, a former Headmaster, conducted the dedication ceremony on Sunday, April 3rd, 1921.

The following inscription is above the window in the Memorial Cloister :—

> *" You that would enter here to worship God,*
>
> *Think of your brothers who before you trod*
>
> *These walls and ways, and did not grudge to give*
>
> *Their lives in war, that you in peace might live.*
>
> *Ask for a heart to follow in the way*
>
> *Of sacrifice and duty.  Pass, and pray."*

Below the window is: *" In memory of Six Hundred and Seventy Five Old Cheltonians who gave their lives in the Great War, 1914-1919. This stone was laid by the Right Hon. Lord Lee of Fareham, G.B.E., K.C.B., on the fourth day of July, 1919.  Egregias animas quæ sanguine nobis hanc patriam peperere suo decorate supermis muneribus."*

CHELTENHAM COLLEGE MEMORIAL

ST. JOHN'S SCHOOL MEMORIAL

# ST. JOHN'S SCHOOL, LEATHERHEAD

*" Quæ sursum sunt quærite."*

WO impressive ceremonies took place on Saturday afternoon, June 19th, 1920. The first was the dedication of a floor Cross in the Chancel of the Chapel, and the second the unveiling of a Cross in the Inner Quadrangle Both Crosses were in memory of the One Hundred and Fifty Old Boys of the School who were killed on War Service.

The Cross in the Chapel was dedicated by the Bishop of Buckingham. This Cross is of brass, with a border of brass on the Chancel floor, and the inscription: "*Our glorious Dead, 1914-1919. All live unto Him.*"

The Cross in the Inner Quadrangle was unveiled by Major H. H. Gordon-Clark, High Sheriff and Deputy Lieutenant, who acted in place of Admiral Jellicoe, who was unable to be present owing to illness. This Cross is in Portland Stone, of simple design, and bears the following inscription in Latin: "*Memtote vos superstites eorum qui ex hac schola progressi disciplina eius minime dedecorata gloriose pro nobis mortui gloriam sibi sempiternam asciverunt, MCMXIV—MCMXIX.*"

The Guard of Honour was supplied by the School Officers' Training Corps, and buglers sounded the "Last Post."

---

# SEDBURGH SCHOOL

*" Duru virum nutrix."*

HE Memorial is a Cloister Court, cut out of the side of the hill on which the School stands, with a quadrangle above the Cloisters.

The Cloister is built of Barnard Castle stone. Five central arches symbolise the "Houses" which existed at the outbreak of the War. They are enriched with the arms of Roger Lupton and Edward VI.

The two main entrances to the Cloister are flanked by large lions' heads carved in bold relief; the only other carving is found in the rich laurel borders that surround the four panels in memory of the Two

Hundred and Fifty Old Boys and Four Masters who gave their lives in the Great War. On each panel is a victor's wreath in low relief and the words "*In Memoriam*," followed by the names, incised in Stancliffe stone and coloured vermilion. The inscription on the Cloister is: "*Their name liveth for evermore.*"

The floor of the Cloister is paved, and each Bay is roofed with a concrete dome. Opposite the central arch a flight of steps leads up to the New Quadrangle, in front of the School Buildings.

The Cloister was designed by J. Hubert Worthington, an Old Sedberghian, of the Royal College of Arts, South Kensington. The builder, E. Harold Pattinson, was also an Old Boy.

The foundation stone was laid on July 31st, 1922, and the Memorial was unveiled by Lieutenant-General Sir Charles Harington, G.B.E., D.S.O., on July 6th, 1924.

SEDBURGH SCHOOL MEMORIAL

38

# WOLVERHAMPTON GRAMMAR SCHOOL

*" Schol · grammat · wulfren · hantunens."*

HE Memorial screen is of carved English Oak in the Renaissance Period style. On the four panels of the screen are carved the names of the One Hundred and Two Old Boys who fell in the Great War. The central panel bears the inscription: " 1914-1919. *Their names liveth for evermore.*"

The screen was designed and executed by Messrs. Bridgman, of Lichfield.

The ceremony took place on February 1st, 1922, Colonel John V. Campbell, V.C., C.M.G., D.S.O., performing the unveiling.

It is situated at the extreme end of the " Big School." The carving is boldly and artistically executed.

WOLVERHAMPTON GRAMMAR SCHOOL MEMORIAL

# CHIGWELL SCHOOL

*" Aut viam inveniam aut faciam."*

HE Memorial is a Chapel of brick and stone, with a porch at the South East End, built to accommodate 350 people. The oak, red bricks and hand-made tiles are of Essex origin or manufacture. The foundation stone was laid on June 23rd, 1923, by Lord Lambourne, and the Chapel was dedicated by the Bishop of Chelmsford on October 10th, 1924, the sentence of dedication being preserved in the School archives. The Head Boy, B. B. Jackson, delivered the keys to the Bishop on his entrance; the Recessional was the Founder's Psalm CXIII. The first and last offertories in the new and old chapels were given to the Public School Cottages for disabled soldiers at Enham.

The Architects were Messrs. Tooley & Foster. Mr. Reginald Hallward designed the Dorsal of the Stalls and the East Window, which represents four scenes from the " Pilgrim's Progress," namely, " At the golden gates," " The Holy City," " Meeting the lions " and " The slough of despond." The design of " The Holy City " contains in the extreme left-hand corner a fragment of glass from the Cathedral at Ypres. On the outside lintels of the two doors are inscribed the words: " *Laudate pueri dominum, laudate nomen domini.*"

The Roll of Honour contains the names of One Master and Seventy Eight Old Boys. After each name is added an appropriate motto in Latin or English, the first being " *Bene mori semper vivere.*"

# BRISTOL GRAMMAR SCHOOL

*" Ex spinis uvas."*

THE Memorial consists of a screen across the transept of the Great Hall, forming a background to the platform dais. The design was carried out by an Old Boy, and the type follows the tradition of the arcaded and vaulted rood screens that are characteristic of the West of England.

The screen is designed in six bays, the two end ones occupied by doorways leading to the East Transept. Over them are the mottoes: *" Dulce et decorum est pro patria mori." " Ex spinis uvas celestes."*

The screen has been executed in oak without artificial colour of any kind by Messrs. R. F. Ridd & Sons, of Bristol. The panelling of the four bays contains the Memorial Tablets in bronze, on which are inscribed the names of the One Hundred and Twenty Old Boys who died. The tablets will be toned by time, the face only of the letters will be kept bright. They are the work of Messrs. Humphreys & Oakes, of Bristol. The dais is furnished with a table and chair of Jacobean date.

A bronze tablet inserted in the panelling of the Hall contains the following inscription: *" This screen was erected by the Old Boys' Society and by the parents and friends of those who gave their lives for King and Country in the Great War. Their name liveth evermore."*

The Memorial was unveiled on October 5th, 1922, by Mr. H. E. Chattock, Chairman of the Governors of the School.

D

# ETON COLLEGE

## *"Floreat Etona."*

OUNDER'S Day, December 6th, 1921, was a memorable occasion in the history of Eton, for on that day was unveiled the great Bronze Frieze by the Provost, Dr. Allington: "In the Name of God let the Memorial of our brothers be unveiled, and let it be perpetually held in honour in this place."

The scholars were grouped in the area between the Chapel Steps and the Central Pathway; Collegers were placed in the space west of the steps, Oppidans on the east, and six Junior Houses on the east of the path leading from the Chapel to the Memorial. The area between the central path and the Lower School were reserved for relatives, while the Masters were behind the Collegers. The space north of the statue was open to local residents.

The Guard of Honour was formed by the Senior available members from each House and was drawn up in front of the colonnade. Fourteen Lance-Corporals removed the veiling from the Bronze Frieze, and the service began at 11.30 a.m. Lloyd's Memorial March, "Honour we owe to the men of old," was played and sung, followed by the hymn "O, Valiant Hearts." The Headmaster read the special prayers; then, during the singing of Psalm xxiii, the procession left the Chapel steps and took up a position in front of the central arch under the Upper School. The procession was formed by the Provost, the Vice-Provost, Viscount Hambleden (representing the Fellows), Headmaster and Lower Master. After the unveiling there was silence for one minute. Then followed the "Last Post" sounded from Weston's Yard by buglers of the Irish Guards. There was a further silence for one minute, after which the trumpeters of the Royal Horse Guards sounded the "Reveille" from the roof of the College Chapel. The last verse of the "School at War" (C.A.A., 1914) was sung, and one verse of the National Anthem. The Coldstream Guards, commanded by Lieutenant Evans, played the Coldstream March.

The Bronze Frieze covers the upper half of the wall from the main entrance of the Upper School to the entrance of the Lower School. The letters inscribed are raised and burnished. The Frieze begins on the

ETON COLLEGE MEMORIAL

right-hand side of the main entrance to the Upper School as follows: "*Gratias agamus domino deo nostro propter hosce fratres nustrus qui pro patria militantes per tenebras transierunt in lucem sanctam.*" The names of the One Thousand One Hundred and Fifty Seven who fell follow, arranged in alphabetical order. On the right and left of the main gateway, on entering the School Yard, are the words: *Bello inde ab anno MCMXIV per quinquennium gestro Etonensium militaverunt quinque millia sexcenti sexaginta occiderunt. Mille et centum quinquaginta septem. Quorum ut fratres sui perpetuo tueantur memoriam. His parietibus inscripta sunt nomina. A.D. MCMXXI.*" And, "*1914 The Names recorded here are those of the 1,157 Etonians who died in the War, in which 5,660 served. Let us always remember their valour and their sacrifice with love and thankfulness, and pray God to make us worthy of them in time to come. 1919.*"

The designers were Messrs. Romaine, Walker & Jenkins.

There is a new boldly-carved oak roof to the colonnade; alterations have been made to the entrance archways and new bronze-work lamps have been fitted. Various other additions have been made as Memorials: (1) A North Window in the Vestry Chapel; (2) a new Choir Vestry; (3) a Golden Book, containing the names of the Fallen; and (4) the Four Tapestries in the Chapel. The Tapestries, designed by Mrs. Akers Douglas, are 14 feet by 8 feet, and represent the boyhood of St. George. The faces of several Etonians were used as models. The Tapestries were made at Merton Abbey on looms erected by William Morris in 1881. The borders were woven by Edward Russel, an apprentice aged 15, and the work was supervised by Mr. Henry Dearle, painter.

The School Roll of Honour contains 1,157 names. On the Service List there are 1,467 names of the wounded, 1,669 mentioned in despatches, 1,999 who gained British Honours, and 591 Foreign Decorations.

---

# CITY OF NORWICH SCHOOL

*" Floreat Norvicum."*

THE Memorial, a painted and carved oak triptych, is placed in the Main Assembly Hall, in a central position on the wall at the back of the platform. The names of Eighty One Old Boys and Three Masters who fell are incised in gold on a dull red background in the centre of the triptych. Normally, the names will be hidden from view by two doors fastened by a broken sword.

CITY OF NORWICH SCHOOL MEMORIAL

The Memorial was designed by and carried out under the supervision of Mr. W. T. Watling, the School Art Master, who also undertook to do the painting and adornments. The gun-metal broken sword was executed by Mr. G. F. Johnson, also of the staff, the wood carving by Mr. Hubert Miller, and the constructional joinery by Messrs. J. S. Smith & Son.

On the inside of the doors appear paintings of Amor, beneath the date " 1914." She is symbolised by a Mother anxiously watching her child setting out into the night. Behind the child, who traverses a path

45

bordered with wild flowers, but obstructed with brambles, can be seen a distant peep of Norwich. The child is carrying a bunch of poppies.

Beneath the date " 1918 " is Dolor, represented by a Mother clasping a bunch of poppies to her breast. She is standing against the night sky and a suggestion of a blood-stained battlefield, but the star of hope shines above her head. She is oblivious of the glorified form of her child, seen in the foreground, his feet immersed in a cluster of blood-stained poppies, his hands outstretched towards the dawn.

On the outside of the doors, beneath the date " 1914," Virtus is depicted, clad in a white robe of purity. In his right hand, exalted, is the hilt of a broken sword—the glowing symbol of Christ's message. Virtus stands with golden wings, surrounded by a beautiful harvest. A scythe—for reward—an overflowing jar—for thrift—a symbolic ship, all recall those happy and flourishing times our men hoped to regain. An anvil, partially obscured, suggests that the world's work is done; a dove is hovering in the background.

Spes is depicted beneath the date " 1918 "; he is looking towards the future aglow with eager demand. His green wings outspread, he stands beside a vision of spring. The anvil and the dove of peace tell of the world's work resumed. An earthen jar awaits the time when the

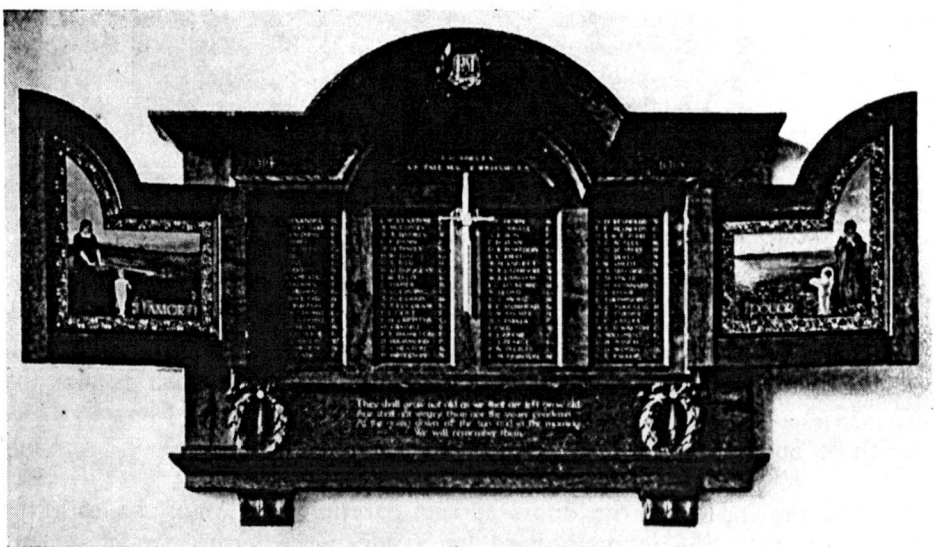

CITY OF NORWICH SCHOOL MEMORIAL

blossoms of promise shall have come to fruition.   The ethereal city in the background symbolises the ideals and aspirations of youth; the dark valley in the middle distance symbolises the path to the greater future, fraught with difficulties and obstacles that man's work must overcome.

The figures thus represented are Amor (Love), Dolor (Sadness), Virtus (Virtue) and Spes (Hope).   Below the doors, always visible, is the inscription :—

*" They shall grow not old as we that are left grow old,*
*Age shall not weary them nor the years condemn;*
*At the going down of the sun and in the morning*
*We will remember them."*

The Memorial was unveiled by the Right Hon. the Lord Mayor of Norwich, and dedicated by the Bishop of Norwich, on Thursday, March 2nd, 1922.   Dr. Blyth stated that the Art Master, Mr. Watling, on his departure to the Front, asked that, should he return, he might be allowed to execute a design for the War Memorial.   The Lord Mayor said that when they remembered that the School was only opened in 1910, they must recognise that the City of Norwich School did its duty most nobly in the great struggle.   Before Christmas, 1914, Eighty Three had volunteered, and before the next year had passed this number had swelled to more than 200.   Upwards of 600 Old Boys took some share in the gigantic struggle, and yet at the outbreak of War very few of the scholars had reached the age of twenty, whilst even at the close not many Old Boys were more than 25.   Considering their comparative youth, the number of distinctions gained is highly creditable.   They were : 1 D.S.O., 6 M.C., 1 D.F.C., 2 D.C.M., 12 M.M., 1 M.M. with bar, 3 M.S.M., 1 D.S.M., 10 mentioned in despatches, and no fewer than 75 commissions.

Prior to dedicating the Memorial, the Bishop stated that he had given prizes on the first occasion after the School opened to many of those who had now fallen.   He was struck by a touch of personal sentiment, for no School master can foretell what will become of his old pupils.

The War Memorial panel doors were opened by the Senior Prefect, A. G. Gooch, and a few moments of silence followed.   Then the " Last Post " was sounded by buglers of the Norfolk Regiment.

The surplus from the Memorial Fund was invested, and the interest is devoted to the purchase of annual prizes.

# CLIFTON COLLEGE

*" Spiritus intus alit."*

A MEMORIAL Gateway erected at the main avenue of the School approach has inscribed upon it Five Hundred and Seventy Eight names, and the words: *" To the memory of 3,063 Cliftonians who served and 578 who fell in the War, 1914-1919."*

It was unveiled on June 30th, 1922, by Field-Marshal the Right Honourable Earl Haig, G.C.B., President of this College.

CLIFTON COLLEGE MEMORIAL

He received the key from the President of the Old Cliftonian Society, Lieutenant-Colonel Sir Francis Younghusband, K.C.S.I., K.C.I.E., and ultimately handed it to the Chairman of the Council, Sir Herbert Warren, K.V.C.O., D.C.L.

A short service was held at the South African War Memorial in the Close, commencing with the hymn " Lord of our Life and God of our salvation." The Collect for All Saints' Day was followed by two prayers, the second of which was the "Pater Noster." Then was sung the hymn "O God our Help in ages past," after which was said the Collect for Easter Day, concluding with the Benediction.

A procession to the Memorial Gateway was formed. After the unveiling the flag on the Gateway was lowered to half-mast, and the buglers of the Officers' Training Corps sounded the "Last Post" and "Reveille."

The procession returned to the South African Memorial for an address by Earl Haig. The O.T.C. then marched from the Close along Guthrie Road and College Road, through the Gateway, Earl Haig taking the salute on the terrace.

> "*From the great Marshal to the last recruit,*
> *These, Clifton, were thy Self, thy Spirit, in Deed,*
> *Thy flower of Chivalry, thy fallen fruit,*
> *And thine immortal Seed.*"

---

# ST. EDMUND'S CANTERBURY.

## "*Exlesiæ Filii.*"

THE existing School Chapel was enlarged in memory of the Sons of the School who gave their lives for King and Country. The East End of the old Chapel was taken down and a new Choir was added and the East End replaced. A tablet in marble was erected on the North Wall of the new Choir and on it inscribed the Fifty Three names of the Fallen.

New Choir Stalls were added and the flooring of the Choir Sanctuary was paved with marble.

The Memorial was dedicated by the Archbishop of Canterbury on October 9th, 1923. The Architect was Mr. Charles Blumfield.

KING'S SCHOOL, CANTERBURY, MEMORIAL

KING'S SCHOOL, CANTERBURY, MEMORIAL

# KING'S SCHOOL, CANTERBURY

## "*Age dum agis.*"

HE Memorial to the One Hundred and Forty Seven Old Boys who gave their lives for King and Country takes the form of a paved court and Memorial Cross situated in front of the famous Norman staircase. Stone steps surround the Cross, and during excavations the Norman bases of the pillars on which the present Schoolroom is built were disclosed.

The Cross was dedicated by the Very Reverend the Dean of Canterbury, and unveiled by Major-General Sir E. E. Carter, K.C.M.G., C.B., M.V.O., on December 19th, 1921. The following inscriptions appear: "*Lord God of Hosts be with us yet, Lest we forget, Lest we forget*" and "*Our Help standeth in the Name of the Lord*"; and below, "*In proud and thankful memory of those boys of King's School who gave their lives for King and Country, 1914-1919.*"

The names of the Fallen are inscribed upon the wall of the Memorial Court under the "Big School," and on the left of the Norman staircase, with the following inscription above them: "*Remember these who gave their lives, 1914-1919.*" This part of the memorial was unveiled by His Grace the Archbishop of Canterbury on November 11th, 1925.

The architect was Sir Herbert Baker, A.R.A.

---

# ST. EDWARD'S SCHOOL, OXFORD

## "*Pietas parantum.*"

N Tuesday, December 16th, 1919, the Memorial Calvary in the Master's Garden was dedicated by the Venerable T. H. Archer-Houblon, Archdeacon of Oxford, who took the service from the Commendation to the Benediction. The "Last Post" was sounded by Corporal Sercombe, while the Guard of Honour stood at the "Present." The robed Clergy and Choir were preceded by the Jeffries Memorial Processional Cross.

On Sunday, December 6th, 1925, the opening of the Memorial Building took place. The Gate of Remembrance has upon it the words "*Alumni Alumnis.*" The unveiling ceremony was performed by General Sir A. Godley, G.C.B., K.C.M.G., G.O.C., of the Southern Command.

ST. EDWARD'S SCHOOL MEMORIAL

# CRYPT SCHOOL, GLOUCESTER

*" Floreat schola cryptiensis."*

THE War Memorial takes the form of a plain brass, mounted on black marble and affixed to the west wall of the Assembly Hall.

The Tablet is surmounted with the School Arms in oxidised silver and enamel. It contains Fifty Eight names. The design was by A. F. Watts, B.A., M.B.E. (a Master at the School), and the work was executed by Messrs. Marshall & Co., of Cheltenham.

The Memorial was unveiled by Lieutenant-Colonel J. H. Collett, D.S.O., C.M.G., who commanded the 5th Gloucesters in France, and dedicated by the Ven. Archdeacon of Norfolk (Rev. A. R. Buckland), both these being formerly scholars at the School. Among those present at the ceremony were the Mayor of Gloucester (Councillor J. O. Roberts), Sir James Bruton, M.P., Mr. W. H. Madge (all Old Cryptians).

The ceremony began with the National Anthem (Westminster Version). The Headmaster (Mr. D. G. Williams, M.A.) read the lesson (Solomon iii, 1-10), and Mr. W. H. Madge, Chairman of the Governors, in the absence of the President of the Old Boys' Club, read the Roll of Honour. The Service Roll (to November, 1921) contained 329 names, and the distinctions gained were: 19 M.C., 6 D.S.O., 8 other British decorations, 22 mentioned in despatches and 1 Croix de Guerre and 1 Medal Militaire.

Lieutenant-Colonel Collett said he came into close contact with many of those whose names were inscribed. It was marvellous how the spirit of lack of selfishness permeated all ranks.

The Archdeacon referred to the Tablet as a bond of Duty between Young and Old, and said that book-learning was not the greater part of School Life; but the formation of character, as preparation for contingencies in their National Life. At the conclusion of the service the hymn " For all the saints " was sung.

CRYPT SCHOOL MEMORIAL

# REPTON SCHOOL

*" Parta vacat culpa."*

THE Memorial was the restoration of the remaining portions of the Old Repton Priory, formerly used as a boarding-house, the clearing of the Old Monastery Garden and the restoration of the Cloister.

A Memorial Cross was also erected in the beautiful garth, and tablets containing the names of the Three Hundred and Fifty Four of the Fallen are erected on the walls of the adjoining cloister.

The Dedication Service was performed by the late Bishop of Southwell, and General T. Burnett Stuart, an Old Boy of the School, unveiled the tablets.

They are the work of Mr. W. A. Forsyth.

REPTON SCHOOL MEMORIAL

# DOVER COLLEGE

*" Non recuso laborem."*

A CARVED English Oak Screen was erected in the Choir of the School Chapel. Recorded on three large panels, which are again divided into two, are the names of the One Hundred and Eighty Five Old Boys who were killed in the War. These panels were dedicated by the Bishop of Dover. The following inscription appears above them: *" These, at the call of King and Country, left all that was dear to them, endured hardness, faced danger and finally passed out of the sight of men by the path of duty and self-sacrifice; giving up their own lives that ours might live in Freedom."* On either side of this inscription are the Arms of the School and the Town of Dover.

DOVER COLLEGE MEMORIAL.

RUGBY SCHOOL MEMORIAL

58

# RUGBY SCHOOL

*" Orando Laborando."*

THE Memorial Fund started at a meeting held on April 4th, 1917, at Drapers' Hall, London, with the following objects :—

    1. The erection of a permanent memorial at Rugby.

    2. Provision for the education at Rugby of the sons of those who fell or were incapacitated in the War.

    3. Application of surplus funds for the sons of Rugbeians financially embarrassed by the War, to be educated at Rugby or other schools, or at preparatory schools.

In 1915 was started the War Benefactions Fund at Rugby, by special gifts of the School Staff. East of the new Big School, the Cross was erected at the Crossways.

The permanent Memorial consists of a Lantern Cross and Chapel. The Cross was designed by Sir Charles Nicholson (O.R., S.H. 81-86) on the lines of the Old English Lantern Crosses, and was unveiled by Lieutenant-General Sir S. M. Harper, K.C.B., D.S.O., on June 19th, 1920. Unveiling the Cross, he said : " French's contemptible little army was mainly officered by Public School Boys. That army held out against overwhelming forces until the resources of the Empire could be mobilised. Undoubtedly the Public Schools contributed largely to our success in this War. It is all the more necessary that our reserves should have some knowledge of the art of self-defence. What unpreparedness for war entails, what unnecessary sacrifices are the result! "

The Memorial Chapel was also designed by Sir C. Nicholson. It is in the north-west angle of the Close, connected with the main south-west door of the School Chapel by a Cloister, and accommodates about 120. The shape is that of a Greek Cross with a five-light window in each arm. The names of the Fallen now number Six Hundred and Eighty Two; they are inscribed on the walls of the two Transepts. Above is the inscription : " *These walls record the names of 682 sons of the School who gave their lives in the Great War of 1914-1918.*" The carved stone Reredos rises in two stages. The upper contains a Pieta, on each side an attendant angel; on the left St. Peter and St. Nicholas (representing sailors), and on the right St. Alban and St. Martin (representing soldiers). The subjects of the windows are the Last Supper, the Crucifixion, the Entombment and the Ascension; at the foot of the last (west) window is a picture of ships returning to port. The five small windows of the Cloister represent Lawrence Sheriff (Founder), St. Oswald, King Alfred, St. Edmund and King Arthur. On the stone in the centre of the Chapel floor is the inscription (slightly altered from the King's Scroll): "*This Chapel commemorates those who, at the call of King and Country, left all that was dear to them, endured hardness, faced danger and finally passed out of the sight of men by the path of duty and self-sacrifice, giving up their own lives that others might live in freedom. Let those who come after see to it that their names be not forgotten.*"

On the outside of the east end of the Chapel are the words: "*In remembrance of our Dead. 1914-1918.*"

RUGBY SCHOOL MEMORIAL

The dedication was performed on July 8th, 1922, by Dr. A. David, Bishop of St. Edmondsbury and Ipswich (former Headmaster); Dr. W. Temple, Bishop of Manchester, gave the address, and Dr. H. A. James, President of St. John's College, Oxford (a former Headmaster), assisted. The order of service was, in brief: Dr. James said the Opening Sentences and Foundation Prayer; the 84th Psalm was chanted; the Headmaster (Mr. W. W. Vaughan, C.V.O.) read the Lessons from Isaiah and Revelations. Then followed the Jubilate and a Prayer. The Bishop of Ipswich used, in dedication, a prayer which was used 100 years previous at the Consecration of the Chapel. " Jesus, where'er Thy people meet " was sung; then followed the address by the Bishop of Manchester.

In a lectern in the Chapel are preserved the seven volumes of Memorials of Rugbeians, and also the Rugby War Register. The lectern, in memory of Lieut. Littleboy, is made of oak, inlaid with walnut, ebony, holly and sycamore; it is octagonal in shape, and surmounted by a bronze figure of an O.T.C. Cadet. The inscription reads: " *God made trial of them and found them worthy of Himself, as gold in the furnace He proved them.*"

---

## CITY OF OXFORD SCHOOL

Formerly The Boys' High School, Oxford.

" *Fortis est veritas.*"

**T**HE Memorial consists of a bronze tablet, on which are the names of the Eighty Old Boys who laid down their lives in the War.

The commemoration service was held in Christ Church Cathedral on April 24th, 1920. The order of service was as follows: Hymn, " O God our Help in ages past "; the sentences St. John xi, 25-26, and St. John xv, 13 were read by the Chaplain. The choir then sang Psalm xxiii. The lesson was from Revelation vii, 14-17. Memorial Prayers were said, followed by the reading of the Eighty names, after which the choir sang the anthem " When the Lord turned again the captivity of Sion " and " Let us with a gladsome mind " to the music by Stanford. The Chaplain then read the versicles and prayers. The hymn " Let saints on earth in concert sing " was sung, followed by the address given by the Very Rev. the

Dean of Christ Church.   After the hymn " For all the Saints who from their labours rest," the Benediction was pronounced.   The service ended with Handel's " Funeral March " and the " Last Post."

The Tablet is the work of the Bromsgrove Guild, and was erected by Messrs. Fletcher.   It is placed on the wall of the Grand Staircase.

This Memorial was unveiled by the Headmaster, Mr. A. W. Cave, M.A., on July 5th, 1920, and was dedicated by the Rev. H. B. Hall. Sir Oswyn Murray, K.C.B., Secretary to the Admiralty and President of the Old Boys' Club, committed the Tablet to the custody of the governing of the School.   In his speech he said: " The Great War has been fought in the Playing Fields and Classrooms of every School throughout the Empire."   The gathering included the Mayor and Corporation of the City of Oxford.

Above the list of names on the Tablet are the words: " *This Tablet was erected to perpetuate the memory of the boys of this School who fell in the War*, 1914-1918," and below, " *Their name liveth for evermore.*"

The School " Service Roll " includes 580 Old Boys, of whom 57 served in the Royal Air Force.   Commissions were held by 311.   The following distinctions were gained: 1 K.C.B., 3 C.B., 1 C.B.E., 9 D.S.O., 3 M.C. with bar, 25 M.C., 16 other medals, and 39 mentioned in despatches.   Foreign distinctions won were: 2 Legion d'Honneur, 4, Croix de Guerre (French), 3 Croix de Guerre (Belgian), 1 Order de la Couronne (Belgian), 2 Silver Medals and 1 Croie di Guerra (Italian).

CITY OF OXFORD SCHOOL MEMORIAL

# MAGDALEN SCHOOL, OXFORD

THE War Memorial at this School is fourfold. First, a Memorial Window in the School Chapel, upon which are the Patron Saints of England, Scotland, Ireland and Wales, with a centre figure, "The Light of the World," from Holman Hunt's picture in St. Paul's Cathedral. The second, a Memorial Brass in the School Chapel, contains the names of Forty Seven Old Boys, to which are to be added the names of two Old Boys who died after the unveiling. The third, an "Honours" Brass in the "Big School," contains a list of 38 Honours, including two V.C.s (one with Bar) and eight D.S.O.s. The fourth was the electric lighting in the School Chapel.

Among the fallen were five Senior Prefects; of these, three held office consecutively, namely, Messrs. Leicester, Callender and Alasden, the first two being voluntary soldiers, and the last a member of the Regular Army.

The Memorial Window and Tablets were unveiled by the President of Magdalen College and Chairman of the School Governors on February 16th, 1920.

The Window and Brasses were designed by Messrs. Mowbray & Co., after a suggestion from the Headmaster.

---

# HURSTPIERPOINT COLLEGE

*" Manhood learning gentleness."*

THERE is at this School a Mural Tablet of ten oak panels bearing the names of the One Hundred and Ten who fell. As a further Memorial, a fine Cricket Pavilion, designed by Mr. J. Hunt and situated on the playing fields adjacent to the School, was erected and opened on July 23rd, 1921. The Rev. E. M. Naine, Provost of Lancing, dedicated both Memorials on that day.

The architect of the Chapel Memorial Tablet was Mr. Temple Moore. On it is the inscription: "1914. *Pro Patria.* 1918. *Vitam dederunt.*" Each name on the tablet occupies a separate scroll, giving a fine effect to the otherwise rather severe design.

The inscription in the Pavilion is: "*This Pavilion was given by the Old Boys in memory of their fellows who gave their lives in the Great War, 1914-1918.*" It was erected with funds collected by the Old Boys.

The day on which the Memorial was opened commenced at 7.30 a.m. with the Requiem Eucharist. At 11.30 a.m. there was a cricket match between the School and a team of ex-Service Old Boys, and a luncheon was given to the subscribers to the War Memorial Fund.

In the Chapel are other memorials; the panel behind the altar is in memory of Mr. F. G. B. Lys, the screen is in memory of W. H. B. Wolstencroft, and the stalls in memory of Mr. D. S. Campbell. The College have also granted a Scholarship.

The following distinctions were gained by Old Boys: 59 M.C.. 8 D.S.O., 4 D.F.C., 19 other British distinctions, and a large number of foreign orders.

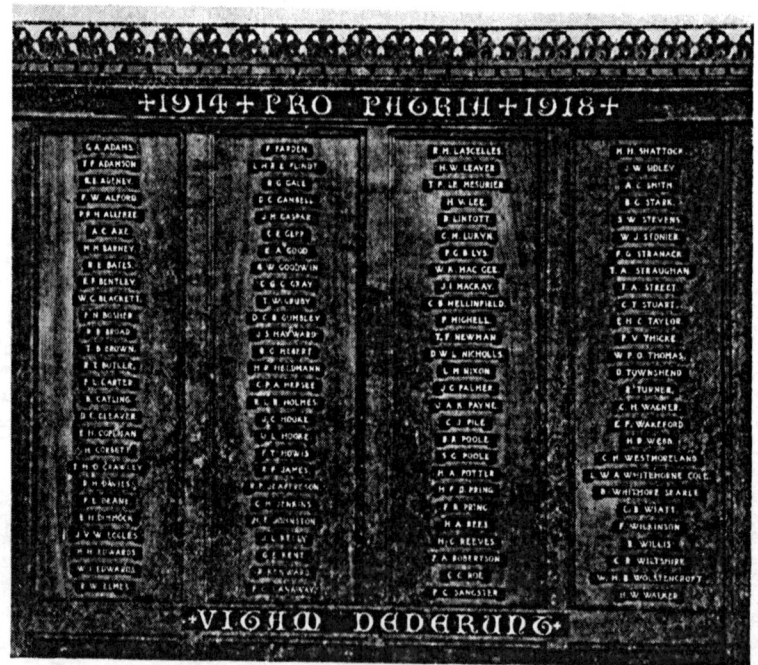

HURSTPIERPOINT COLLEGE MEMORIAL

MEMORIAL CRICKET PAVILION, HURSTPIERPOINT COLLEGE

# MONKTON COMBE SCHOOL

*" Verbum tuum veritas "*

HE Memorial Chapel was dedicated on June 25th, 1925. The Headmaster conducted the first part of the service; Dr. Edwyn Bevan read the lesson. The Lord Bishop of Bath and Wells performed the act of dedication and then proceeded to unveil the Memorial Tablet in the Chapel, while the Guard of Honour, supplied by the School O.T.C., remained with heads bowed and arms reversed.

The architects were Professor Beresford-Pite, F.R.I.B.A., and Mr. J. Hodges, A.R.I.B.A.

MONKTON COMBE SCHOOL MEMORIAL

# NEWCASTLE-UNDER-LYME SCHOOL

*" Schola novi castelli nunquam non nova."*

THE Panelling of the Big School in British Oak, the erection of an Organ and a Dais and a Memorial Tablet form the Memorial at this School. It was unveiled by Colonel J. V. Campbell, V.C., C.M.G., D.S.O., and dedicated by the Bishop of Stepney, Dr. Henry Mosley, (an Old Boy of the School) on Founder's Day, June 29th, 1923. Colonel Campbell said: " When you see this tablet, remember the brave lads who gave up their lives. Lead a life of unselfishness and self-sacrifice, try to live up to their example; cherish their memory." The Bishop of Stepney, in his address, referred to " Good comradeship in the Communion of Saints."

The Roll of Honour contains Ninety One names.

The architect for the Memorial was Mr. W. T. Loveday, A.R.I.B.A., of Rugby.

STONYHURST MEMORIAL

# STONYHURST

*" Quant je puis."*

HIS artistic Memorial consists of an Altar Shrine, Marble Reredos in low relief, and a Crucifix in Gothic Style, the whole surmounted by a large Oriel Window at the end of the long School Gallery. The Memorial was unveiled by Colonel Walter Maxwell-Scott, C.B., D.S.O., on June 27th, 1922. The service began with the Great Academies.

The following stanza, referring to the Memorial, is from the prologue:—

*" Five sermons on the stone, they'll tell their message year by year*

*Of men who fought on stricken fields for a fair dream they knew,*

*A dream that lurked in the eyes of death, they read and did not fear,*

*And gave their gift of youth to God to make the dream come true."*

Cardinal Bourne said that such memorials pointed the way to that discharge of duty, the training for which was the main object of education. The order of the unveiling ceremony was as follows: An address, and the unveiling by Colonel W. J. Maxwell-Scott; the Volley, " Last Post " and " De Profundis "; the Blessing by His Lordship Bishop John Vaughan (wearing the famous cope from Henry VII's Chapel at Westminster), assisted by Father Leo Parker. Then came the " Feu de joie " and the Stonyhurst Chorus, followed by a procession past the Shrine, led by the O.T.C.

Colonel W. J. Maxwell-Scott said that the qualities of a good soldier were courage and determination. Many acts of bravery were unknown and went unsung. They would listen to the " Reveille " with the safe assurance that they would meet their friends again.

The inscription on the tablet at the foot of the Shrine is: *" Pray for the eternal welfare of the Stonyhurst men who died for their Country in the Great War of 1914-1919. May they rest in peace."*

The figures at the Cross are representative of the Navy, Infantry, Air Force and Gunnery. The meaning of the figures is the teaching of St. Paul that all Christians are at one with Christ, sharing His life through the gift of Grace (His life in us).

> " *Swords lightly drawn from war-worn sheath,*
>
> *Lips still in age-long prayer*
>
> *And final act of faith, Sleep on!*
>
> *To wake when fall the stars and sun,*
>
> *At God's last trumpet blare.*"
>
> —*Francis Cowper (Syntax I).*

The architects for the Memorial were Messrs. E. Kirby & Sons, of Liverpool. The sculptor was Mr. Gilbert Ledward.

It is interesting to note that in addition to the Altar Shrine, a Science Wing containing fully-equipped laboratories, was erected. Several Bursaries were founded to assist in the education of sons of Stonyhurst men killed in the War.

Among the distinctions won were three Victoria Crosses. Lieutenant M. J. Dease, of the Royal Fusiliers, was the first man to gain the Victoria Cross in the Great War. This proud distinction thus belongs to a Stonyhurst man. He was killed on August 23rd, 1914, and was buried in St. Symphorien Military Cemetery (near Mons), plot 5, Row B, grave 2. As there were two V.C.s prior to the War, the record of the School is now five. Service Roll includes 1,012 names; 167 were killed.

# KING'S SCHOOL, ROCHESTER

THE War Memorial Window in the Lady Chapel, and the Sanctuary Lamp, were formally unveiled and dedicated on Saturday, December 11th, 1920. The robed clergy present were the Bishop of Rochester, attended by Rev. E. Powell, Sacrist, as Chaplain; the Dean, Dr. Storrs; the Archdeacon, Canon C. F. Burney; the Headmaster and the Precentor, Rev. R. John Stone. The procession of clergy and choir moved to the Lady Chapel after Brahm's "Requiem" had been played.

General Graham then unveiled the Window, and the Sanctuary Lamp, presented by the Patriarch of Jerusalem, was dedicated by the Dean. The "Last Post" and "Reveille" were sounded by buglers of the O.T.C., afer which the Bishop gave the Benediction.

The Roll of Honour contains Fifty Nine names, which are engraved on a tablet under the window. In the top windows, from left to right, are figures of St. George, King Arthur and St. Michael, while in the lower windows are figures of St. Peter, St. John, the Resurrection and the three Marys.

The following coats of arms appear: Top, Henry VIII; Lower, the School Arms, the Arms of the County of Kent and the City of Rochester. There is also the following inscription: " *As by man came Death, by man came also the Resurrection of the Dead.*"

Above the tablet on which are the names of the Fallen are the words " *Bello partem adepti,*" while below are the words " *In pace requiescant.*"

# CRANBROOK SCHOOL

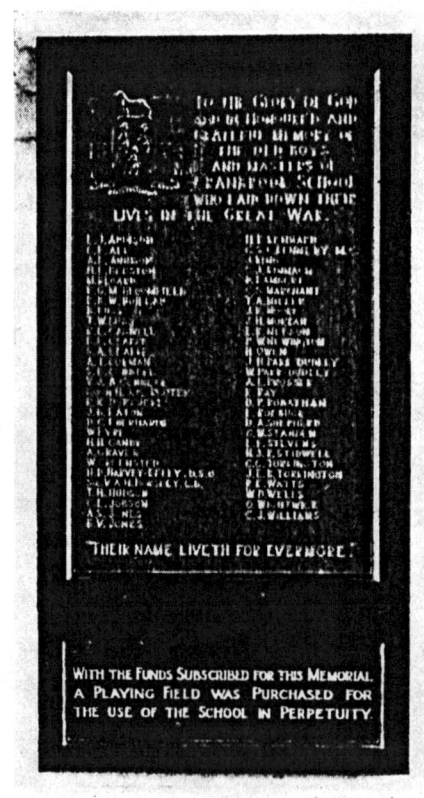

COLONEL W. C. HORSLEY unveiled the War Memorial Tablet in June, 1921, during the Speech Day celebrations.

On the Tablet, which is situated in the " Big School," are inscribed the names of the Fifty Seven Old Boys who fell in the War, with the year of the Foundation—1574— the School Crest and inscription: " *To the Glory of God, in honoured and grateful memory of the Old Boys and Masters of Cranbrook School who laid down their lives in the Great War.*"

Below the two columns of the names are the words: " *Their name liveth for evermore.*" " *With the funds subscribed for this Memorial a Playing Field was purchased for the use of the School in perpetuity.*"

# TRENT COLLEGE, DERBY

*" Fons vitæ sapientia."*

THE College War Memorial is in three parts; the first, Oak Panels round the Communion Table in the Chapel, on which appear the names of the One Hundred and One Old Boys who were killed in the War, and underneath, the inscription: *" To those sons of Trent who loved our brotherhood, and at the call of duty laid down their lives in the Great War,* 1914-1918."

The second part of the Memorial was a Headmaster's House with a garden and four acres of land. Over the entrance to the house is inscribed: " 1914. *In memory of the brave.* 1918." *" Pro nobis, pro patria, pro mundo." " Within this quiet garden close, though o'er all lands our graves lie spread, still do we live, and walk with those whose thoughts are with the Dead."*

The other Memorial, a Gate of Remembrance, has been constructed in the form of a lych gate, and bears over it the following inscription: *" Hic amor, hic patria, nec aspera terrebant." " They gave us peace by their warfare and life by their death."*

The Memorials were unveiled by General Sir C. Harington, G.O.C., Northern Command. The architect was Mr. E. S. Wimperis, of London.

The number of Old Boys who served in the forces was 763, and a number of Scholarships were founded for the sons of those who fell.

---

# EASTBOURNE COLLEGE

*"Ex oriente salus."*

HE Dedication Service was conducted by the Rev. A. H. Streeten, M.A., M.C. (O.E।)., Minor Canon of St. Paul's, assisted by the Rev. C. Crowden, D.D. (Headmaster at the School from 1888-1895), and the Rev. E. H. S. Hunt, M.A., the School Chaplain, on Sunday, June 28th, 1925.

The "Toc H" Lamp of Remembrance was lit by Major-General Sir Arnold F. Sillem, K.C.M.G., C.B. (O.E.), at the end of the Chapel Service, and Lieutenant-General Sir Charles H. Harington, G.B.E., K.C.B., D.S.O., opened the Memorial Tower. The ceremonial concluded with the breaking of the College Flag on the flagstaff on the top of the Tower and the sounding of the "Last Post" and "Reveille" by buglers of the College O.T.C.

The wrought-iron gates at the east and west ends of the Memorial Building have inscribed upon them: "*In Memoriam*, 1914-1918." The ground floor is occupied by a Memorial Hall, the first floor by Senior and Junior Libraries, the second floor by four Music Rooms, and two other floors complete the Tower. The south block contains the Armoury and Drill Hall, five Classrooms and a Workshop. The north block will contain three Physics Laboratories, one large Chemistry Laboratory, a Balance Room, two Private Rooms for Science Masters and four Classrooms.

The tablets on the North and South Walls contain the names of the One Hundred and Sixty Five who fell. On the South, the centre panel bears the words: "*To the memory of those Members of this School who died in the Great War, 1914-1918. This Tower was erected in token of sorrow for their loss, of pride in their valour, and in full assurance that the remembrance of their heroism will inspire those who fill their places with the same courage and self-devotion.*"

On the two outer panels of each tablet are replicas of the Battle Sword in bronze.

On the North, the centre panel bears the words: "*My sword I give to him that shall succeed in my pilgrimage, and my courage and skill to him that can get it. My marks and scars I carry with me to be a witness for me that I have fought his battles. Who will now be my Rewarder?"*

The Tower was designed by Messrs. Sydney Tatchell and G. C. Wilson, FF.R.I.B.A. (O.E.).

EASTBOURNE COLLEGE, THE MEMORIAL TOWER
*(From College Road)*

EASTBOURNE COLLEGE MEMORIAL GATEWAY

EASTERN ENTRANCE OF THE MEMORIAL TOWER

EASTBOURNE COLLEGE : GENERAL VIEW, WAR MEMORIAL BUILDINGS

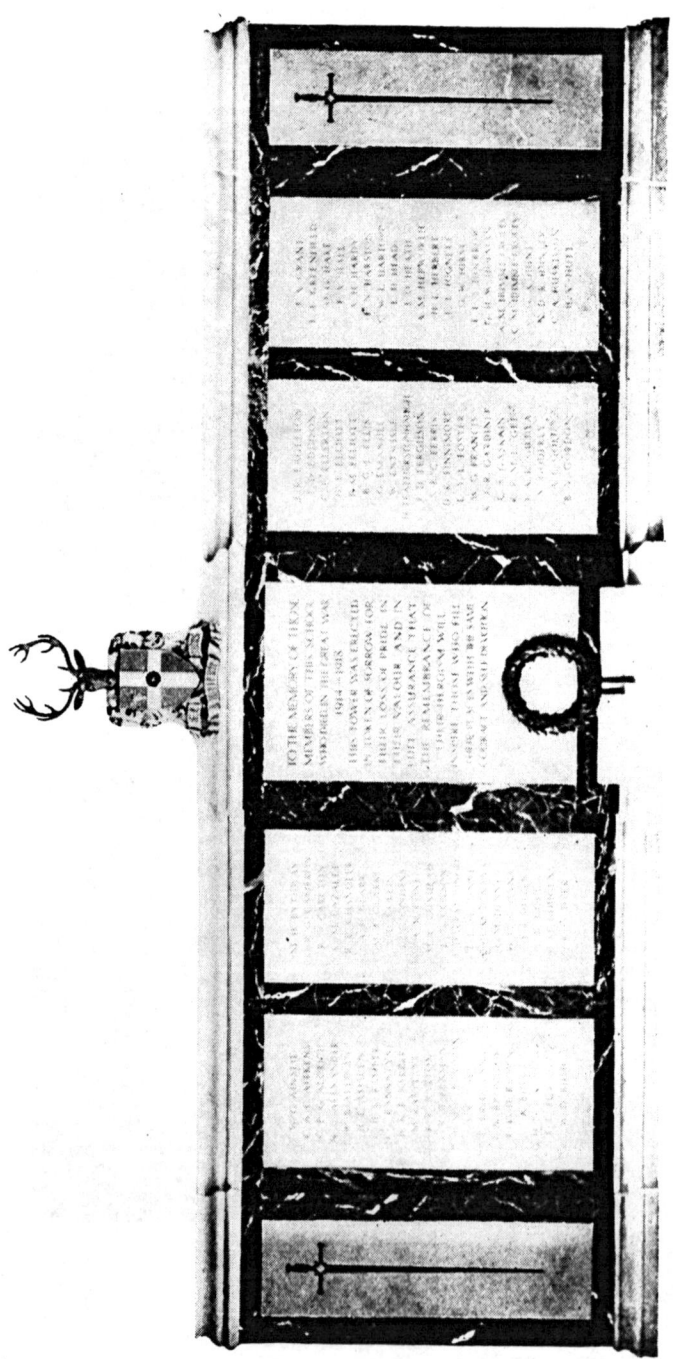

EASTBOURNE COLLEGE MEMORIAL TABLET—ROLL OF HONOUR (SOUTH PANEL.)

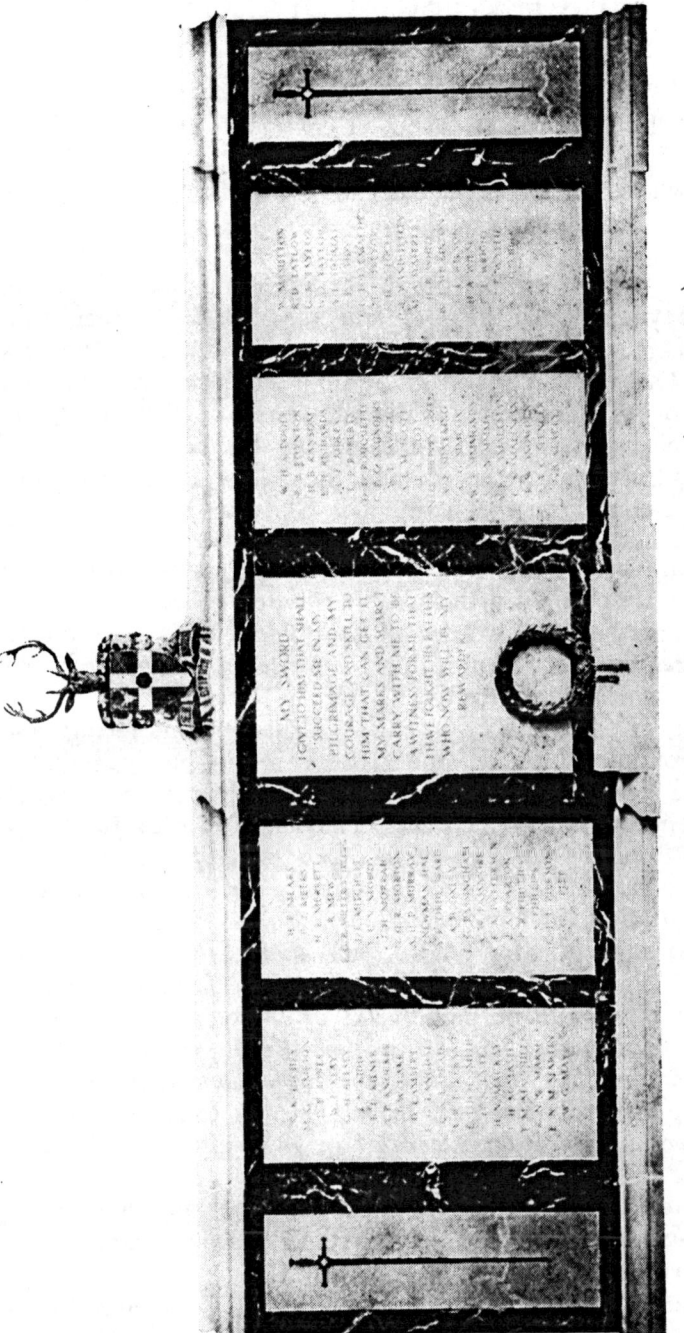

EASTBOURNE COLLEGE MEMORIAL TABLET—ROLL OF HONOUR (NORTH PANEL)

# WINCHESTER COLLEGE

*" Manners makyth man."*

THE War Memorial Cloister was opened on May 31st, 1924, by His Royal Highness the Duke of Connaught, who entered the Cloister through the Meads Doorway— the East Door.

The service began with Hymn 95 in the School Hymn Book, "*Finita jam sunt proclia*"; then followed the Psalm cxxii, the Lesson from Hebrews xi, 13-16, Four Prayers and the Blessing. The unveiling and dedication sentences were pronounced by Bishop Talbot, of Winchester. Viscount Grey of Falloden then gave an address, which was followed by the singing of the National Anthem. Two minutes' silence was observed, and the "Last Post" was sounded. The service concluded with the hymn "O God our Help in ages past."

In the centre of the Cloister, between the grass squares and where the four paved ways of the Garth meet, is situated an octagonal monolith, on which are inscribed the words: "*Esto fidelis usque ad mortem et dabo tibi coronam vitæ.*" From this base rises a stone shaft crowned with a Cross, on which is inscribed in Greek: "*Christ is Risen.*" On each side of the Cross is the figure of a sentinel Crusader, one facing east, one facing west. An inscription of stone letters, set in knapped flints, runs in a continuous band round the walls of the Cloister, nine feet from the ground. The words inscribed are: *Thanks be to God for the service of these Five Hundred Wykehamists, who were found faithful unto death amid the manifold chances of the Great War. In the day of battle they forgat not God, Who created them to do His will, nor their Country, the stronghold of freedom, nor their School, the mother of godliness and discipline. Strong in this threefold faith they went forth from home and kindred to the battlefields of the world and, treading the path of duty and sacrifice, laid down their lives for mankind. Thou, therefore, for whom they died, seek not thine own, but serve as they served, and in peace or in war bear thyself ever as Christ's soldier, gentle in all things, valiant in action, steadfast in adversity.*"

In the outside North Wall, close to the north-east angle, stands a Craftsmen's Stone, on which is inscribed the following names:—
Sir Herbert Baker, A.R.A. (the Architect).
Alfred Turner, A.R.A. (Sculptor of Central Cross and Crusaders).

WINCHESTER COLLEGE MEMORIAL

Charles Wheeler (Carver of St. Mary and the Bas Reliefs).
George K. Gray (Designer of the Emblems).
Lawrence Turner (Painter of the Emblems).
A. E. Clarke (Master Foreman, of Winchester).
Messrs. Holloway Brothers (the Builders).

Below the names is written: " *Non sibi sed deo et mortuis* " (Not for thee, but for God and the Dead), which exactly describes the zeal and interest taken by the craftsmen in the work they undertook.

On each wall of the Cloister are two name tablets, eight in all. Entering the Cloister by the Mead's Gate (in the middle of the East Wall of the Cloister), and turning to the right, there is the first name tablet, on which is inscribed: " *On the seas, Heligoland Bight, Falkland Islands, Dogger Bank, Dardanelles, Jutland, Tigris, Zeebrugge, Dwina River, Archangel.* " Then the North-East Corner is reached; this is known as the " Indian Corner." Continuing along the North Wall there is the " Peace relief " and the North-West (Dominion) Corner. Passing along the South Wall there is the South African (Boer War) Memorial Gateway and the South-West (Australian) Corner. The " Victory Door," leading to the Sick House, Gymnasium and Rackets Court is passed, and finally the South-East (African) Corner. Turning north to the Mead's Gate, there is the last tablet, commemorating the battles on land.

The North-East Corner contains black marble paving from Budh-Gaya (India); the North-West Corner, Canadian Marble from Texada Isle (British Columbia); the South-West Corner, a five-star Cross in syenite from New Zealand, and the South-East Corner, granite from Table Mountain, South Africa. The paving in the Mead's Gate contains gift stones from Ypres, and on the outside of the Gateway is a statue of St. Mary and a monogram. There are also tablets, on which are the inscriptions: " *Foundation stone laid 15th July, 1922.* " " *Cloister opened 31st May, 1924.* "

The badges of 120 regiments, in which Old Wykehamists served, are emblazoned on the corbels and tie-beams. On the oak struts of the roof, over the arches, are four badges of regiments closely associated with Winchester, supported by figures of angels. The regiments are: The Rifle Brigade, King's Royal Rifles, Hampshire Regiment, and the Royal Artillery.

The three central figures of the Reredos in the Chapel are not part of the War Memorial, but the Reredos was reconstructed and a stone altar, designed by Mr. W. D. Caroe, was placed in the Chapel.

Grants were made for the sons of the Fallen, and four Memorial Volumes were published by Messrs. Warren & Son. The Roll of Honour in the Chapel was the work of Graily Hewitt, B.A., of Lincoln's Inn, and his assistants.

Two thousand three hundred and thirty Old Boys of the School served in the Forces; 480 were wounded and 870 gained distinctions, which included 4 V.C.s.

---

# LANCASTER ROYAL GRAMMAR SCHOOL

*" Præsis ut prosis."*

HE Memorial takes the form of a Brass Tablet containing the names of the Eighty Nine Fallen. It is placed in the "Big School" in the centre of the wall facing the dais. The central panel of dedication is inscribed thus: *" To the Glory of God and in honoured memory of the Old Lancastrians who gave their lives for their King and Country in the Great War, 1914-1918."*

The Tablet was unveiled by Lieutenant-Colonel C. M. Bateman, D.S.O., on July 5th, 1922.

Other parts of the War Memorial Scheme are a Memorial Library, for which plans have been prepared by Mr. H. Littler, of Preston, and the Playing Field.

---

# BROMSGROVE SCHOOL

*" Deo Regi Vincimo."*

HE Memorial is to take the form of a new School Chapel, and in it will be placed a list of the Eighty Nine names of the Fallen. It is hoped to commence building operations in 1927.

DOWNSIDE SCHOOL MEMORIAL

# DOWNSIDE SCHOOL

N the preface of the Dom Lucius Graham's book, "Downside with the War," is a beautiful poem, complete list of all Gregorians who served in His Majesty's Forces, a list of War Captains, especially mentioning Dom Stephen Rawlinson, and, after the lists of those who fell, the prisoners of war and the Foreign and British Orders gained, appear the "Memoirs."

> "*And Downside will tell of the story*
> *Through ages to be*
> *Of our heroes who, crowned with glory,*
> *Died worthy of thee.*"

There is erected in the School grounds a Memorial Cross on which are inscribed the names of the One Hundred and Seven Fallen.

The actual War Memorial is the completion of the Nave of the Abbey Church. The task was difficult, as it meant erecting a new Nave to link up with Garner's Choir and the existing Chapels, but the architect, Sir Giles Gilbert Scott, has succeeded in expressing his own personality and enhancing the character of the earlier work. The style is early Gothic, the arches are light and limber in grace without the severity of the late Gothic style.

The ceremonies formed a "Triduum"—from July 25th to July 27th, 1925. On the first day was the Hallowing of the Great Memorial Nave; on the second, the Thanksgiving for those who survived the War, and on the third the Requiem for those who fell, and the unveiling of the Memorial Tablets.

On Saturday, July 25th—Feast of St. James the Apostle—His Eminence Cardinal Bourne sang pontifical mass (high) wearing the pallium. In the sanctuary were present His Eminence Cardinal Gasquet, His Grace the Archbishop of Cardiff, the Bishop of Lancaster and Bishops Vaughan, Butt and Keatinge. In the choir were the Abbot and Community, the Bishop and Chapter of Clifton, the Abbots of Belmont and Buckfast, Abbot Ford and Mgr. Barnes and Pyke. Fathers Bede Jarrett, Daniel Meyer, Guardian O.F.M. Bristol and Prior Wincaton, O.D.C., were also present. After the Gospel, the Bishop of Clifton preached. "Euge Bone" was sung, followed by the Papal Blessing and

DOWNSIDE SCHOOL MEMORIAL
NAVE INTERIOR

DOWNSIDE, THE MEMORIAL CROSS

the Indulgence.  At the Offertory the School sang "O Felix Roma."
The Choir was conducted by Dom. Thomas, and the organ played by
Dom. Gregory Murray.

On Sunday, July 26th, the Bishop of Clifton sang the Mass.

On Monday, July 27th, Dr. Keatinge, Bishop-in-Ordinary to Army
and R.A.F., sang the Requiem.  The other ministers had been Army
Chaplains, namely, Doms. S. Rawlinson Young, Paul Brockfield, Richard
Darey and Ambrose Aguis.

His Eminence Cardinal Gasquet assisted in the Sanctuary, while the
O.T.C., who were in uniform, were in the Nave and formed a Guard of
Honour round the Catafalque.  After Mass all assembled outside the
Church, where the Memorial Tablets, whereon One Hundred and Ten
names of the Fallen are inscribed, was unveiled by Sir Hugh Clifford,
heavy rain falling during the ceremony.

Two members of the Sacred College attended, namely, Cardinal
Bourne and Cardinal Gasquel, of Santa Maria, in Campitelli.  It was
with regret that the absence of the Abbots of Ampleforth, Douai and
Fort Augustus had to be recorded.

---

# NORTHAMPTON TOWN AND COUNTY SCHOOL

ON Old Boys' Day, Saturday, July 5th, 1924, the War
Memorial Tablet was unveiled by Colonel G. S. Eunson,
who is an Old Boy of the School.  The dedication was by
the Rural Dean, Canon F. S. Keysell.

The Tablet was designed by Mr. G. H. Stevenson,
an Old Boy, and on it are inscribed the names of the Ninety
Two Old Boys who fell in the War.  The Tablet is situated at the end
of the Hall under the clock and faces the dais.

The names stand out well on a background of red, and the Tablet
harmonises with the panelling of the Hall.  The following inscription
appears : " *To the Glory of God and in affectionate remembrance of the
Old Boys who fell in the Great War, 1914-1918.*"  " *Mors est janus
vitæ.*"

# PORTSMOUTH GRAMMAR SCHOOL

HE unveiling of the Memorial Tablet took place in 1922 by Admiral Sir Sydney Freemantle, commanding at Portsmouth. There are upon the tablet One Hundred and Twenty Six names of those who made the sacrifice for Freedom. Surrounded by a laurel wreath are the dates 1914-1919 in scroll design. Above all is the School Arms. The lower part on each side carries crests, and centrally the inscription: "*These sons of the School, serving their country by land, sea and air in the Great War, gave their lives in defence of liberty and right.*"

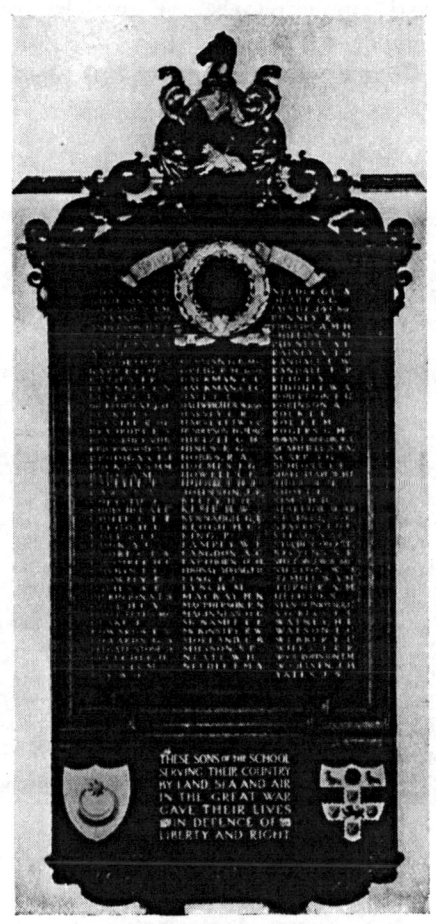

PORTSMOUTH GRAMMAR SCHOOL MEMORIAL

# EXETER SCHOOL

*" Sigillum scholæ scoti johannis intra civitatem Exon."*

THE Memorial was dedicated by the Rev. the Honourable F. L. Courtenay. It consists of the Reredos, and panelling of the Chancel of the School Chapel carried out in British oak.

The names of the Seventy who fell in the War are recorded upon panels, on which appears the following inscription: *" In memory of the Old Boys of Exeter School who gave their lives for their Country and for us in the Great War."*

EXETER SCHOOL MEMORIAL

# HEREFORD CATHEDRAL SCHOOL

THE Brass Memorial Tablet is placed in the Lady Chapel of Hereford Cathedral. An oak tablet is also erected in the School Library. The architects were Messrs. Nicholson & Clarke, of Hereford. There are Sixty Nine names on the Roll of Honour. The Dean of Hereford, the Very Rev. R. W. Waterfield, conducted the unveiling and dedicatory service on December 16th, 1921. The ceremony was attended by a large number of Old Boys and relatives, and was mostly of a civic and ecclesiastical character.

The Service Roll contains 485 names, and the following distinctions were won: 9 D.S.O., 38 M.C., 9 Foreign Orders, 2 C.B., 3 C.M.G., 1 C.S.I. and 120 other British Orders.

The Tablet bears the School Crest, and below, the words: "*To the Glory of God and to the Revered Memory of the former members of Hereford Cathedral School who gave their lives for their Country in the Great War, 1914-1918. Their name liveth for evermore.*"

After the two columns of names are the words: "*Dulce et decorum est pro patria mori.*"

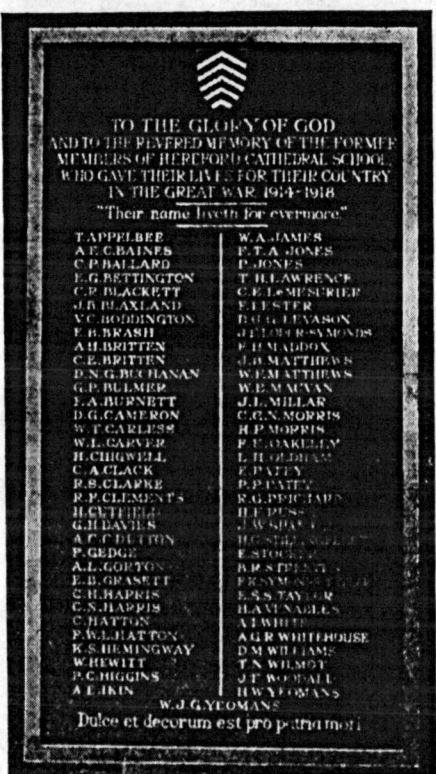

TONBRIDGE SCHOOL MEMORIAL

# TONBRIDGE SCHOOL

*" Deus dat incrementum."*

O N Saturday, October 10th, 1925, the Gate of Remembrance, leading from the Ante-Chapel into the Chapel, was unveiled by Major-General Sir William Edmund Ironside, K.C.B., C.M.G., D.S.O. (O.T.), and dedicated by the Right Rev. Bishop Henry Russell Wakefield, C.B.E., D.D. (O.T.), formerly Bishop of Birmingham. The School, the Headmaster, and Masters entitled to be so, were in uniform. Mr. Hilton, whose son is at the School, kindly made all provision for the unveiling, and presented to the School the two Union Jacks specially made to veil the Memorial.

The Gate of Remembrance was designed by Mr. Henry Wilson. The bronze group represents St. George, with a belted sword indicating that his fighting days are over; on his right an Angel presents a youth to him; on his left another Angel offers the Garland of Glory. Above this group is the figure of the Divine Mother, and, above her, the Son descended from the Cross. The arms of the United Kingdom and Skinners' Company and the School are on either side of the figure of the Mother. The arms of Rochester and Canterbury are on the spandrils decorated with roses and vine leaves.

Below this group are panels containing the names of the Four Hundred and Fifteen Old Boys and Three Masters who gave their lives, surmounted by the inscription: *" Mementote in Christo hujus scholæ alumnorum, qui sui immemores pro patria occubuere."*

The Gate piers are crowned with the arms of the Colonies, and across the opening is written: *" They gave us peace by their warfare and by their death life."*

The Roll of Honour Portrait Gallery contains photographs of all but ten of those who gave their lives.

An educational scheme for the education at Tonbridge of the sons of the Fallen was instituted in 1918.

# ROSSALL SCHOOL

*" Mens agitat molem."*

TWO dates will be pre-eminent in the annals of this School —1894, the fiftieth anniversary of the foundation, and 1925, when, on June 26th, the Memorial was dedicated to the honour of the Two Hundred and Ninety Seven Rossallians who fell in the Great War.

The Service Roll contains at least 1,600 names, of whom two gained the V.C., 54 D.S.O. (9 with bar), 154 M.C. (13 with bar), 7 Air Force Crosses, 69 other British decorations and 65 Foreign decorations.

The dedication was performed by the Archbishop of York, the Right Rev. Cosmo Gordon-Lang, D.D., assisted by the Bishops of Warrington, Burnley, Whalley and Hulme (the latter Chairman of the Council) and Bishop Price (O.R.). Canon Olivier acted as Chaplain to the Archbishop.

The service began with the Easter Hymn, " The strife is o'er, the battle won." The versicles and special collects were intoned by the Headmaster, followed by Psalm xlvi and the lesson from Revelation xxi, 1-7, read by the late Headmaster, Dr. Way.

The Memorial Chapel was then dedicated, with the organ and window " and all other works now given to increase the beauty of His worship in this place." The choir then gave Dr. E. C. Bairstow's setting of the words " Save us, O Lord, waking; guard us sleeping," after which special prayers for the Fallen and for all that mourn were said by the Bishop of Hulme. Then followed the hymn " O Valiant Hearts."

The Archbishop preached the first sermon from the Memorial Pulpit from the text, Matthew xxiv, 44: " Be ye also ready." " We must never let the mist of disillusionment blind our eyes to the greatness of the light that then shone upon our English life. The generation since the War has need to be reminded of that heritage of trust and of honour into which they have entered. I shall always think that the spirit of our Public Schools rose to its highest power in the flame of sacrifice which lit up those four fateful years. These English boys must merit the famous words of Pericles, 'They fled from shame, but with their bodies they endured the battle, and so in a moment, at the supreme moment of their fortune, passed from the place, not of their fear but of their glory.' If the old place of the Public School and University men is passing their sun is setting in splendour on the fields of France and Flanders. Therefore, 'Be ye also ready.'" In concluding, the Archbishop said: "You will be found ready—men who will find their motive for work, not in wealth, but in service."

The choir then sang as an anthem Rudyard Kipling's "Recessional" to the setting by Dr. E. T. Sweeting (a Master at the School from 1882 to 1897), and the service concluded with the Blessing pronounced by the Archbishop, Stainer's "Sevenfold Amen" and Beethoven's Second Symphony.

ROSSALL SCHOOL MEMORIAL

95

The existing Chapel was enlarged and beautified, the work being entrusted to Sir Robert Lorimer, A.R.A. The south transept gable was rebuilt and a second bay inserted. In the centre of the east wall of this new bay an apsidal recess was formed, in which was placed the War Memorial Altar. On the north and south walls are oak panels bearing the names of the Two Hundred and Ninety Seven who fell. On one panel is the inscription: "*To the Glory of God and in memory of 297 Rossalians who, in the years 1914 to 1919, died for their Country.*" On the other panel is written: "*So they passed over, and all the trumpets sounded for them on the other side.*"

The whole of the Chapel has been re-seated with stalls of native oak. A gallery has been added, and the new organ placed therein. There have also been added a new oak pulpit, reredos and chancel panelling. The wood carving was carried out by Messrs. W. & A. Clow, of Edinburgh (who also carried out the carving in the Knights of the Thistle Chapel, Edinburgh, and the choir of Dunblane Cathedral). The design on the pulpit—a figure of St. John the Baptist—is carved in one block of oak by Mrs. Meredith Williams, who also modelled the figure of St. George in the south transept.

At the end of one of the pews is carved the figure of a wild ass wearing a football-cap. The ends of the pews in the Chancel have upon them the signs of St. Matthew and St. John.

The east window was given by the Fletcher family in memory of their father, Ralph, and their brother, Leonard, both Old Rossallians. The window illustrates "The Life of our Lord" in the aspects of the Crucifixion, Resurrection and Ascension. The scene in the Carpenter's Shop has a special significance. In the large sext-foils are the Four and Twenty Elders, with the Virgin and St. John the Baptist on thrones. The latter is the patron saint of Rossall.

The windows in the Memorial transept are the Apse windows—simple figures on quarry grounds. The centre figure is "Christ in His Majesty" and on either side are figures of St. George and St. Christopher. Beneath the figures are the shields of England and Rossall in a design of oak leaves.

The three-light window is designed on the Elizabethan hymn "Ah! my sweet home, Jerusalem." In it are depicted the City of God, the entrance of Warriors into Blessedness, meeting the Virgin with her choir,

St. Ambrose, St. Augustine, Simeon, Zachary, David with a harp, St. George and the Holy Innocents. At the top of the central light is the figure of " Christ in Glory."

The new organ was built by Messrs. Harrison & Harrison, of Durham; the case was designed by Sir Robert Lorimer. There are three manuals, CC to A, 58 notes, two and a half octaves of radiating, and concave pedals CCC to F, 30 notes; speaking stops 26 and couplers 8. There is a total of 34 drawn-stops. The draw-stop jambs are at an angle of 45 degrees to the keyboards. Solid ivory heads are used. The action is tubular pneumatic, except the manual to pedal couplers, which will be mechanical. C equals 517 vibrations per second at 60 degrees Fahrenheit. The blowing is done by discus fans and an electric motor, made by Messrs. Watkins & Watson, of London.

---

# WYGGESTON GRAMMAR SCHOOL.

*" Labore et Honore."*

THE Memorial takes the form of a Cenotaph, which was unveiled on Monday, July 10th, 1922, by Major-General H. L. Croker, C.B., C.M.G., and dedicated by the Lord Bishop of Peterborough.

The architect was Colonel J. C. Baines, an Old Wyggestonian.

The Roll of Honour contains Two Hundred and Two names, and has upon it the following inscription: " *The Roll of the Masters and Old Boys of the Wyggeston Grammar School who have given their lives for their King and Country.*"

The War Memorial Fund was used for helping pupils proceeding to the Universities, preference being given to the sons of men who fought in the War.

# DERBY SCHOOL

*" Vita hominis sine literis mors est."*

**A** BEAUTIFUL obelisk formed of a single column of Portland stone is the Memorial at this School. It stands in front of the main entrance to the School and on it are inscribed Sixty Nine names; two more are yet to be added. The inscription on the centre of the base is: *"To the memory of the Old Boys of Derby School who fell in the Great War, 1914-1918."*

The Memorial obelisk and the planning and laying out of the forecourt were the design of Sir Reginald Blomfield, R.A.

The unveiling ceremony was held on Armistice Day, November 11th, 1921. The service commenced with the hymns " All people that on earth do dwell " and " For all the Saints." Then followed an address by the Bishop of Derby, in which he said : " A School Memorial was —to him, at least—the most moving of all memorials. It went to the roots of humanity. On a similar spirit of sacrifice and comradeship a world peace might be built."

Between two ranks of scholars the congregation proceeded to the Memorial, where the Great Silence was observed. The Headmaster read the Roll of Honour, and Lieutenant-Colonel G. A. Lewis, C.M.G. (an Old Derbeian) who was in command of the 5th Sherwood Foresters in France, unveiled the Memorial. He said that the Great Silence was the method of keeping in their minds the moment when the enemy realised the failure of their bid for world-power.

Alderman Laurie, the Chairman of the Governors, stated that 62 per cent. of the Old Boys who served gained commissions, 20 per cent. laid down their lives, 70 per cent. gained decorations, and 54 were mentioned in despatches.

The Bishop of Derby then dedicated the Memorial, and the O.T.C. buglers sounded the " Last Post " and the " Reveille."

The Cadet Corps was then reviewed by Lieutenant-Colonel Lewis.

A Scholarship Fund has been formed for the education of relatives of the Fallen.

DERBY SCHOOL MEMORIAL

# HYMERS COLLEGE, HULL

*" High merit, high reward."*

THE new Memorial Hall was formally opened on Armistice Day, November 11th, 1924, by the Right Hon. Lord Gorell, C.B.E., M.C., M.A., who unlocked the door of the Hall with a silver key handed to him by the architect.

The Memorial Tablet was unveiled by H. R. Ferraby, the son of an Old Hymerian who fell in the War.

The Memorial Building was designed by Mr. John Bilson, F.S.A., the architect of the original School Buildings. The Hall is 54 feet 9 inches long and 29 feet wide, and will accommodate about 300 people. The floor is of oak, the walls are panelled with oak up to the window sills, and the open timber roof is of pitch-pine left in its natural colour.

An open porch outside the south entrance of the main building gives access to a wide corridor, which leads to the Hall. This corridor has a marble floor, an enriched plaster ceiling, and its walls are panelled entirely in oak. The tablet is placed in a recess in one of the side walls of the corridor, and is a columned and pedimented structure framing the three panels which bear the inscriptions. The panels are of bronze and were executed by the Bromsgrove Guild. Inscribed on the centre panel are the words: *" Remember those of this School who, at the call of King and Country, left all that was dear to them, endured hardness, faced danger, and by the path of duty and self-sacrifice passed out of the sight of men into the safe keeping of God, giving up their own lives that others might live in freedom and peace. 1914-1918."*

The panels on either side bear the names of the Fallen, One Hundred and Seventeen in all.

The carving in oak has been executed by Mr. George Haughton, of Worcester; the School Arms in the pediment were painted by Mrs. Anderson (the Art Mistress of the School). Three Windows on the opposite side of the corridor are the work of Mr. J. C. N. Bewsey, and contain in the upper lights the Arms of the Empire and its dependencies. In the lower lights are represented the Three Virtues, and in the side lights the Arms of the towns prominent in the War. The quarries in the background are covered with the badges of representative north-country regiments.

A Memorial Scholarship was instituted, to be known as the " Hymers College Memorial Scholarship."

HYMERS COLLEGE MEMORIAL

# DENSTONE COLLEGE

*" Lignum crucis arbor scientiæ."*

THE Memorial was designed by Sir Aston Webb & Son; the sculptor was Mr. Alfred Drury, R.A. On an approach of three steps is a plinth of Portland stone, 12 feet high, on the face of which are the words: "*Laus deo. In memory of the boys of Denstone who gave their lives in the Great War. R.I.P.*" On two sides of the pedestal are wreaths in bronze encircling the dates " 1914 " and " 1919." On the top of the plinth, looking out from the centre of the Lonsdale Quadrangle, is a figure in bronze of St. George, clad in full armour. The statue is 8 feet high. The figure is holding a sword by the blade so that the hilt is stretched as a cross over the countryside of wood and meadowland. The face expresses tenderness and strength.

In the Ante-Chapel have been placed stone tablets, on which are inscribed the names of the One Hundred and Seventy who fell in the War. In the canopy above is the School Crest.

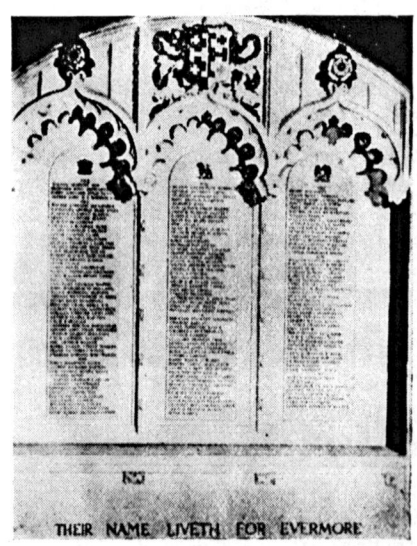

THEIR NAME LIVETH FOR EVERMORE

The unveiling ceremonies took place on June 25th, 1925, when Colonel C. P. Heywood, C.M.G., D.S.O., Chief Staff Officer of the

Aldershot Command and a grandson of Sir Percival Heywood, Bart., the Founder of the College, performed the unveiling. The Memorial was dedicated by the Bishop of Lichfield.

The service commenced with " Sons of St. Chad," sung to music played by the 2nd Battalion North Staffordshire Regimental Band. Then the Headmaster read the lesson from Wisdom iii, 1-9, and prayers were said by the Provost. The Rev. Prebendary F. A. Hibbert, who was Headmaster during the War period, read the Roll of Honour. The " Last Post " was then sounded, followed by a short silence, and the " Reveille." Colonel Heywood then said: " We do well to honour those who fell in the Great War, and the Roll of Remembrance of their sacrifice will broadcast its message far and near, now and hereafter. As a nation we came through it strained almost to breaking point, but not broken. Let us remember those years, 1914-1918, how in that great crisis the British Empire went through united. Was not this the message of all War Memorials? Were they not signs pointing with pride to the past, to the future with confidence? May its tale of duty nobly done inspire us and those who come after us with high ideals of life and conduct! "

Wreaths were laid during the playing of Elgar's " Pomp and Circumstance." The hymn " O Valiant Hearts " was sung, and the Benediction and the National Anthem closed the ceremonies.

---

# SUTTON VALENCE

HE Memorial Tablet, erected in the Main Hall of the School, was unveiled on Friday, June 29th, 1923, by Viscount Chelmsford, G.C.S.I., ex-Viceroy of India, and dedicated by the Headmaster, the Rev. W. W. Holdgate.

The ceremony took place after the annual prize distribution. Mr. C. C. Rogers, Chairman of the Old Suttonians' Association, referred to the Old Suttonians in every part of the world who placed their services at the disposal of their King and Country—in Canada, Australia, New Zealand, South Africa and far-off Alaska. One travelled 3,600 miles by a dog train to enlist. Out of the 613 Old Boys who left the School, between 1883 and 1917, 187 (or

30 per cent.) joined the Forces. The total Service List was 209. Thirty decorations were won, including 11 D.S.O., 13 M.C., 1 D.F.C. and 1 M.M.

Mr. Rogers then read the names of the Fallen, and the hymn " For men who heard their Country's call " was sung, followed by a prayer. Viscount Chelmsford pulled aside the Union Jack, revealing a Bronze Tablet, on which are inscribed the names of the Forty Two Fallen, surmounted by the School Crest. Above the names is written: " *To the memory of those Suttonians who gave their lives in the War, 1914-1918, this Memorial has been erected by their Schoolfellows.* " Below the names are the words: " *Their name liveth for evermore.* "

SUTTON VALENCE MEMORIAL

Viscount Chelmsford then said: " There never was a war when those words, ' We who survive,' connoted so much." He wondered whether they remembered the story of Valiant's death from " Pilgrim's Progress "—" So he passed over, and all the trumpets sounded for him on the other side. Clarion call of victory, of pride, of triumph."

At the conclusion of the ceremony the hymn " Praise my soul the King of Heaven " was sung and the " Last Post " was sounded.

A short musical programme was given by the Scholars under the direction of Dr. Henniker.

# KINGSWOOD SCHOOL

HE School Memorial takes the form of a Chapel in Gothic style of architecture from designs by Messrs. Gunton & Gunton, of London. The Roll of Honour contains One Hundred and Sixteen names. The Chapel was opened by the Rev. Marshall Hartley, Chairman of the Governors, on June 23rd, 1922.

KINGSWOOD SCHOOL MEMORIAL.

---

# GRESHAM'S SCHOOL

*" All Worship be to God only."*

WING to building reconstruction and consequent difficulties, no definite War Memorial is yet in existence. The Chapel has several new adornments, which will be included in the Memorial.

# LEIGHTON PARK SCHOOL

THERE are two forms of Memorials at this School. One is a War Memorial Board erected in the School Hall by the Governors. This Board is made of English oak and the names of Twenty Eight who fell are inscribed upon it, let into the panel in black ebony, with the following inscription: " *They died for great ideals* " at the foot, and the dates " 1914," " 1918 " at the top corners.

The other form of Memorial was a Scholarship for £50 a year for three years for sons of Old Boys, and a " Place of Remembrance," both given by the Old Boys' Association. The Place of Remembrance is situated opposite the School Hall; on the raised terrace is the Helio-chronometer, situated on a pillar on which is a brass plate with the words: " *Erected by Old Leightonians in memory of their comrades who gave their lives in the Great War and to commemorate the foundation of a Memorial Scholarship.*"

There was no public opening, but every year, about Armistice Day, attention is drawn to the duty of those now living, so to live as to prevent war in the future; and mention is made of those Old Boys whose names appear on the Tablet.

This Memorial of a small school is unique in its simplicity, and it is well that a quiet place of remembrance be set aside for contemplation of the greater problems of life; to remember that in the midst of life we are in death. Those few moments of thought will, in generations to come, count much for happiness in after years, both to the boys them-selves and to the nations of the earth.

The architects were Messrs. F. D. Rowntree and R. Thorp, and the builders Messrs. Nicholls & Sons, of Gloucester. The Sundial was supplied by Messrs. Fenning & Co., of Hammersmith, and the Helio-chronometer by Messrs. Negretti & Zambra, of London. The Sundial brickwork and paving stone were supplied by Messrs. Goodall & Co., of St. Mary's Butts. It is interesting to note that the boys of the School actually helped in the erection of the Place of Remembrance, for they laid the stone paving. The Oak Panel was supplied by Mr. A. R. Smee in association with Messrs. White, Allom & Co.

LEIGHTON PARK SCHOOL—GARDEN OF REMEMBRANCE

# MARLBOROUGH  COLLEGE

*" Virtute Studio Ludo."*

THE Memorial Hall stands on the ground to the west of the main College buildings, joined to the Chapel (designed by the late G. F. Bodley) by stone steps leading down to a brick-paved forecourt.

In the centre of this forecourt is a hexagonal-shaped pool, with a floor of blue and gold mosaic. Round the wide surrounds of the pond are six flower-pots especially designed to represent the six years of the War (1914-1920).

The front terrace is of York stone, with one square of green Connemara marble in the axis of each entrance door to the Memorial Hall. The facade towards the forecourt forms two entrances, separated by eight stone columns. The entrance doors to the Hall have bronze ornamental handles.

The vestibule is 19 feet square, with a flat-domed ceiling. The paving here is of slate and Portland stone. Seven steps lead to a square opening, bordered with Hopton Wood stone, while on the lintel, in scarlet letters, is the solitary word *" Remember."* The inner oak lobby gives access, through leather-covered doors, to the ambulatory circle, situated behind the seats in the Hall. All the interior ballustrades, lamp-shades and seven $18\frac{1}{2}$ feet windows are in oak. Beneath these windows are Commemorative Tablets cut in Ancaster stone by Mr. Lawrence Turner, an Old Boy of the School.

These Tablets, situated on the back wall of the circle, are tinted grey and red, and contain the names of Seven Hundred and Thirty Three Old Boys, Seven Assistant Masters and Nine members of the College Staff who died in the War, thus making a total Death Roll of Seven Hundred and Forty Nine.

Three thousand four hundred and eighteen served in the War, of whom 3 gained the V.C., 232 the D.S.O., 425 the M.C., 6 the D.S.C., 1 the G.C.B., 13 the K.C.B., 2 the G.C.M.G., 9 the K.C.M.G., 2 the K.C.I.E., 1 the K.C.V.O., and 2 Baronetcies.

To the right of the porticos of the front of the Hall is a rose garden, approached by a little brick gate-house. Above the archway is the inscription, in Greek characters, meaning : " We lie over the whole earth, but in this garden we still walk with those that remember the dead."

Within the Hall, the auditorium is semi-circular in shape, with tier upon tier of Indian greywood seats. Above the Proscenium is a cherub holding the College Crest.

The blue stage curtains are trimmed with gold, black and ivory, with the College Arms in silk. The heraldic colourings contrast with the blue-green silver colour of the window curtains.

Field-Marshal Sir Henry Wilson was, at the time of his assassination, President of the Old Boys' Club, and Lady Wilson, his widow, was present at the opening ceremony on May 23rd, 1925. During a fanfare of trumpets by Lancers, the doors of the Hall were unlocked by His Royal Highness the Duke of Connaught, K.C.B., to whom the architect, Mr. W. G. Newton, an Old Marlburian, and the builder, Mr. H. T. Holloway, were presented.

A Guard of Honour of 100, under Major C. I. F. Boughey, was drawn up on the terrace.

MARLBOROUGH COLLEGE MEMORIAL HALL

The service in the Chapel was conducted by the Chaplain, the Rev. J. M. Lupton, D.D., as follows: Hymn, " Now thank we all our God," versicles and responses; Psalm cxxii and the lesson from Ecclesiastes xliv, 1-15, read by Dr. Cyril Norwood; Croft's Anthem, " I am the Resurrection "; two prayers of a dedicatory character; hymn, " For all the Saints," concluding with the Benediction.

The Bishop of Salisbury said: " This passionate loyalty to our old schools is a mighty moral force in the land. It stands at the back of all those best things which our Public Schools have given."

His Royal Highness said: " They set an example of Duty, Patriotism and Chivalry. I am sure that those who follow after will show that same spirit."

MARLBOROUGH COLLEGE MEMORIAL HALL—INTERIOR

The Headmaster then said: " May it never come to pass that there will ever walk in that garden English men or boys who do not pay honour, gratitude and faithful memory to the Fallen. Did I not feel no sacrifice is in vain, had I not faith that Death shall be swallowed up in Victory! "

After the singing of the National Anthem, the School lined the Bath Road Drive, and the Rev. A. P. Wickham (Senior Prefect in 1874) and Mr. C. G. Furnivall (Senior Prefect, 1925) were introduced to the Duke of Connaught.

The first charge upon the Memorial Fund is for the Education of the sons of the Fallen.

The opening Concert in the new Hall was on May 23rd, 1925, when the following artists took part: The Salisbury Singers, Mrs. F. J. Hill (violinist), Mr. John Coates (tenor) and Miss Carmen Hill (soprano). Mr. B. Mason and Dr. J. W. Ivimey were the accompanists.

On Sunday, May 24th, Dr. Ivimey gave a fine rendering of the " Hallelujah Chorus," the sermon on this occasion being preached by the Bishop of Winchester. The text chosen was 1 Peter ii, 4-5.

The Bishop said: " To be a part of one great strength that moves and cannot die! The Memory of the Dead is in our hands, only our lives can make it. Ye are as living stones built upon a spiritual house. This Memorial, after all, is yours."

---

## CAMBRIDGE COUNTY HIGH SCHOOL FOR BOYS

*" Virtute et fide."*

THE War Memorial Tablet was unveiled and dedicated by the Rev. C. J. N. Child, M.A., former Headmaster of the School, on May 1st, 1924.

It is situated at the end of the School Hall and consists of three central panels and two larger side panels, surmounted by the School Crest and Motto, with the dates " 1914 " and " 1919." The whole is in an oak frame. There are Eighty Nine names inscribed on the panels. The inscription above the names on the centre panels is: "*These died for Britain,*" and below the names: "*Their spirit endureth for ever.*" The architect was Mr. I. Buckerfield.

The following is a short synopsis of the service: Hymn, "O Valiant Hearts"; three prayers, the first being the "Pater Noster"; then the lesson from Wisdom ii, 23 and iii, 5; then followed the prayer, "Remember O Lord," and unveiling and dedication of the Memorial. After the Nunc Dimitis came the address and the hymn "For all the saints." Except during the lesson, the assembly remained standing throughout the service.

CAMBRIDGE COUNTY HIGH SCHOOL MEMORIAL

# ST. GEORGE'S SCHOOL, HARPENDEN

*" Levavi Oculos."*

HE War Memorial Extension to the Chapel was dedicated by the Bishop of Kensington on February 17th, 1923. As part of the ceremony, Captain Evans, the Antarctic explorer, lit the Lamp of Maintenance in memory of the Fallen. This lamp had been acquired by the School from Talbot House (" Toc H ") in recognition of interest in social service.

Proceeding to the Altar steps, Captain Evans said : " I light this lamp in token of our undying memory of that bright flame of sacrifice, lit up for all generations by our elder brethren in the years of the Great War, and in token of the high and sacred duty, falling upon us all, to keep that light burning ever more brightly for the glory of God in Christ and in service of humanity."

The Bishop of Kensington then made an appeal that " In these days after War troubles the spirit of forgetfulness of self might be recaptured."

MEMORIAL TO SEVEN CAPTAINS OF THE SCHOOL

113

During the years 1914-1918 many memorials have been executed at the School, the first being the "Monk" Reredos by Mr. Edmund Hunter, early in 1915, commemorating the first Georgian to give up his life. Two windows designed by Mr. Alec Hunter (Old Georgian) were erected to the memory of three School Captains—the "Thomas" Window (1917) and the "Powers and Birch" Window (February, 1923).

The actual Roll of Honour, in the South Transept, on which the names are inscribed, was dedicated by the Headmaster, the Rev. Cecil Grant, on November 1st, 1919. The names and records of the Fallen, together with the full roll of all who served, are contained within twelve symbolic columns. These columns of carved wood covered with gesso are highly coloured and represent the diverse activities of the human spirit, leading through sacrifice to victory.

Over the columns is a frieze, on which white figures stand out in relief upon a background of blue, tinged more and more with rose as it nears the centre. The figures are of soldiers, sailors and women; the most central of them are in attitudes of devotion before the figure of Christ Triumphant, which surmounts the whole composition.

The frieze is interrupted in the centre, a space being left for an original painting of the Crucifixion. At present a Memling reproduction occupies the space.

The Christ Triumphant is in white relief upon a golden sun—the Sun of Righteousness—circumscribed by a rainbow, the symbol of reconstruction after storm. Beneath the Christ, but above the level of the frieze, stretch a pair of wings, upon which are the words: "*Sub umbra alarum tuarum*," and below the Crucifixion: "*Ad dei gloriam atque ut georgiani grati in sæcula sæculorum partis in bello magno scholæ sint memores.*"

Below this latter inscription is an unfinished space occupied by more colour reproductions, and still lower the School Motto: "*Levavi oculos.*"

Underneath the columns, running along the bottom, are the words: "*That they may be known upon earth. 1914-1918. Thy saving help among all nations.*"

Above the Roll are silk flags with the initials and regimental crest of each of the Dead, worked by their families.

Another work which is considered part of the War Memorial is a Wall Painting by Alec Hunter, occupying the wall of the east end of the Old School Room, in memory of the Seven School Captains who gave up their lives in the War, six of whom held the post in succession. It depicts Sir Galahad coming upon a procession of Guilds, Crafts and Husbandmen issuing from a cathedral. The knight is kneeling on the left of the painting, and has his eyes fixed upon a figure of Christ which appears hovering over the procession.

Mr. H. W. Horsley was the architect for the addition to the west end of the Chapel and for the Cloisters, which are to be completed in the near future.

Old Boys.—Number of Boys who served, 90; killed 19 (including two who died on Service); wounded, 18 (excluding those subsequently killed). 1 O.B.E., 2 M.B.E., 7 M.C. (1 with bar), 1 D.F.C., 1 Serbian Merit Medal, 6 mentioned in despatches.

Staff.—Served, 12; killed, 3. 1 M.C., 1 Croix de Guerre, 1 mentioned in despatches.

ST. GEORGE'S SCHOOL MEMORIAL

# UPPINGHAM SCHOOL

HE Memorial takes the form of a Shrine in the Chapel and the erection of the Great Hall. The Shrine, which records the names of the Four Hundred and Forty Seven Old Boys who fell in the War, was dedicated by the Bishop of Southampton on October 16th, 1921.

The Hall Memorial was unveiled by Lieutenant-General Sir C. E. Harington, G.B.E., K.C.B., D.S.O., on Dominion Day, July 1st, 1924. The architects were Mr. Ernest Newton & Sons. The late Mr. Ernest Newton, who died before the opening of the Hall, was an Old Uppingham Boy; his work was completed by his two sons.

UPPINGHAM SCHOOL MEMORIAL

At the opening service the band of the 5th Battalion Leicestershire Regiment played " See the Conquering Hero Comes " for the arrival of Generals Sir P. S. Wilkinson, C.B., K.C.M.G., and Sir Charles Harington, who were accompanied by Major F. Latham, D.S.O., commanding the Leicestershire Regiment depôt.

In the Hall the hymn, " O God our help in ages past," was sung with an orchestral accompaniment, conducted by Mr. R. S. Bennett, M.A., A.R.C.O., the School Music and Choir Master. Prayers were read by the Headmaster, and the speeches followed. The Headmaster said: " The Duty and Service—two splendid words—which inspired them were eternal in value, and in life, and these words must be the future watchword of the School, just as they had been of her sons in the past."

General Harington, in his address, said: " I was asked, after the Battle of Messines, to what success was attributed, and I thought there were three reasons, each beginning with a ' T '—the first, Trust; the second, Training; and the third, Thoroughness, all of which I consider good watchwords in life."

UPPINGHAM SCHOOL MEMORIAL—INTERIOR

At 3 p.m. the 470 members of the O.T.C. on parade, under the command of their officers, were inspected. Wireless and signalling operations were carried out, and the whole parade was marked by a spirit of thoroughness.

The Service Roll contains nearly 3,000 names.

UPPINGHAM SCHOOL MEMORIAL SHRINE

# ROYAL GRAMMAR SCHOOL, NEWCASTLE-ON-TYNE

THE Organ, erected as a Memorial to those One Hundred and Sixty Two Old Boys who died fighting for their Country, was unveiled by Major-General Montgomery at a ceremony in the School Hall on Friday, June 1st, 1923. Upon panels are inscribed the names and the words:

"*Dulce et decorum est pro patria mori*" and "*Hujus scholæ alumni qui pro patria decertantes haud indecoræ morti occuberunt.*" The carving is the work of Mr. Appleby of the School Staff, and the Memorial is the generous gift of Sir Arthur and Lady Sutherland.

Sir Alfred Palmer, Bart., was the Chairman at the ceremony, and the Lord Bishop of Newcastle dedicated the Organ. The lay clerks and choristers of Newcastle Cathedral rendered the " Russian Contakion," and Mr. William Ellis, Mus. Bac., F.R.C.O., played Chopin's " Funeral March " and gave a recital at the end of the ceremony.

Sir Arthur Sutherland quoted in his speech, as a message of sympathy to the bereaved parents, the immortal words of Abraham Lincoln: " I pray that our Heavenly Father may assuage the anguish of your bereavement and leave you only the cherished memory of the loved and lost, and the solemn pride that must be yours to have laid so costly a sacrifice upon the Altar of Freedom."

The following is a specification of the Organ: A two-manual and pedal organ of compass manual CC to C, 61 notes; pedal CCC to F, 30 notes. It embraces the following stops:—

Great Organ.—Double-stopped Diapason, Open Diapason, Solicional, Hohl Flute, Principal, Octave Quint, Super Octave.

Swell Organ.—Contra Fagotto, Oboe, Open Diapason, Rohr Flute, Gamba, Voix Celestes, Harmonic Flute, Dulciana Mixture, three ranks.

Pedal Organ.—Bourdon, Dolce Bass, Bass Flute.

Couples.—Great to Pedal, Swell to Pedal, Swell to Great, Swell Octave, Swell Sub-Octave, Swell to Great Octave, Swell to Great Sub-Octave, and Tremulent to Swell. Two combination pedals to Great and Pedal Organs, two composition pedals to Swell Organ.

The action is Binns' Tubular Pneumatic and the blowing is by electricity. The Organ was built by the firm of Messrs. Binns, of Leeds, to the specification of Alderman A. T. Robinson; the architects for the case were Messrs. Dunn, Hanson & Fenwicke, of Newcastle-on-Tyne.

ROYAL GRAMMAR SCHOOL MEMORIAL

# WELLINGTON COLLEGE

*" Heroes Herorum Filii."*

HE Memorial consists of a marble column, which is black surmounted by a white figure of St. George slaying the Dragon; the column is mounted on a white base and has a moulded plinth. In front of the column stands an unfurled Union Jack painted in its proper colours, in transparent paint, allowing the marble to show through like silk.

The walls of the apse in the chapel are covered with dove-coloured marble, panelled with white. The floor is of black and white marble and around the white cornice is the following: *" Their Name Liveth for Evermore."* The inscription below this is: *" To honour those Boys, Masters and Servants of this College who served and died for England in the Great War."* On the black slab beneath the flag are the following words: *" Heroes Herorum Filii,"* and on the base between the green marble wreaths is *" Amen." " MCMXIV—MCMXIX."*

The design was by Sir Edwin Lutyens, R.A. An illuminated manuscript book contains the names of the Seven Hundred and Seventeen men who fell; this book is placed immediately behind the Memorial column on a lectern.

Major-General Sir John Capper, K.C.B., undertook the panelling and decoration of the Old Hall in memory of his son.

A large sum was set aside for the formation of Scholarships, and the balance founded a War Exhibition Fund.

The magnificent Memorial was opened by His Royal Highness the Duke of Connaught, K.G., on October 24th, 1922.

The Service was in two parts: (1) The Memorial Service and (2) The Service of Dedication.

The Memorial Service began with the " Dead March in Saul," by Handel, and then followed the hymn, " O Valiant Hearts." Psalm XXVII was sung, followed by the lesson from St. John v, 24, read by Mr. Vaughan, a former Headmaster of the College. Then followed prayers, and the " Last Post " and " Reveillé " were sounded, and thus ended the Memorial Service.

The Dedication Service began with the hymn, " For all the Saints," followed by the lesson from Wisdom iii, 1-6, read by Mr. Malim, the present Headmaster. The Monument was then unveiled and a prayer of dedication was said. An anthem was sung, the words being "He that shall endure to the end the same shall be saved." The collect of the Foundation of the College was pronounced and the Benediction followed by Dr. Pollock, Bishop of Norwich. This service was terminated by Schubert's "Solemn March."

There were three Headmasters present at this ceremony: Mr. Vaughan, Dr. Pollock, and Mr. Malim, the present Master.

The following are extracts from the sermon preached by Dr. Pollock, Bishop of Norwich, whose text was Revelation xiv, 5: "Without fault before the Throne."

"There have been only five Masters of Wellington College. I stand in the middle, familiar alike with the two who came before me and those who have followed, into whose mourning I am permitted to enter to-day. Nor can I enter this chapel without thinking that here we set our aims more surely, more highly, than in seeking for our boys the spirit of wisdom and understanding . . . 'and to crown all the fear of the Lord.' This, the Prophet's exposition of the activities of the Spirit of God, as you are aware, comes into the great collect of the Confirmation Service; the thought that reminds me of my happiest associations with the hundreds of my own old pupils, alive or dead, as I think of the spiritual link between us when those confirmation days used to make us not only allies and friends but, best of all, friends in the Lord."

"England must not allow, at home or abroad, the comrades of the trenches to be rivals now, who only grasp at the spoils of victory or the stolen fruit of self-contained aims. There are hundreds and hundreds of Wellingtonians who have, one by one, on our far-flung battlefields, given of their best for the salvation of their country; they have adorned the history of their School and enriched its traditions, and now stand, redeemed by the Blood of the Lamb, without fault before the Throne of God."

> "They climbed the steep ascent of heaven
>     Through peril, toil and pain;
> O God, to us may grace be given
>     To follow in their train."

The Roll of Honour contains among the names those of Seven Masters and Eleven Servants who gave their lives.

WELLINGTON COLLEGE MEMORIAL

123

# BRADFIELD COLLEGE

A MEMORIAL CROSS of Portland stone is placed in the Quadrangle in front of " Big School," and opposite is the School Chapel. A paved pathway, bordered by roses, leads up to the Cross.

The fine engraving on the Cross embodies a design of grapes and foliage, while on the sides and three-tier base are inscribed the names of the Two Hundred and Fifty Seven Old Boys who fell. On the face of the Cross is the inscription : " *Pro Deo et patria. MCMXV.*" The number of the Fallen was so large that names have even been inscribed on the facets which surround the octagonal base of the Memorial.

On the south wall of the Chancel, in a simple frame, is placed the Roll of Honour, and immediately beneath it a " Toc H " lamp. Above is the flag of St. Andrew, the patron saint of the College. On either side of the Roll are golden figures of cherubs, while opposite are two similar ones bearing British flags. Along the lower walls of the Chancel are placed Battlefield Crosses, actually taken from the graves of fallen Old Boys whose graves now bear head-stones supplied by the Imperial War Graves Commission. On the south wall are placed seven crosses and on the north wall eleven; the names on all are quite legible. 500 Old Boys were reported wounded and 33 missing, while 1,400 served in the Forces.

The new Playing Fields and Pavilion were part of the War Memorial.

# ST. EDMUND'S COLLEGE, WARE

*" Avita pro fide."*

SPEECH Day, July 1st, 1924, was the day set aside for the unveiling of the War Memorial—a stained-glass Window and Bronze Tablet—to the memory of Seventy sons of St. Edmund's who gave their lives in defence of all that we Englishmen hold most dear—Freedom and Justice— a sacred cause.

The Galilee Chapel porch is the position chosen for the Bronze Tablet. This Chapel was the gift of His Eminence Cardinal Bourne, and a fine portrait of the Cardinal, painted by Sir John Lavery, R.A., was presented to the College by Colonel the Master of Sempill.

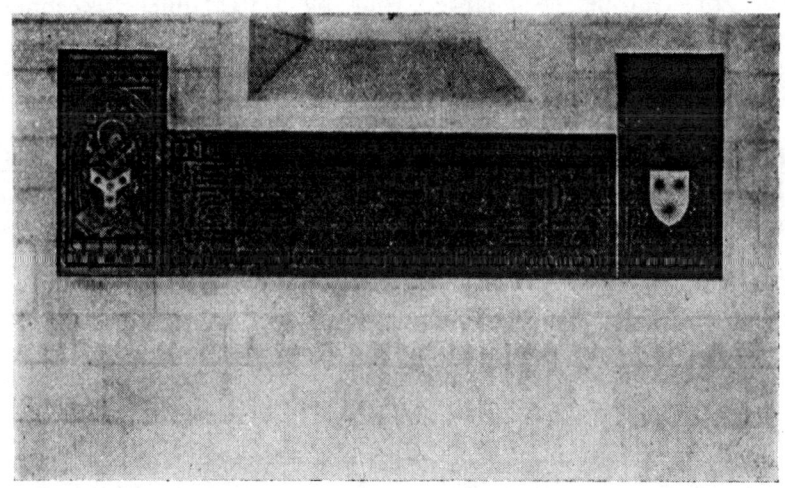

ST. EDMUND'S COLLEGE ROLL OF HONOUR

Among those present at the unveiling ceremony were Cardinal Bourne, the Bishop of Brentwood, King Manoel of Portugal, Sir H. Termingham, the Hon. Mrs. Forbes-Sempill, Canon Burton, Colonel Casson, and the Earl and Countess of Denbigh.

A system of lay houses has been re-adopted by the School. The chief houses are Talbot's and Challoner's, named respectively after Bishop James Talbot, who brought the School to "Old Hall" in 1769, and Bishop Challoner, who opened the School at Strandon in 1749. Each house will accommodate fifty lay scholars. Douglas House, built by Bishop Douglas in 1795, is entirely for boys who intend to follow an ecclesiastical vocation.

Some six scholarships were founded during the year 1924, two of £50 per annum for the whole period of the school career, guaranteed by the Old Boys' Association.

The Guard of Honour was inspected by the Earl of Denbigh, who also unveiled the Tablet. This was the gift of the Old Boys' Society, who also repaired the fabric of Pugin's beautiful Church. Lord Denbigh said : " We had hopes that a war would not again deface the history of Europe, but there is still a lot of human nature about, and in the face of the uncertainties of life, of power and the use of power, it is well that England should ever be ready. Not by apathy, not by forgetfulness, can the peace of Europe be guarded, but by watchfulness, keenness and readiness to sacrifice."

The Galilee Chapel allows the whole School to participate in the Liturgical Services of the Collegiate Chapel. The magnificent altar, above a plain table of alabaster, possesses a superb reredos in gold and red, the central panel is devoted to Our Lady of Pity, and in the side panels are figures of St. George and St. Peter.

Later in the day a Latin Play was performed in the New Hall. The play, entitled " Sauropolemopompus," was written by the Rev. R. Knox, M.A., it being produced by the Rev. A. B. Purdie, M.A.

---

ST. EDMUND'S COLLEGE MEMORIAL ALTAR
IN THE GALILEE CHAPEL

# DEAN CLOSE SCHOOL, CHELTENHAM

*" Verbum Dei Lucerna."*

IN years to come, November 1st, 1923, will be a memorable day to all Old Boys who retain any regard for the School, for on that day the New Chapel, the School Memorial, was dedicated by the Bishop of Gloucester. Dr. Flecker met the Bishop at the door, and the procession entered whilst the twenty-fourth Psalm was being sung. The Roll of Honour, containing One Hundred and Twenty names, was read by Mr. Ellam, and buglers sounded the "Last Post" and "Reveille." Then followed the hymn "All things are Thine," a shortened form of Evening Prayer, and the anthem "Glorious and powerful God." Archdeacon Gardner read the lesson, and the Bishop preached his sermon from the text "Except the Lord build a house." After the sermon the hymn "For all the Saints" was sung, and the service concluded with the Benediction and the first stanza of James Ellroy Flecker's version of the National Anthem.

The Annual Commemoration will take place on All Saints' Day. The first Commemoration Service was held in the evening of the day of dedication, when the Bishop of Chelmsford was the preacher.

The Service Roll of the School contains 663 names; 66 M.C., 9 D.S.O. and 2 C.M.G. were included in the decorations won.

The Chapel is of red brick with stone tracery windows. The decadence of stonecraft in Gloucestershire made the cost of the local product prohibitive. The building is 100 feet long, the Chancel has a breadth of 25 feet and the North Nave of 30 feet, while the ridge of the roof is 54 feet above the ground. The axis of the building is north and south. There are six large windows on the south side and five on the north. The middle bay of the Nave, on the north side, will contain the organ, and behind it a vestry. The heating apparatus is in the basement of the vestry. Fine canopy woodwork will be placed between the brickwork of the bay windows. It is hoped that the east and west windows and the remaining eleven smaller windows will all be of stained glass.

The building is so constructed that there is a very pleasing echo, reminiscent of some of our older abbeys.

Mr. L. Barnard was the architect for the exterior of the Chapel, and Mr. A. L. Iredale was responsible for the interior furnishing.

DEAN CLOSE SCHOOL MEMORIAL

---

# TETTENHALL COLLEGE

*" Timor Domine initium sapientæ"*

REMEMBRANCE DAY, November 11th, 1921, began with the ordinary routine of the College. At 11 a.m. the whole School gathered in the "Big School" to observe the National Two Minutes' Silence. Half an hour later the School assembled in the Chapel for a short service, conducted by the Headmaster. The main function of the day was the unfurling, by Mrs. Bulloch, of the Flag she had kindly presented to the School.

The ceremony took place at the Playing Field at Newbridge, the verandah of the New Pavilion acting as a platform. Dr. Lees said that the idea of giving the playing field had originated among the Old Boys, and also described the plans they had for improving the gift. He appealed for funds to pay off the mortgage which still remained on the field.

The Senior Boy presented a bouquet to Mrs. Bulloch, who proceeded to unfurl and haul up the Flag. The Headmaster thanked her for the generous gift, and Mr. Whalley seconded the unanimous vote of thanks. Mr. Butler was the donor of the Flagstaff, accessories, and a similar vote of thanks to him was seconded by Mr. Hall. The Senior Boy expressed gratitude to Dr. Lees for presiding, and the vote of thanks was seconded by Mr. Morley.

In the evening a firework display was given, and a supper followed in the decorated dining hall. The Headmaster proposed the toasts of " The King " and " The Fallen Old Boys," the latter being drank in silence. After toasts had been proposed to those who had helped, the Staff and the Prefects, Dr. Lees rose to propose " The Headmaster," a toast received with musical honours by the whole School.

The following is the address given by Mrs. Bulloch on presenting the Flag to the School : —

" Mr. Chairman, Mr. Headmaster, Staff, Boys of Tettenhall College, Ladies and Gentlemen. It is a great privilege to present this Flag to the School, and I am glad that the Flag hung in the College Chapel this morning. It gives it the spiritual significance I want it to hold for all generations of Tettenhall Boys. You will see that you have the School Colours, about which I need hardly speak because I know what an inspiration they always are to all of you. I am glad to feel that your Colours will go to the top of the mast for every match you play, and I hope that in all your sport, as well as in all your lives, you will nail your colours to the mast and never lower them, or disgrace them for any consideration whatsoever. I want to call your attention to the emblem on this Flag. There is your own Coat of Arms—and I think the present and recent generations of Tettenhallians have done a great deal to bring honour and respect to that fine Coat of Arms—instituted over 58 years ago. The other emblem is of particular importance on this Remembrance

Day—it is just a simple laurel wreath, the simplest and most honourable symbol of tribute we can give to the memory of our Old Boys who made for us the Great Sacrifice in the War. As this is a Memorial Flag, I think it is only right that this symbol should find a place on it. It encircles the words " Tettenhall College," and underneath a motto that I know is often used in the College. The spirit of it has certainly made the letters " T.C." stand for a spirit that can endure to the end. It is my own motto, and knowing the spirit of Tettenhall College, I have presumed to give it to you as a watchword that may help you in your sport, in your work, in your whole life. Remember that this was the motto that enabled you to carry on during the dreadful years of war. Before I finish I wish to thank Miss Williamson and Mr. Williams for the very great help they gave me in preparing this Flag. Their work has been very considerable. I have now the honour to ask the Headmaster to accept the Flag and undertake its custody on behalf of the School, as my tribute, not only to the Old Boys who have fallen, but to a School where such a fine spirit exists and where so much is done to make our boys worthy citizens of a great and glorious Empire."

TETTENHALL COLLEGE MEMORIAL

# WELLINGBOROUGH SCHOOL

*" Salus in arduis."*

HIS dignified Memorial, a Chapel in the English Renaissance style, was planned by Mr. Talbot Brown, the Architect.

The Memorial Chapel was dedicated by the Bishop of Peterborough on Commemoration Day, November 14th, 1924.

Massive oak panelling surrounds the Sanctuary. The School Arms and Motto are emblazoned above a suitable inscription and the five panels recording the names of the One Hundred and Eighty One who fell in the War, of which number Four were Masters.

The Communion rails are of oak, as is the organ screen, which is carved and gilded. The organ is situated on the North Wall of the Chapel.

Various adornments were made to the Chapel; on the roof are the monograms and arms of Canterbury, Peterborough, the Universities of Oxford and Cambridge, London and Manchester; the East Window portrays St. Michael, St. George, St. Joan, St. Martin of Tours, St. Alban and the Warrior Saints of France and England, surmounted by the arms of Peterborough and the School.

Mr. Knight made the Altar furniture, which is of bronze gilded after the Italian Renaissance style. The frontal Altar cloth is of blue and gold brocade, while the pavement of the Chancel is of black marble. The carpet is a fine example of Afghan work.

Two points during the service were of note : the fine rendering of Psalm XLVI and the sounding of the " Last Post " by Bugler C. C. Ellis.

One Thousand and Sixty Old Boys served in the Forces.

WELLINGBOROUGH MEMORIAL CHAPEL —INTERIOR

# DURHAM SCHOOL

*" Schola Dunelmensis."*

THE Memorial takes the form of a School Chapel in the Gothic style, the present buildings being two-thirds of the complete design. The Chapel, designed by the late W. H. Brierley, of York, was dedicated on September 30th, 1926, by the Bishop of Durham, assisted by the Dean of Durham, and the Headmaster. After the First Lesson the Ninety Eight names of those on the Roll of Honour were read by the Headmaster.

The words of the dedication were pronounced by the Bishop, who preached a sermon, in which he said: " The dedication of this Memorial Chapel must be a matter of genuine satisfaction to all connected with Durham School. It is a matter of real regret that the eminent architect had not lived to see its dedication. This Chapel will perpetuate the names of the Old Dunelmians who fought and fell in the Great War. Their names are carved on the columns—we recall them as we knew

DURHAM SCHOOL MEMORIAL CHAPEL

them, in the beauty and ardour of boyhood—we recall them in the budding glory of manhood. The proudest works of man crumble and fall to dust. There is that in us which can rise out of the perishing and lay firm hold on the Everlasting. In the flux of time we can anchor on the Rock of Ages."

At the end of the service, after the singing of the National Anthem, the "Last Post" was sounded by four of the School Buglers stationed in the west doorway. During the service the sun shone directly into the Chapel and brought the message of cheerfulness and hope.

> *"They shall not grow old, as we that are left grow old,*
> *Age shall not wither nor the years condemn,*
> *At the going down of the sun and in the morning*
> *We will remember them."*

Many gifts have been presented to the Chapel, in the nature of Memorials, by families who lost relatives in the War. Among these gifts are: A Window, A Bible, the Altar with Chalice, Paten and Cross Candlesticks, a Kneeling Desk, Alms Dish, an Altar Book and the Organ and East Window.

DURHAM SCHOOL MEMORIAL CHAPEL—INTERIOR

# MALVERN COLLEGE

*" Sapiens qui prospicit."*

THE bronze figure of St. George in the Quadrangle was executed by Mr. Alfred Drury, R.A. As the patron saint of Chivalry, and representing England, it is the symbol of the best qualities in the character of English manhood and those most worth while striving for. The pedestal is of Portland stone, Gothic in character: it was designed in keeping with the general style of architecture of the buildings and stands about 20 feet high. On the front of the pedestal is the College Crest, and below it the words: *" To our brothers, 1914-1919."* On the back of the pedestal is a small representation of St. George and the Dragon.

The panels in the Chapel, nine in number, are placed on the north wall; the lettering on them is in inlaid white hollywood. Above these panels are three small tablets, the centre one bearing the inscription: *" Here are recorded the names of 457 members of this College who gave their lives for their Country in the Great War "* and the College Coat of Arms. The side tablets bear the dates " 1914 " and " 1918." They were designed by Mr. W. J. Blomfield.

The Dedication Service was conducted on Saturday, July 8th, 1922, by the Bishop of Worcester, who was accompanied by Archdeacon James (former Headmaster). The first part of the service was held in the Chapel. The anthem was " Comes at times a stillness as of even." It was followed by an address, in which the Bishop of Worcester said: " The loss sustained by the War can only be described as the wiping out of a generation; those who are left have to take up a double duty. There remains a great task of recovery, to see that everything is done to make the world better, purer, happier and more united. Those who died had the vision, those who live have the work to do."

After this address the congregation joined in the ceremony at the statue which was unveiled by Admiral Sir F. C. Doveton Sturdee, one hundred Cadets forming the Guard of Honour. The Admiral said: " I unveil this Memorial to the glory of God and in memory of those young men who volunteered for the Front and laid down their lives in defence of their Country." Subsequently he urged his hearers not to forget the sacrifice made in building up our vast Empire, and to assist in maintaining the Empire for the good of civilisation.

Buglers sounded the " Last Post " and " Reveille," and the Bishop of Worcester pronounced the Benediction. Wreaths were laid at the foot of the Memorial by relatives, scholars and Old Boys.

MALVERN COLLEGE MEMORIAL

K

# CHARTERHOUSE SCHOOL

*" Deo dante dedi."*

A VERY beautiful Chapel has been built to the designs of Sir Giles Gilbert Scott, R.A., on a hill adjoining the School grounds at Godalming.

On the foundation stone, which was laid by the Right Rev. Dr. Randall, Archbishop of Canterbury, on June 7th, 1922, is inscribed: *" Deo dante dederunt."* Over the south-west door, inside the Chapel, is inscribed: *" They went everyone straight forward "*; over the south-east door: *" Empti estis pretio "*; over the north-west door: *" Of thine own we have given thee,"* and over the north-east door: *" Absentes adsunt."*

Some of the panelling and seating of the Chapel, and the case of the organ has yet to be completed.

The east end of the Chapel, including the Reredos and Sarcophagus, was the gift of Sir Henry Seymour King, a Governor.

The Cloisters are the School's South African War Memorial.

A portion of the Memorial Fund is set aside for the purpose of providing education at Charterhouse for the sons of Carthusians killed in the War.

On June 18th, 1927, the anniversary of the occupation of Charterhouse at Godalming in 1872, the new Chapel was consecrated. About 2,000 persons were present at the ceremony. The Guard of Honour, formed by the O.T.C., was inspected by Field-Marshal Lord Plumer, who later unveiled the Screens near the west end of the Chapel, which bear the names of the Six Hundred and Eighty Six Carthusians who fell. Altogether 3,000 Carthusians served.

The Bishops of Southwell, Guiana, Monmouth, Newcastle, and Sheffield, the Bishop Designate of Guildford, Bishop Talbot (late Bishop of Winchester), the Bishop of Winchester and the Archbishop of Canterbury took part in the service of consecration. Lord Plumer spoke of the War as a complete vindication of the English Public School training in enabling unexperienced soldiers to take responsible posts successfully: " The Memorial Chapel is a tribute to the past and an inspiration for the future. . . ."

After the hymn, " For all the Saints," was sung to the tune of Dr. Vaughan Williams, the Bishop of Winchester consecrated the building and gave an address. Bishop Talbot (O.C.) offered a prayer, and the Archbishop of Canterbury pronounced the Blessing.

In the evening Dr. H. G. Ley, Precentor of Eton, gave a recital on the new organ, and three numbers of Brahms' " Requiem " were sung by the choir.

It is interesting to note that the old Chapel was consecrated by the then Bishop of Winchester about one hundred years ago.

CHARTERHOUSE SCHOOL MEMORIAL CHAPEL

# HARROW SCHOOL

*"Donorum Dei dispensatio fidelis."*

HE War Memorial Building commemorating the names of the Six Hundred of Harrow's Sons who were killed in the War, was opened on Thursday, June 3rd, 1926. It had taken five years to erect. The architect was Mr. Herbert Baker.

The Memorial consists of an arcade and dome-shaped Shrine opposite the Chapel. The names of the Fallen are inscribed on the stone walls, and at the end of the Shrine is a Cenotaph, on which is a drawn sword. Around is an inscription in gold from Mr. Arkwright's hymn, "O Valiant Hearts." A bronze Cross, inlaid in black marble, is let into the paving in front of the Shrine. A stone balustrade reaches from over the Shrine terrace to the platform outside the Speech Room;

HARROW SCHOOL MEMORIAL BUILDING

the double staircase leads to the Upper Hall, and to the Fitch War Memorial Room—the gift of Lady Fitch in memory of her son. The Roll of Honour in gold is the gift of Mr. H. Yates Thompson.

The construction work was done by Holloway Brothers, and the joiner's work by Mr. A. Brockett and Mr. W. Penfold.

The service in the Chapel was attended by the Prime Minister (Mr. Stanley Baldwin), the Archbishop of Canterbury, the Dean of York (Dr. Lionel Ford, former Headmaster), Mrs. Butler (widow of Dr. Butler, late Master of Trinity College, Cambridge), and Dr. Cyril Norwood (the present Headmaster).

Dr. P. C. Buck played on the organ Chopin's " Prelude in E Minor." The hymn, " O God our Help in ages past," was sung. The Dean of York took the special prayers, followed by Dr. Cyril Norwood reading the lesson from Romans viii, 18-37. Psalms cxxi and cxii were sung by the choir, prayers were recited, and the hymn, " O Valiant Hearts," terminated this service.

HARROW SCHOOL MEMORIAL SHRINE

The second part was held at the Shrine, which was dedicated by the Archbishop of Canterbury, who concluded with the words: " And for our brother Harrovians who died the Death of Honour, let us make our prayers in the spirit of fellowship and hope." The Prime Minister, in his speech, quoted the words of Socrates: " And now the time is come for us to go our ways; I go to death, and you to life, and which of us hath the better lot is known to none but God." " There is a strange leaven at work to-day; it is devoting itself to social enquiry." "There is one question: ' Have we died in vain?'" The answer would depend on what superstructure they could build on the foundation that had been cemented in their blood.

The " Last Post " was sounded by buglers of the Royal Fusiliers, a two-minutes' silence was followed by the " Reveille," and the Archbishop pronounced the Benediction.

A large sum of money has been set apart for assisting the education of the sons of Old Harrovians.

---

# CRANLEIGH SCHOOL

Motto: " *Ex cultu robur.*"

THIS Memorial takes three forms; the first a Cenotaph, designed by Sir Edwin Cooper, situated in front of the School. This was erected by the Right Honourable Viscount Devonport, an Old Cranleighan, and was unveiled by Field-Marshal Sir W. Robertson, G.C.B., K.C.V.O., D.S.O., G.C.M.G., on July 26th, 1921. The names of the One Hundred and Thirty Eight who fell in the War are upon the sides of the Cenotaph. Above the list are the words: " *Ex cultu robur,*" and below: " *To the honoured memory of the Old Cranleighans who made the supreme sacrifice,* 1914-1918."

The Cricket Pavilion, erected in the School Playing Fields near the School by the Old Cranleighans' Society, was opened on July 28th, 1923, by Lieutenant-Colonel C. F. H. Greenwood, D.S.O., O.B.E., an Old Cranleighan also.

The third form of the Memorial were many alterations to the School Chapel, performed by members of the School Council.

CRANLEIGH SCHOOL MEMORIAL

# PERSE SCHOOL, CAMBRIDGE

*" Qui facit per alium facit per se."*

THE Memorial is in two portions, one a new playing field adjoining the old field and comprising ten or eleven acres; two, an oak tablet in the School Hall.

The Oak Tablet contains the names of the Eighty Five fallen, and above the names are the Coat of Arms and the School Motto, with the following inscription: "*These died for England.*" Below the names is the inscription: "*Their spirit endureth for ever.*" The tablet was unveiled by General Lord Horne in the presence of the Bishop of Ely, the Chairman of the Governors, the Headmaster, Scholars and relatives of the fallen, on May 25th, 1921. It was the work of Mr. Cyrus Johnson.

The playing fields form the main Memorial, and they have already been levelled and laid out, and it is hoped that they will be opened for cricket during 1927. The new fields, the property of the Trustees of the Perse School Tercentenary and the War Memorial Fund, which will shortly be known as "The Perse School Commemoration Trust," of which the Chairman will be Mr. Harold P. Cooke, will, together with the old fields, comprise nearly twenty acres.

---

# EPSOM COLLEGE

*" Deo non fortuna."*

A MEMORIAL Tablet has been in existence for some time in the Old School Chapel. On it are inscribed the names of the One Hundred and Thirty Eight who fell in the War. Above the five columns of names, in the centre, is the School Crest; on the left-hand side "*Pro patria,*" and on the right "*MCMXIV—MCMXVIII.*" The Roll of Honour contains One Hundred and Forty Five names—seven names are to be added to the Tablet when it is moved to the new Nave. The Nave has been added as a further Memorial from designs by Arthur Blomfield, M.A., and was dedicated by the Bishop of Winchester on February 21st, 1925.

EPSOM COLLEGE MEMORIAL

# KING EDWARD'S SCHOOL, BIRMINGHAM

*" Domine salvum fac regem."*

THE Memorial consists of eight Bronze Tablets, on which are inscribed the full names, rank and unit of each of the Two Hundred and Forty Seven killed in action or who died on service. The unveiling ceremony was conducted by Lieutenant-Colonel Sir John Barnsley on December 16th, 1920.

The Tablets, executed by the Birmingham Guild of Applied Arts, were placed in the great corridor leading to "Big School," which was designed by Sir Charles Barry about 1836. They were placed in this position in case the School should move into the country.

The Tablets themselves are in arched panels separated by pillars. Over each are the words "*Deo Laus.*" The first panel bears the School Coat of Arms and under it the inscription: "*These sons of the School, at their Country's call, gave their lives in the cause of liberty and right, 1914-1919.*"

KING EDWARD'S SCHOOL MEMORIAL

As a further memorial an Organ will be erected in the " Big School " during 1927.

About One Thousand Four Hundred and Eleven Old Boys served in the forces.

---

# KING'S SCHOOL, ELY

THE Memorial takes the form of an English Oak Wall Tablet placed in the Dining Hall. The designers were Messrs. Maile & Co., of Euston Road, London. The number of names inscribed on the Roll of Honour is Twenty Four. Special gifts of Communion Plate, Altar Vases and Candlesticks were made to the School Chapel.

KING'S SCHOOL MEMORIAL TABLET

# KING'S SCHOOL, CHESTER

*" Rex dedit, benedicat Deus."*

HE foundation of this School dates back to King Henry VIII—the founder of Trinity College, Cambridge.

The School Memorial consists of Bronze Tablets containing the names of Fifty Seven Old Boys of the School, and One Master, who fell in the War.

The Tablets were designed by Mr. C. H. Minshull (an Old Boy) and were cast by the Birmingham Guild.

The unveiling took place on July 29th, 1920, by Lieutenant-General Sir H. M. B. de Lisle, K.C.B., K.C.M.G., D.S.O., G.O.C., of the Western Command.

A Memorial Window, designed and executed by Messrs. Powell (makers of the windows in Liverpool Cathedral and of the Great East Window in the School Refectory) was also unveiled. This Window is symbolic of the virtues of " Valour," " Loyalty," " Patriotism " and

KING'S COLLEGE MEMORIAL

"Self-Sacrifice." In the centre light is King Arthur, with the legend: "*Such a sleep they sleep,*" and "*The men I love.*" The four other lights are filled, from left to right, by Sir Lancelot, with the inscription: "*A man with strength and will to right the wrong*"; Sir Galahad and the inscription: "*If I lose myself I save myself*"; King Arthur has on his right Sir Boras, with the inscription: "*Ever loyal man and true,*" and lastly, Sir Tristan, with his cry: "*Fear God, Honour the King.*" The upper lights have heraldic devices presenting the armorial bearings of the School, the City of Chester, the Episcopal Diocese and the Universities of Oxford and Cambridge. The smaller enrichments are the Fleur de Lys, the Portcullis, Tudor Rose, a Crown and Royal Cypher—all commemorative of the foundation of the School.

The opening of the Memorial was of military, ecclesiastical and civic nature, and there was a large attendance of Old Boys and relatives of the Fallen.

---

# HAILEYBURY COLLEGE

*"Sursum corda."*

THE actual Memorial is not yet completed. It is to include a New Dining Hall, to the north of the Quadrangle.

The names of the Five Hundred and Seventy Two who fell are carved on the marble Cloisters of the Quadrangle, and the names are also on the Roll of Honour in the School Library.

A stone Cross, designed by Sir Reginald Blomfield, R.A., an Old Haileyburian, has been erected in the centre of the terrace opposite the west door of the Chapel. It has upon it a Sword of gilded brass, upon which are the words: "*Vobis parta quies.*" The Cross itself is similar to those which were erected in the War Cemeteries in France, and stands upon a hexagonal base; it was unveiled by General Sir A. J. Godley, K.C.B., K.C.M.G., and dedicated by the Bishop of Southwell, Dr. Hoskyns, on July 7th, 1923. Both were Old Boys of the School. The following words appear on the plinth: "*In remembrance of those who did their duty; even unto death. 1914-1918.*"

The Endowment Fund also provided for Closed Exhibitions and Scholarships.

HAILEYBURY COLLEGE MEMORIAL

# IPSWICH SCHOOL

*" Semper eadem."*

THIS School is also known as Queen Elizabeth's School, Ipswich, thus showing its early foundation. The Mural Tablet Memorial, which was designed by Mr. H. Munro-Cautley, an Old Boy, is placed on the east wall of the south transept of the School Chapel. The carving was done by Mr. Saunders, stonemason, of Ipswich.

Lieutenant-General Sir E. A. H. Alderson, K.C.B., unveiled the Tablet at 2.15 p.m. on July 29th, 1922.

The Tablet is of stone, and on it, in three columns, are inscribed the names of the Seventy One Old Boys who fell in the War. On the top of the Tablet is a lion crouching upon flags, cannons, cannon balls and other instruments of destruction. Between the figure of the lion and the list of names is the inscription: "*When the power of the city shall seem great to you, consider then that it was purchased by valiant men and by men who knew their duty* "—Pericles. Below the names, at the sides, are the dates " 1914 " and " 1918," while in the centre is a wreath encircling the words: "*To the Glory of God and in proud Remembrance of the Old Boys of this School who gave their lives for their Country in the Great War.*"

The opening service was conducted by Rev. A. A. L. Gedge (O.I.). It began with sentences from the Burial Service, followed by the hymn " How bright these glorious spirits shine." Then followed four special prayers, including the " Pater Noster." Lieutenant-General Sir E. A. H. Alderson gave an address, in which he said: " This is a day memorable indeed in the history of the School, and one poignant in the hearts of many. To have a high ideal—do not be afraid; if a very high ideal of life and conduct comes within your vision—keep it, train yourself to it. Your ideal will be shining before you till it leads you to the golden gate. The five secrets of influence in the world are: Absolute straightness, absence of " side," sympathy, sense of humour, faith, and a high ideal may be added as a sixth."

The Tablet was then unveiled, and after the reading of the list of names Stainer's anthem " God so loved the world " was sung, and the service closed with the Benediction and National Anthem.

Four hundred and thirteen Old Boys served in the War, who won the following distinctions: 30 M.C. (2 with bar), 11 D.S.O. (1 with bar), 1 M.M., 1 D.F.C., 2 D.C.M., 3 C.M.G., 2 K.C.B., 4 O.B.E., 2 M.B.E., 10 mentioned in despatches, 2 Croix de Guerre and 1 Serbian Order of the White Eagle.

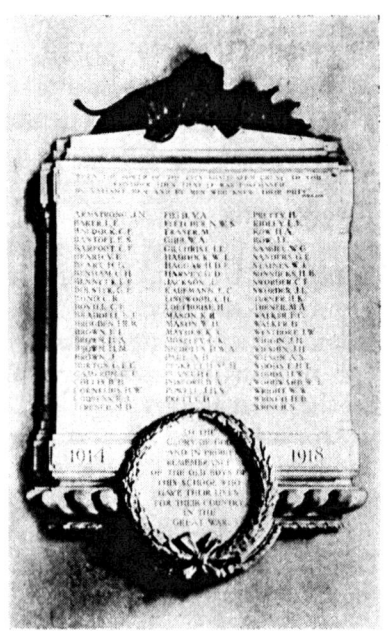

IPSWICH SCHOOL MEMORIAL TABLET

# SILCOATES SCHOOL

*" Clarior ex ignibus."*

ON Founder's Day, July 23rd, 1920—the centenary date of the School—there was unveiled in the entrance hall a large bronze Memorial Tablet, mounted on oak, recording the names of the Forty One (including Two Masters) on the Roll of Honour. The inscription is: *" This Tablet is erected by the boys present in Silcoates School on the occasion of the School Centenary, July, 1920." " In proud and loving memory of the Old Boys who fell in the Great War, 1914-1918."*

The Tablet was unveiled by Mrs. J. Stubley, of Batley, the mother of one of those named on the Roll.

When the School Chapel is completed the Tablet will be moved from its present site to a place in the Chapel.

The architects were Messrs. Maile & Son, of London.

SILCOATES SCHOOL MEMORIAL TABLET

# WEYMOUTH COLLEGE

*" Perseverando vincimus."*

HE Commemoration Day at this College was on Monday, July 25th, 1921. On this day, at 2.15 p.m., the simple and beautiful Memorial, set up in the College Chapel to the memory of the Eighty Four Old Boys who died as warriors in the Great War, was unveiled and dedicated.

The Memorial consists of Choir Stalls on the north and south sides of the College Chapel; there are eleven panels below the window on the west side; a central panel on the north side bears the College Arms and a corresponding panel on the south side, a carved shield of dedication with the inscription: *" To the memory of Old Weymouthians who fell fighting for their Country in the Great War, 1914-1919."* *" These Stalls are dedicated by their Schoolfellows past and present."* *" Perseverando vincimus."*

WEYMOUTH COLLEGE MEMORIAL

154

The panels at the west end of the Chapel are made of English oak; the wide upper moulding and band bears a design of the vine, oak, rose, etc. The centre panel in the upper half has upon it the College Arms; in the lower half there is written: "*To the Glory of God and in honoured memory of the Weymouthians who gave their lives for us, 1914-1919.*" "*Us they trusted, we the task inherit.*"

Below the central panels is a seat bearing the inscription: "*In memory of Francis Ritson, Captain Dorsetshire Regiment, killed in action June 17th, 1917.*" This seat was presented by Mrs. Ritson in

WEYMOUTH COLLEGE MEMORIAL PANELS

memory of her husband, and was designed by Mr. Basil Stallybrass, of Plymouth, and carved by Miss Pinwill, of Plymouth. Miss Pinwill also carved the Memorial Stalls, designed by Mr. H. W. Crickmay, architect, of Weymouth.

General Sir William Onslow, K.C.M.G., after a few soldierly phrases, unveiled the fine oak screen and choir pews. The dedicatory prayer was pronounced by Canon F. B. Sowter, assisted by Rev. F. E. Coryton and Rev. E. V. Tanner, M.C., the College Chaplain. The Headmaster, Mr. R. Conway, M.A., read the first lesson, and the Head Prefect, Mr. Lart, the second lesson. Canon Sowter's address dealt with " Service, sacrifice and immortality." He said : " The greatness of our heritage is the measure of our responsibility." The ceremony ended with the National Anthem and the hymn, " Soldiers of Christ Arise."

The Cadets, Scouts and Wolf Cubs were inspected.

The " Service Roll " of the College contains about 300 names.

---

# OAKHAM SCHOOL

*" Quasi cusores."*

THE Foundation Stone of the School Chapel was laid in July, 1924. The Chapel is built in the Gothic style, in keeping with the neighbouring Church in the parish, which is in the perpendicular form. The plan of the Chapel consists of a broad Nave with narrow aisles, which lead to the Narthex, or Ante-Chapel, at the west end. Over the Narthex is the Gallery for the Organ and Choir. The two shallow transepts between the Nave and the Chancel lead to an Apse, which is half a hexagon. The walls and windows are in Weldon stone, the roof and seatings in natural English oak. The accommodation is for 300 boys. The sculpture on the West Door symbolises the sacrifices, suffering and endurance of the War. It is the work of Mr. F. W. Sargant and was presented by his brother, the Headmaster. The inscription is : *" This Chapel was erected to the Glory of God and in memory of the Old Oakhamians who fell in the Great War, 1914-1919."*

On each side are the Memorial panels, with the inscription: "*Others they saved, themselves they did not save; therefore more glorious were the lives they gave.*" The books in the Chapel were the gift of the family of Dr. Wood (Headmaster, 1846-75), and valuable service was given on the Memorial Committee by Mr. Jerwood.

The Chapel was dedicated by the Bishop of Peterborough on October 29th, 1925. The sermon was preached by the Right Rev. J. G. F. Day (O.O.), Lord Bishop of Ossory, from the text "Let your light so shine" (Matt. v, 16).

The Roll of Honour contains Sixty Eight names.

Messrs. G. S. Streatfield & Atwell, of London, designed the Chapel, and the builders were Messrs. E. Bowman & Sons.

OAKHAM SCHOOL MEMORIAL CHAPEL - WEST DOOR

ST. LAWRENCE COLLEGE MEMORIAL CHAPEL.

ST. LAWRENCE COLLEGE MEMORIAL CHAPEL—INTERIOR

# ST. LAWRENCE COLLEGE, RAMSGATE

*" In bono vince."*

THIS College was formerly known as the South Eastern College, and changed its name in 1906 to St. Lawrence College. Its Memorial is a new School Chapel, now completed and dedicated by the Archbishop of Canterbury on Wednesday, June 8th, 1927.

In his address, the Archbishop spoke of the influences and associations of such a stately and beautiful edifice as being inestimable. He also referred to the new spirit which Arnold, of Rugby, introduced into English Public Schools by making the School Chapel the focus of its life.

The architect for the Chapel was Sir Aston Webb. The Old Boys' Club provided the Choir Stalls, Pulpit and Lectern; the Masters' Stalls are the gift of the father of three Old Boys who came safely through the War.

There is a Memorial Tablet at the School recording the names of the One Hundred and Thirty Two Old Boys who gave their lives in the Great War. This Tablet is of white marble with a surround of black and white Sicilian marble, veined, and surmounting it is the School Crest flanked by flags. There is inscribed on the Tablet: "*In honoured memory of the Old Boys of St. Lawrence College who gave their lives for their Country in the Great War, 1914-1919*"; and below: "*Never heroic heart was offered to death in vain. Erected by their Schoolfellows.*"

The names are arranged in three columns, and after each name is the rank and regiment. The Tablet will be moved later from the Library to the Chapel.

As a further part of the Memorial, there are Bursaries at the School to provide for the education of brothers and children of those who fell; there is also a new Library, as yet incomplete.

The following distinctions were gained by Old Boys: 1 V.C., 1 C.B., 3 C.M.G., 1 C.I.E., 5 C.B.E., 1 D.S.C., 2 D.C.M., 1 M.M., 23 D.S.O. (2 with bars), 1 M.S.M., 77 M.C. (5 with bars), 127 mentioned in despatches, 2 M.R.V.O., 13 O.B.E., 4 M.B.E., and many Foreign Orders.

# SHERBORNE SCHOOL

*" Dieu et mon droit."*

HE existing Chapel, particularly the Chancel, was greatly enlarged, and a new School staircase added. A commemorative Mural Tablet records the names of the Two Hundred and Eighteen Old Boys who died in the War. The designs were by Sir R. Blomfield, R.A.

The Chapel had been thrown out of porportion by the addition of the North Aisle in 1877, so that the addition to the Chapel has made the length proportionate to the breadth. The new Ante-Chapel and staircase are in a simple and dignified design, and were carried out in Ham Hill stone, a local product.

The Dedicatory Tablet, also of Hopton Wood stone, is placed between two windows. It records that : *" This Chapel was enlarged and this Ante-Chapel added in 1920-22 in loving memory of those Shirburnians who laid down their lives in the Great War, 1914-18. Nor love thy life, nor hate, but what thou liv'st live well: How long or short permit to Heaven."*

The inscriptions and the names of the Fallen are in plain letters of noble appearance.

Bishop Whitehead, of Madras (an Old Boy of the School), dedicated the Memorials on July 5th, 1922, when the order of service was as follows : Hymn, " Jesus lives, no longer now "; the Bishop's procession to the west end of the Chapel to receive the petition for consecration from the Headmaster; the " Pater Noster " and several versicles, said by the Bishop; Psalm xxiv, sung by the choir, and " Come Holy Ghost our souls inspire," sung with all kneeling; several prayers, followed by the sentence of consecration read by the Chancellor and ordered to be kept in the registry of the diocese; hymn, " Jesus where'er Thy people meet," followed by the Bishop's address; hymn, " O Valiant Hearts " and three Dedicatory Prayers; the reading of the Roll of Honour by the

Headmaster and the Dedication by the Bishop, concluding with the "Last Post." The clergy then passed down the staircase—the "Via sacra" of Remembrance. The hymn "Now thank we all our God" preceded the episcopal Benediction.

The Service Roll of the School contains 1,157 names, and the following distinctions were gained: 2 V.C., 58 D.S.O. (1 with two bars, 1 with one bar), 76 M.C. (3 with two bars, 8 with one bar), 3 Air Force Medals, 43 Foreign Distinctions, 137 mentioned in despatches, and 55 other British Orders.

---

# SHREWSBURY SCHOOL

*"Intus Sic Recte Ne Labore."*

THIS Memorial is situated at the meeting-place of all the avenues leading from the School. A bronze figure of Sir Philip Sydney in armour is situated on a rectangular plinth; beneath the figure is a bronze relief of "A scene in the trenches," above which is the legend "*Scholæ meæ alumnos agnosto.*" At the foot of the statue are the words "*Philippus Sidney Salopiensis,*" and on the back is a relief of Sir Philip Sydney's death at Zutphen.

The Memorial was unveiled by Lieutenant-General Sir Harold Walker, K.C.B., K.C.M.G., D.S.O. (O.S.), on May 24th, 1923, and dedicated by the Bishop of Chester (O.S.). It is interesting to note that the Burgomaster of Zutphen in person laid a wreath on the Memorial.

Mr. Brook-Kitchen was the architect; his design was a most happy one, commemorating and embodying the great Scholar, History Maker and Courtier of Elizabethan Times: a character-sublime, and fearless unto death—very dear to the hearts of Englishmen. The work was executed by Messrs. Foster & Dicksee; A. B. Burton, founder, and A. G. Walker, sculptor.

The Roll of Honour contains Three Hundred and Twenty Two names, inscribed on each side of the plinth. The School Arms are on the front below the relief.

SHREWSBURY SCHOOL MEMORIAL

163

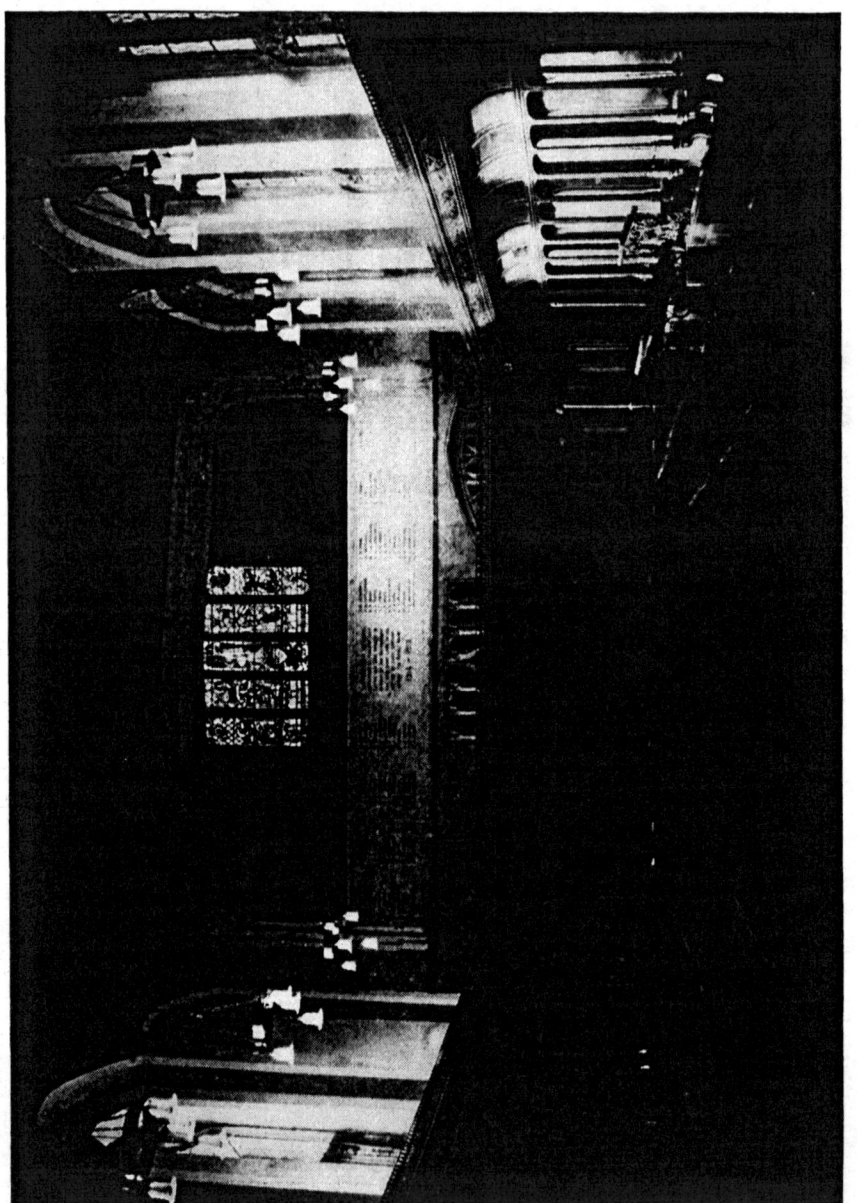

WARWICK SCHOOL MEMORIAL

WARWICK SCHOOL MEMORIAL WINDOW

# WARWICK SCHOOL

*" Altiora peto."*

THE School's War Memorial was dedicated by the Archdeacon of Coventry, the Venerable C. M. Blagden, on Armistice Day, November 11th, 1925.

The Memorial is in two parts: The Gallery and Vestry, for which the architect was Mr. E. P. Trepass, added to the west end of the existing Chapel; and the special West Window, the gift of the Headmaster and Mrs. Pyne in memory of their son, Eric Wilfred Pyne.

On the central stone in the front of the Gallery are inscribed the words: *" The extension of the Chapel, consisting of Gallery and Vestry, has been erected in memory of Old Warwickians who lost their lives in the service of their Country during the Great War, 1914-1918."* On either side are the names of the Eighty Four Boys and Masters who died.

The West Window, which was designed by Mr. F. H. Spear, of the Royal School of Art, has many interesting features; it is a five-light, executed chiefly in red and blue with traceries. At the bottom is inscribed the School Motto, *" Altiora peto,"* and above it the Coat of Arms.

The central light has a figure of Edward the Confessor as a founder and patron saint of the School. On the right is the figure of King Henry VIII, the chief patron, and on the left that of Ethelfreda, Lady of the Mercians and daughter of King Alfred, the founder of Warwick Castle, and an early foundress of the School. On both the outer lights are legendary scenes from the life of Edward the Confessor. Under the left and right central lights are the dates " 1914 " and " 1918 " and the inscription: *" In memoriam Eric Wilfred Pyne donum dederunt parentes."* The whole design is inter-twined with English oak, giving place to the emblem of sacrifice at the top—a pelican feeding its young with blood from her own breast—a well-thought-out conception from the emblems of the history of its patrons and founders to the symbol of the supreme sacrifice.

Eventually two stained-glass windows will be placed in the Vestry. They are the gifts of Alderman S. Flavel and Sir Michael Lakin, and will contain figures of St. Nicholas, the patron saint of sailors, and St. George, the patron saint of soldiers.

The ceremonial service was conducted to the special setting of Psalm cxxv, by the Rev. F. Tibbits, an Old Boy of the School. The Headmaster, H. P. Pyne, M.A., B.Sc., read the lesson from Revelation xxi. The Rev. P. H. Croxier (O.W.) took the special prayers, assisted by the School Chaplain, the Rev. R. G. E. Bowers, M.A. The Archdeacon of Coventry gave his address from the text, Deuteronomy viii, 2: " Ye shall remember."

Wreaths were laid on behalf of the Headmaster, the Old Boys' Club, and the Officers and Cadets of the O.T.C.

---

# READING SCHOOL

*" Ars mercede viget."*

THE Memorial Service commenced with the hymn " Jesus Lives," followed by a few sentences from the Burial Service; then the Psalm xxiii and the lesson (Wisdom iii, 1-10) read by the Headmaster. The choir sang the well-known and ever-beautiful anthem by the late Dr. Hayden Keeton, " Blest are the departed."

After special versicles and prayers, Harwood's fine Easter anthem, " Christ being raised from the dead dieth no more," was sung, and Lieutenant-Colonel Leslie Wilson, D.S.O., M.P., unveiled the tablet, which contains the Eighty Three names of the Fallen. This tablet was dedicated by Rev. H. A. Smith-Masters (an Old Boy and Vicar of Hagbourne). Then came the hymn " Ye holy angels bright," followed by the Benediction. The " Last Post " was sounded and a verse of the National Anthem closed the fitting service.

The Memorial Tablet, which forms the centre of the Gothic Oak Panelling round the east end of the Chapel, was unveiled on February 18th, 1922.

Lieutenant-Colonel Wilson said that during the War he commanded three Companies of Miners, and one of Public School and 'Varsity men, and he still believed that the great comradeship formed in the trenches in France and Flanders will endure. The finest memorial to those who gave everything was for all classes to work together for the good of the Country and Empire.

The inscription above the names, which are in five panels, is: "1914-1918." "*Lest we forget.*" On the left is the School Crest, and on the right that of Henry I, founder of the School; both these crests are encircled in wreaths. Fine tracery in the form of leaves appears over each name panel, below which are the words: "*Their name liveth evermore.*"

The " Service Roll " contains the names of 500 Old Boys, of whom 43 gained distinctions.

READING SCHOOL MEMORIAL TABLET

# STAMFORD SCHOOL

*" Me Spede."*

HE War Memorial Fund was opened in April, 1919, the Honorary Secretary being Mr. Albert E. Dolby. At present the Old Schoolroom, which originally formed part of St. Paul's Church, has been used for educational purposes. It is now intended to transform it into the School Chapel and rebuild some of the classrooms in the summer of 1927. The plans, prepared by Mr. W. Pywell, F.R.I.B.A., have been adopted. The names of those killed in the War will be inscribed on tablets in the Chancel. The scheme will be a fitting tribute to the memory of the Old Boys and Assistant Masters who offered the supreme sacrifice during the years 1914-1919 " By Land, by Sea and Air."

# WHITGIFT GRAMMAR SCHOOL, CROYDON

*" Vincit qui patitur."*

THE two Memorials are the Cross and the Mural Tablet. The Cross is situated on the oval lawn in front of the School Buildings and near the entrance tower. It is made of Hopton Wood stone, slightly fawn-coloured, smooth and finely finished. It consists of two platforms, upon which is an octagonal block, the total height being 19 feet. The centre panel has the words: "*In remembrance of our Dead*, 1914-1919. *Vincit qui patitur.*" The four adjacent panels are deeply graven and bear the arms of Whitgift, Canterbury, Croydon and Surrey. The design of the Cross was suggested by the Whitgift Arms, described in Heraldry as " fleury."

The Mural Tablet is placed opposite the Tower door on the wall of the " Big School." In the centre are inscribed these words: "*In piam memoriam Whitgiftensium qui in magno bello terra marique mortem oppetentes de patria bene meriti sunt majorem hac dilectionem nemo habet ut animam suam ponat quis pro amicis.*" Above these words, which are in heavy gold lettering, are the Royal Coat of Arms, and on either side those of Canterbury and Croydon. In the four corners are the Arms of England, Scotland, Ireland and Wales. A border of Laurels and Tudor Roses enhances the five panels, which have the names inscribed on them in black. The Roll of Honour contains Two Hundred and Fifty One names. The whole is hand-painted on vellum.

The sculptors of the Cross were Messrs. Ebbutt, of Croydon, and the Mural Tablet was executed by Messrs. Pratt, of London. Great assistance in the designs was rendered by Mr. A. Talbot Smith and Mr. H. Berney. The Tablet was dedicated by the Archbishop of Canterbury on March 11th, 1922.

---

WHITGIFT GRAMMAR SCHOOL MEMORIAL

171

ST. ALBAN'S SCHOOL MEMORIAL

# ST. ALBANS SCHOOL

*" Mediocria firma."*

HIS Memorial at present consists of a Cross of English pattern and modern Ecclesiastical type. The Cross was unveiled by General Duncan, C.B., C.M.G., C.V.O., D.S.O., commanding East Anglican Division, and consecrated by Rev. H. Woolley, V.C., M.C., on Speech Day, February 16th, 1925.

The Rev. Woolley was Chaplain to the O.T.C. Camp, and is a late Captain of the 9th Battalion of the London Regiment. He won his V.C. at Hill 60 while still a Private.

The Memorial stands on the north side of the old Monastery Gateway. On the plinth is inscribed: " 1914-1918. *Greater love hath no man than this.*" On the front of the octagonal plinth is a bronze plate with the inscription: " *In memory of 48 officers and 37 other ranks, former members of the School, who gave their lives in the Great War, 1914-1918.*"

In the eight cusped panels appear the names of the Eighty Five who fell.

The masonry was executed by Mr. C. T. Alderton, of Harpenden, and the builder was Mr. A. W. Sharp, of St. Albans.

---

# CARLISLE GRAMMAR SCHOOL

*" Be just and fear not."*

HE foundation of this School dates back to 1188, when the authorities made a payment to the Church of Carlisle.

The Old Carliol's War Memorial was unveiled on Speech Day, July 28th, 1921, before the prize-giving. The Dean of Carlisle presided, supported by Sir Robert Allison, who unveiled the Memorial. After the unveiling there was one minute's silence, followed by the sounding of the " Last Post."

The Memorial is an Oak Panel of classic design, on which are three copper plates recording the names of the Eighty Nine who died. The design was by Mr. H. E. Ayris, A.R.I.B.A.

The inscription on the tablet, encircled by a wreath, is: " *Pro patria. 1914-1918. In grateful memory of the Old Carliols who died for King and Country in the Great War.*"

The Memorial Book, which also records the names of the Fallen, is kept in a locker in the central panelling of the Memorial. It is handsomely bound in leather, with the inscriptions in gilt. There are two names on each page. The parchment leaves are illuminated in colours by Mr. Rae, the Art Master at the School.

There are some 300 names on the Service Roll, and the distinctions gained include 6 M.C., 4 M.M. 5 D.S.O., 1 Croix de Guerre and 5 mentioned in despatches.

In the School Memorial Register is the following poem, written by Mr. A. C. Frost when he was in the VIth Form of the School:—

" *These deathless dead have shared the pains of Christ,*
   *Valiant and stainless and earth-consummate,*
*To save all honour, life they sacrificed*
   *Below the thund'rous chariot wheels of Fate.*
*Why mourn, why dim the glittering stars with grief?*
   *Here is no shame, O World, no darkness hence,*
*But purest dawn and Spring of greener leaf;*
   *Their high fulfilment and magnificence.*
*Let praises surge along the years, and now*
   *Heart-shaken nations kneel in vast thanksgiving;*
*The Dead have consecrated all fair things,*
   *And find beyond the memory of living*
*Glory of Time's green chaplet on the brow,*
   *And splendour in the Brotherhood of Kings*"

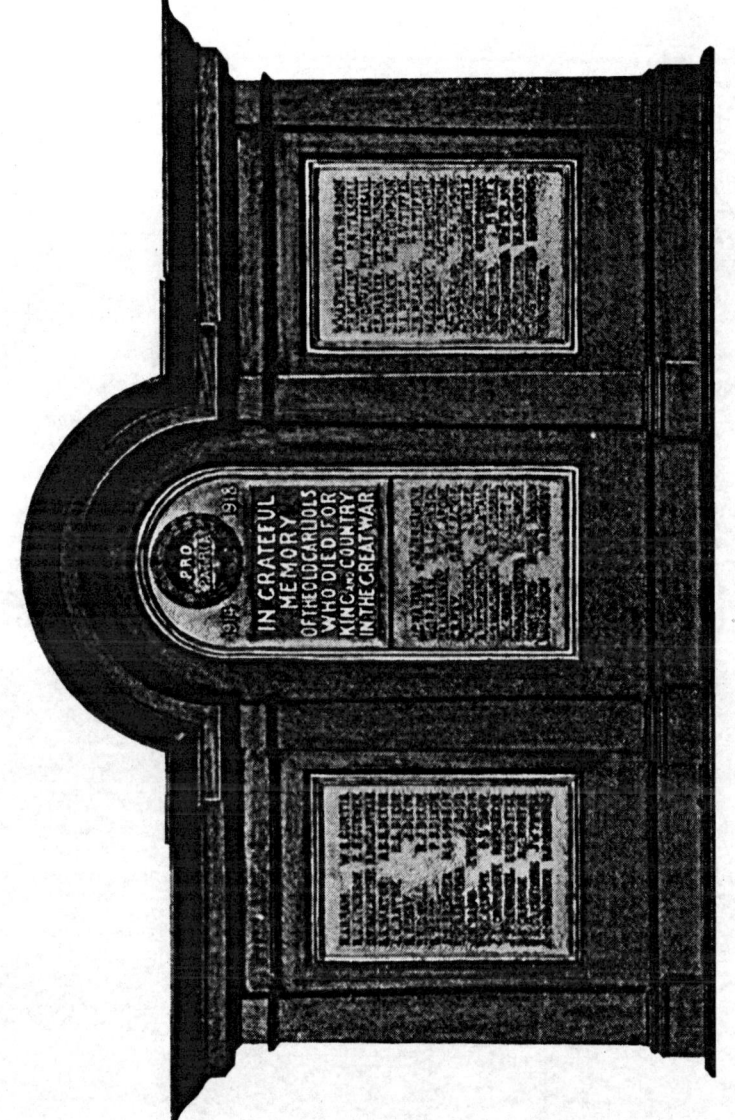

CARLISLE GRAMMAR SCHOOL MEMORIAL TABLET

WAKEFIELD GRAMMAR SCHOOL MEMORIAL

176

# WAKEFIELD GRAMMAR SCHOOL

*" Turpe nescire."*

THE Memorial Service was held in Wakefield Cathedral at 2.30 p.m. on Wednesday, October 5th, 1921. The sermon was preached by the Rev. John Clayton, M.A., Superintendent of the Church Army Huts in the Ypres sector, 1917, and Vicar of Wetwang, York. After the Recessional Hymn Mr. C. H. Head, M.A., unveiled the Memorial Monument at the School. Mr. M. H. Peacock, M.A., B.Mus., Headmaster of the School from 1884 to 1910, read the Roll of Honour of the Eighty Two names of those who fell. The Lord Bishop of Wakefield pronounced the Dedication Prayer, ending with the words: " Is it nothing to you, all ye that pass by? "

The Monument is a bronze statue of a Bugler, emblematical of the King's Own Yorkshire Light Infantry, to which so many of the Fallen belonged. The statue stands upon a plinth with columns on either side; in the centre is a School Crest, and under this a rapier-like sword. At the foot of the column is the following inscription: *" Their name liveth for evermore."*

Mr. C. H. Head, who unveiled the Memorial, was second Master at the School, and had trained most of the Old Boys whose names appeared on the Roll of Honour.

The architect was an Old Boy of the School—Mr. Harold Watson, F.R.I.B.A.

ST BEE'S SCHOOL MEMORIAL

# ST. BEE'S SCHOOL

## " *Expecta Dominum.*"

THE Memorial takes the form of an Obelisk of Portland stone. The central part is a plain column, above which is a Cross within a garlanded wreath, symbolic of Victory. The column rests upon a plinth with marble panels on each of the four sides.

One side-panel has upon it the School Crest. The front one has the words: " *To the glorious memory of Old St. Beghians who fell in the Great War.*" The third states that " *The names of the Fallen are recorded in the School Chapel,*" and the fourth records that this " *Memorial was erected June 20th, 1921.*" Below the plinth are three steps, and above the four marble panels are laurel wreaths.

Inside the School Chapel are two brasses; on one is recorded the names of the One Hundred and Eighty Two Old Boys who fell, on the other the names of the Three Masters who gave their lives.

The Architects were J. Whitehead & Sons, of Kennington Oval, London; the firm of Morris & Co., of London, supplied the brasses.

Both forms of Memorial were unveiled by the Bishop of Carlisle on June 30th, 1921.

---

# NOTTINGHAM HIGH SCHOOL

## " *Lauda finem.*"

THE unveiling of the Memorial took place on Armistice Day, 1922. It was dedicated by the Bishop of Newcastle (Dr. Wild) and unveiled by the Duke of Portland.

The Memorial is a bronze statue of a young officer, standing, in the action of beckoning his men to attack.

The figure rests upon the plinth, under which are three moulded steps. Two sides of the plinth carry bronze tablets, on which are inscribed the names of One Hundred and Ninety Eight Old Boys who fell in the War. The front and back sides of the plinth are carved with inscriptions.

On the front, deeply inscribed in a shield, is: "*To the Glory of God. In lasting and grateful memory of those former members of this School who, by the sacrifice of their lives for the cause of their Country in the Great War*, 1914-1918, *ennobled the traditions which they had here received*."

It is surmounted by the coat of arms of Nottingham and the School Crest. The inscription on the back of the plinth is: "*God gave them a great duty to do, and they did it. Te deum laudamus*."

The Memorial stands in the centre of the entrance to the School from Aboretum Street. The School Buildings, with the fifteenth-century facade, form an imposing background. The design was the work of Colonel A. W. Boswill, F.R.I.B.A., D.S.O. (an Old Boy of the School); the sculptor was Mr. Henry Poole, A.R.A., of Chelsea; the bronze was cast by T. W. Singer & Sons, of Frome, and the stone work was executed by Mr. John Burton, of Nottingham.

The School list of distinctions contains two Victoria Crosses.

NOTTINGHAM HIGH SCHOOL MEMORIAL

# LIVERPOOL COLLEGE

*" Non solum ingenis, verum etiam virtutis."*

HE Memorial consists of a Mural Tablet, in which are inserted five panels containing the names of One Hundred and Twenty Six Old Boys who gave their lives for their King and Country. The Tablet is the work of Mr. W. N. Adams, A.R.I.B.A. It was unveiled by Colonel I. M. McMaster, C.M.G., V.D., I.D., on February 14th, 1922, amid a large gathering of relations and scholars.

Above the list of names appears the following inscription: *" They died for their Country and are honoured by their friends."* Below the names is the following: *" MCMXIV. In memoria æterna erit justus. MCMXXVIII."*

LIVERPOOL COLLEGE MEMORIAL TABLET

LEYS SCHOOL MEMORIAL

# LEYS SCHOOL, CAMBRIDGE

THIS Memorial takes the form of a Mural Tablet in stone, on which are four panels with a central canopied figure of St. George in armour. The four panels hold the names of the One Hundred and Forty Nine Old Boys who gave their lives in the Great War.

The architect was Mr. G. P. Hutchinson, of Messrs. James Cowell & Sons (Whitefriars), Ltd., Wigmore Street, London.

H.R.H. the Duke of York unveiled this Tablet on July 6th, 1922.

This tablet is placed on the external wall of the Chapel under the east window. Under the statue of St. George is the inscription: "*To the immortal memory of Old Leysians who fell in the War of 1914-1919*," while along the bottom of the Tablet, under the name panels, appear the following words: "*My marks and scars I carry with me to be a witness for me that I have fought His battles, Who now will be my rewarder.*"

---

# PLYMOUTH COLLEGE AND MANNAMEAD SCHOOL

### "*L'Union fait la Force.*"

AN unstained carved oak tablet, 9 feet high and 5 feet wide, is the Memorial here. The main panel, 6 feet by 4 feet, contains the names of One Hundred and Twelve of the Fallen, together with their rank and regiment. On either side are carved pilasters of classic design supporting a pediment bearing the Plymouth Coat of Arms, and the dates "1914-1919" and a frieze with the inscription: "*To the memory of those boys of Plymouth College and Mannamead School who laid down their lives in the Great War.*" The Tablet is situated on the East Wall of the "Big School" amid the "Honours" Boards of the College, and has upon it the words: "*Fasti splendidi facti.*"

The Tablet was designed by Mr. M. Alton Bazeley, an Old Plymothian, and it was unveiled by Lord St. Levan on Wednesday, October 6th, 1921. After removing the Union Jack, Lord St. Levan said that such Memorials were meant in one sense to show sympathy with the relatives of the Fallen. He said that he did not think that there could be too many Memorials. Relatives could not forget, but with the present-day needs it was essential that a visible Memorial should be erected to prevent others from forgetting. They died to save England, they set the example, and Memorials were signs pointing out the way of Duty. They wanted to keep England a free country, and it rested with the coming generation to do it.

Buglers of the Royal Marine Light Infantry sounded the " Last Post " and " Reveille," and thus the brief ceremony ended.

A Memorial Scholarship has been founded, tenable at a University.

---

## MERCHANT TAYLORS' SCHOOL, CROSBY.

Motto : " *Concordia parvæ res crescunt.*"

HE Memorial consists of a Mural Brass Tablet with five panels, mounted on black Belgian marble on green Westmorland stone. The Tablet is about 9 feet square and bears the following inscription on the top pediment, surmounted by the School Crest : " *In memory of those Old Boys of Merchant Taylors' School, Crosby, who gave their lives in the Great War, 1914-1919.*"

The unveiling took place on Tuesday, October 2nd, 1923. The Rev. Canon S. C. Armour, D.D., of Liverpool Cathedral and Headmaster at the School from 1863 to 1903, performed the ceremony.

The Roll of Honour contains One Hundred and Fifty Five names.

The architect was Lionel Budden, M.A., A.R.I.B.A., an Old Crosbian, who also designed the War Memorial at Birkenhead and the Liverpool Cenotaph.

MERCHANT TAYLORS' SCHOOL, CROSBY
MEMORIAL TABLET

# ST. PETER'S SCHOOL, YORK

*" Super antiquas vias."*

THE Lord Bishop of Carlisle (O.P.) dedicated the War Memorial on Sunday July 3rd, 1921. The Memorial, to the Seventy Eight Boys from this School who made the Great Sacrifice, consists of Scholarship Exhibitions to the value of £500, a new Gallery and lobby to the " Big Hall," and an Oak Tablet in the apse of the lobby, inscribed : *" In memory of Peterites who fought for right and justice in the Great War, 1914-1918."* This Tablet was dedicated by the Lord Bishop of Carlisle on June 29th, 1920.

The Great Hall St Peter's School York

The oak front of the Gallery, which seats 160 boys, is a design of panels, the centre one bearing the School Crest (Cross Keys) and a Latin motto meaning " Along the old paths."

The Tablet in the north wall of the Chapel contains the names of the Fallen, with incised letters. The School Coat of Arms in gilt and silver surmounts this side, with scrolls in the design of oak leaves. At the foot is an epitaph from Simonides, the Greek poet, in the original Greek. The translation is:

" If to die nobly is life's greatest test
To us of all her boons Fate gave the best;
We died and won a praise that cannot die
Eager to crown our land with liberty."

The architect for the whole of the Memorial was Mr. F. T. Penty (O.P.), and the builder was Mr. Watson, of York. Mr. T. Bellerby was responsible for the woodwork in the Chapel and the Hall, and Mr. Holtby for the new seating in the Hall. Mr. Atkinson laid the flooring in the " Big Hall," and Mr. Milburn was the sculptor of the Tablet.

---

# KELLY COLLEGE, TAVISTOCK

*" Fortitor occupa portum."*

HERE were two erections in memory of those Sixty Old Boys who fell in the War. A Cornish granite Cross was erected in the College grounds, bearing on its base the words: " *In proud and loving memory of our glorious dead. 1914-1919.*"

Bronze Tablets were erected in the College Chapel bearing the names of the Fallen in two columns, above which is the School Crest and the following words: " *In memory of the following Old Kelleians who died on service, 1914-1919.*"

The above Memorials were dedicated on July 28th, 1920, by the Venerable Archdeacon of Plymouth. Most of the money collected for the Memorial Fund has been devoted to the foundation of Scholarships in perpetuity for the sons of those who gave their lives in the Great War.

KELLY COLLEGE MEMORIAL

# LEEDS GRAMMAR SCHOOL

*" Nullius non mater disiplinæ."*

AT this School a Memorial Swimming Bath is nearing completion. The building is of stone with a Memorial Entrance Porch, lighted by a central lantern and four stained-glass windows, representing the Arms of the School, Leeds, St. George and St. Wilfred, the latter being the patron saint of the School Chapel. Inside the porch the names of the One Hundred and Twenty Three Fallen are carved in stone.

The Bath is seventy-five feet long and has thirty dressing-boxes, two big changing-rooms and a fine gallery.

A filtration plant, which will clean the water in six hours, and also heating apparatus, is being installed.

The windows of the Bath are fitted with " Vita-glass," which admits the ultra-violet rays, so necessary to vitality.

The building was designed by Messrs. Austin & Pailey, of Lancaster.

The building is situated opposite the Headmaster's study, forming a court, which includes a lawn and a tennis court.

VIEW OF THE MEMORIAL SWIMMING BATH
(UNDER CONSTRUCTION)

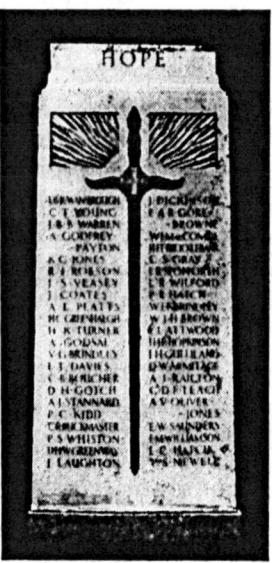

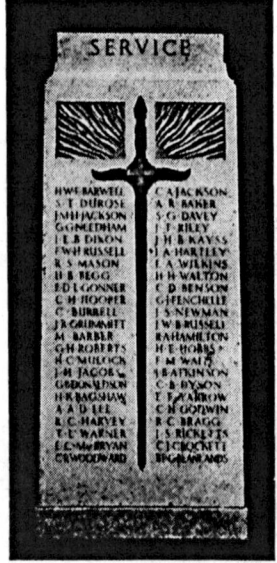

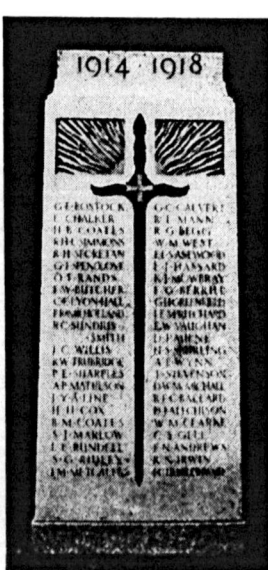

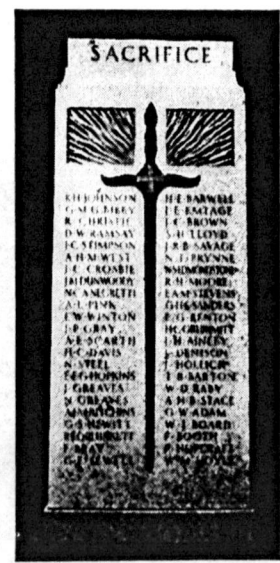

**OUNDLE SCHOOL MEMORIAL TABLETS**

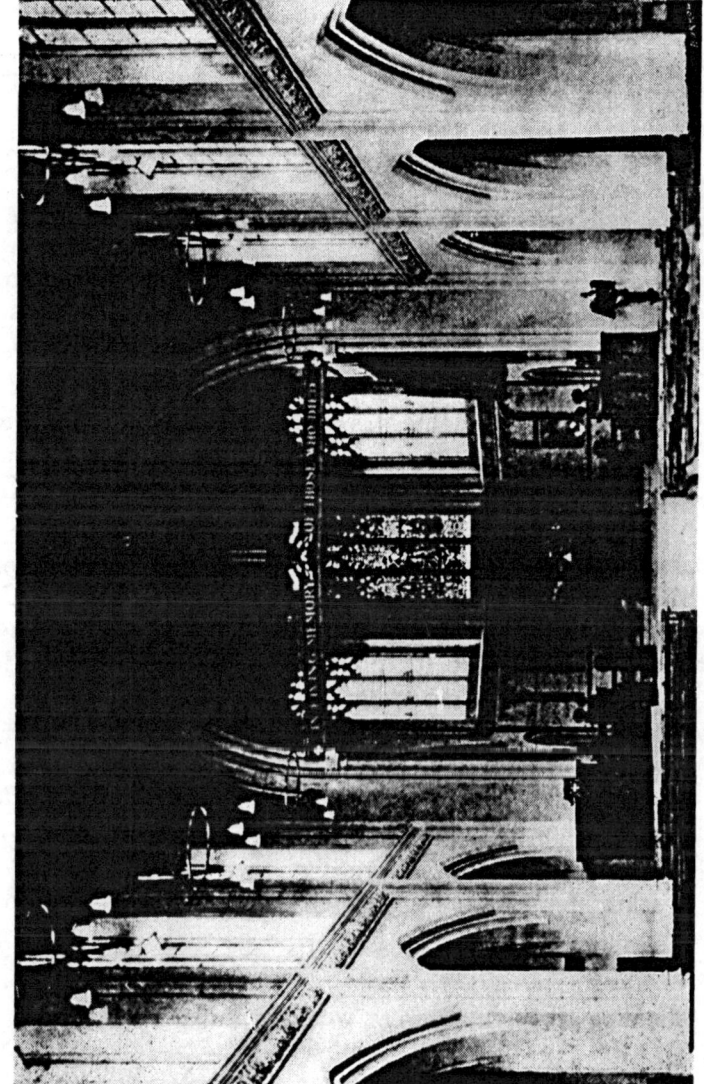

OUNDLE SCHOOL MEMORIAL CHAPEL

# OUNDLE SCHOOL

*" God grant Grace."*

PRELIMINARY meeting was held at Oundle and a further meeting at the Grocers' Hall, London, on July 19th, 1919, when the War Memorial Fund was inaugurated under the presidency of the Master of the Grocers' Company.

The Chapel Foundation Stone was well and truly laid by Colonel R. H. Harvey (Master of the Grocers' Company) in July, 1922. The architect was A. C. Blomfield, M.A., F.R.I.B.A.

The Consecration Ceremony was conducted by the Right Rev. Dr. Woods, Bishop of Peterborough, on November 22nd, 1923. The Bishop dedicated, on Whit-Sunday, May 23rd, 1926, the five Memorial Tablets.

The Chapel has a metal Rood Beam across the Chancel, on which are inscribed the words: *" In living memory of those who died."* The sentence of Consecration of the Chapel, after being signed by the Bishop, was ordered to be preserved in the archives of the School. The beautiful Altar Cloth in the Chapel was the gift of Mrs. M. W. Brown.

The Memorial Tablets are five in number, each bearing a superscription, the centre one, " 1914-1918," the other four, *" Faith," " Hope," " Service," " Sacrifice,"* as emblems of the ideal Christian life. Each tablet has upon it a sword with a cross on its hilt, and rays of sunshine radiating therefrom. On these tablets are inscribed the names of the Two Hundred and Twenty Four who gave their lives in the War.

The following distinctions were won: 3 V.C., 29 D.S.O., 3 D.S.C., 2 A.F.C., 4 D.F.C., 115 M.C. (6 with bars).

# ROYSSE SCHOOL, ABINGDON

JOHN ROYSSE, Mercer and Citizen of London, founded this School in 1563. It belongs to the Governors of Christ's Hospital, a local body, whose foundation is derived from the Abbots of Abingdon. A tablet on the exterior of the south wall of the Chapel is inscribed thus: "*Cum pia memoria Joannis Roysse huiusce scholæ fundatoris hoc saxum posuit. Joannis Thornhill Morland, M.A., J.P., abendonensis opidi præfectus. iii. Kal. Sext. anno salutis MDCCCCI.*"

Inside the Chapel in the centre of the north wall is a Memorial Brass Tablet surmounted by the School Crest and the inscription: "*Misericordias Domine in æternum cantabo.*" Below this is written: "*In memory of those who gave their lives in the War, 1914-1919.*" Then follows, in two columns, the Seventy Three names of the Fallen, with their regiments and distinctions gained. These include 4 M.C. (one with bar) and 1 Croix de Guerre.

This Tablet was executed by A. R. Mowbray & Co., of Oxford, and dedicated by the Master of Pembroke College, Oxford, on Founder's Day, June 18th, 1920.

On the west wall of the interior of the Chapel, opposite to the Lectern, is a small Brass Tablet "*In memory of Allan Murray Austin, Royal Navy, Paymaster H.M.S. Hawke, lost on October 15th, 1914. Faithful unto death.*" This is of special interest, as there are very few references to be found at our Public Schools to boys who served in the Navy.

The balance of the Memorial Fund is being used in the decoration of the Chapel and in providing further additions to the School, as opportunity occurs.

The fittings of the Chapel are in oak; six Corbels of the roof beams have crests in colours, and the Altar Cloth bears in rich embroidery the words: " *Called to be Saints.*"   Stained-glass windows will be added as a further Memorial.

---

# KING EDWARD VI SCHOOL, SOUTHAMPTON

*" Dieu et mon droit."*

AT noon on Founders' Day, June 4th, 1923, was unveiled the School Memorial, a Mural Tablet flanked by two pillars and surmounted by a pediment with the arms of King Edward VI thereon, situated in the Hall.   In the centre of the Tablet is a large panel with three columns containing the Fifty names of the Fallen, and the inscription above the names: " *Their name liveth evermore.*"

The service was conducted by the Headmaster, memorial being dedicated by the Lord Bishop of Winchester, the Right Rev. E. S. Talbot, D.D., and unveiled by the Lord Lieutenant of Hampshire, Major-General the Right Hon. J. E. B. Seely, P.C., C.B., C.M.G., D.S.O.   The compositions of several Old Boys were used in the service, notably the General Thanksgiving of Bishop Reynolds (at the School 1608-1615) and the Hymns " For all the Saints," by Bishop Mant (1784-1789), and " O God our Help in ages past," by Isaac Watts (1678-1690).   Mr. Danbury, Captain of the School, read the lesson.   Colonel Perkings, C.B.E., D.L.M., and Alderman S. G. Kimber were present, and also spoke.

KING EDWARD VI. SCHOOL MEMORIAL

# FELSTEAD SCHOOL

*" Garde ta foy."*

THE Memorial is in two parts. The first is a Screen and Window in the School Chapel, both the work of Mr. F. O. Salisbury. They were unveiled by General Sir H. G. Ruggles-Brise, K.C.M.G., in June, 1921. On the Screen are panels containing the Two Hundred and Twenty Five names of the Fallen. In the centre is a carving of St. George and the Dragon, and underneath the inscription: *" Thanks be to God for those who fought and died."*

The other portion of the Memorial is a block of buildings comprising a Library and a Museum, opened by General Lord Horne, G.C.B., K.C.M.G., in June, 1924. The architects were Messrs. Grant & Chetwood.

FELSTEAD SCHOOL MEMORIAL SCREEN

FELSTEAD MEMORIAL LIBRARY AND MUSEUM

# KING EDWARD VII SCHOOL, SHEFFIELD

*" Fac recte nil time."*

HE Memorial consists of a bronze tablet and a simple Memorial Cross. The tablet, erected by the Old Boys' Association, has been placed over the dais in the Assembly Hall. It contains the Eighty Nine names of the Fallen, and the inscription: *" Erected to the glorious memory of the Sheffield Old Edwardians who fell in the Great War ":* and below, " *They battled that we might be free."*

The Cross, which has been hewn out of Cornish granite, stands in the School Grounds, and has on the base of the plinth the inscription: "1914-1918. *Our Glorious Dead."*

The unveiling was performed by the Lord Mayor of Sheffield, Alderman C. Simpson, and the dedication by the Bishop of Sheffield on November 26th, 1921. The impressiveness of the scene was intense. The Guard of Honour was supplied by the School O.T.C., and the buglers and drummers of the Hallamshires, under Drum-Major Boswell, after the dull muffled sound of the drums, sounded the " Last Post " and " Reveille."

The Lord Mayor, in his address, said that since the School was opened in 1905, 500 of the 850 Boys who had passed through had served in the forces, of whom Eighty Seven Boys and Two Masters gave their lives. The Rev. E. A. Berrisford, M.C., President of the Old Boys' Association, presented the Memorials to the School, on whose behalf they were accepted by Alderman Styring.

The Bishop of Sheffield recalled a memory of 1914, for in that year he presented the prizes to the School; only seven years later he dedicated a Memorial Cross to the honour of many of them. To the present generation he addressed this exhortation : " Be hopeful for the future."

# RADLEY COLLEGE

## *" Sicut Columbæ."*

N Archway has been erected in memory of the Two Hundred and Nineteen Old Boys, Seven Masters and Eight Servants who gave their lives for King and Country during the Great War. The Memorial was designed by Sir Thomas Graham Jackson and was unveiled by Sir William Robertson on May 31st, 1922.

The Service of Dedication was performed by the Bishop of Oxford, who said: " The Righteous shall be held in everlasting remembrance." The choir, standing on the Archway, sang " Jerusalem the Golden," accompanied by the Band of the Oxford and Bucks Light Infantry.

RADLEY COLLEGE MEMORIAL ARCHWAY

199

The inscription on the Archway bears the words: "*In proud and grateful memory of all those who gave their lives in the Great War.*"

One Thousand Two Hundred Old Boys served in the War, and over Two Hundred obtained Decorations.

---

# BLOXHAM SCHOOL

*"Justorum semita lux splendens."*

BLOXHAM'S great founder was Rev. P. R. Egerton, who continued the work of Rev. Nathanial Woodard, a curate in London, whose remains are buried under the Altar of Lancing College, which he founded. He also founded Ardingly College and Hurstpierpoint School.

The War Memorial at Bloxham's is composed of a central panel of oak with a dedicatory inscription, surmounted by a silver Crucifix and the School Crest. On either side are panels, each bearing Thirty Eight names, giving a total of Seventy Six who fell.

The Memorial is situated on the north wall of the School Chapel, just east of the Screen, and was unveiled on All Saints' Day, November 1st, 1920, by Colonel H. A. R. May, C.B., of the Artists' Rifles, an Old Boy. The Headmaster, vested in cope and standing before the Altar, said the dedicatory prayers and two collects; then the hymn, " In our day of thanksgiving," was sung while all knelt. Colonel May, after a short address, unveiled the Memorial, and the Headmaster dedicated it in the name of the Holy Trinity, "To the honoured memory of the Old Boys of this School who gave their lives for their Country in the Great War," and commended their souls to the keeping of their Heavenly Father.

Bugles sounded the "Last Post," and a roll of drums heralded the "Reveille." The Roll of Honour is hung in the Chapel Cloister together with a photograph of each of the Fallen, flanked by colour portraits of Field-Marshal Haig and Admiral Beatty, being copies of the portraits painted by Chevalier Taylor—an old Bloxhamist—for the Lord Mayor and Corporation of London.

BLOXHAM SCHOOL MEMORIAL

# TAUNTON SCHOOL

*" Ora et labora."*

THE Memorial Fund at this School was commenced on November 27th, 1918, and by December, 1921, a sufficient sum had been collected for placing a three-light stained-glass Window in the Chapel, to the memory of the Old Boys who were killed. The Window was unveiled by Rev. D. J. Hiley, H.C.F.

In 1922, a testimonial subscribed for the retiring Headmaster, Dr. Whittaker, was presented by him to the War Memorial Fund, and a Memorial Hall containing Chemical, Physical and Biological Laboratories was constructed. The designs of Mr. Vincent Harris, of London, were accepted, and Messrs. R. G. Spiner, of Taunton, carried out his plans.

TAUNTON SCHOOL MEMORIAL HALL

In the entrance hall, directly opposite the main entrance, is a Memorial Screen bearing the School Arms and the inscription: "*Thanks be to God for the Old Boys of Taunton School who were faithful unto death. 1914-1919.*" Above the Screen hangs a star light, which shines when any other light is burning in the building. Four slabs of Portland Stone in the Hall bear the names of the One Hundred and Sixty Five Old Boys who gave their lives for the great cause.

The Memorial Building was opened by Lord Eustace Percy, M.P., President of the Board of Education, on October 6th, 1925.

---

# LANCING COLLEGE

*" Beati mundo corde."*

A SUPERB Gothic War Memorial Cloister at Lancing College was opened by H.R.H. Prince Henry, K.G., G.C.V.O., on Saturday, June 25th, 1927.

Its approximate cost is £10,000, and it forms a beautiful and harmonious addition to the noble College Chapel, a stately pile on the Downs above Shoreham, which is a landmark for miles around. Situated on the south side of the edifice, the Cloister is formed of Sussex sandstone, brought from Scaynes Hill, near Haywards Heath. It is over 100 feet in length and is in seven bays. The fine ornamentation of the vaulting, known as fan tracery, is very lovely work. The eastern extremity of the Cloister, where there is a beautiful light depicting St. George and the Dragon, extends just beyond the entrance to the crypt, where so many generations of Lancing boys worshipped before the Chapel itself was opened.

Immediately beyond it is the tomb of the founder of the College, the Rev. Nathaniel Woodard, where also rest the bodies of two sons, George Herbert Woodard and William Blatchford Woodard. At the west end of the Cloister there are steps leading up to the Chapel and to the College itself.

The names and regiments of the One Hundred and Fifty Six sons of Lancing, and also the Masters, who made the supreme sacrifice of life in the Great War, are artistically recorded in blue characters in seven groups, inscribed on the outer walls of the inner recesses. The Cloister has a flat asphalted roof.

It is worthy of note that the entire work has been carried out by the College Staff of masons and others employed on the College buildings. Mr. W. Browne, the Clerk of the Works, who has been here for twenty-five years, has during the whole of his life been connected with Gothic church work, and before coming to Lancing he was engaged on the magnificent new Hove Parish Church, where he was general foreman. He and Mr. Dick Gale, who laid all the stone, were presented to the Prince.

There was a considerable amount of excavation required to clear the site for the Memorial, and the pupils of Lancing College themselves assisted in carrying out this task.

The Cloister was the design of the late Mr. Temple Moore. The Foundation Stone was laid in June, 1921. There were many more present on Saturday, which, by a happy coincidence, was " Old Boys' Day."

The public proceedings commenced with the inspection of the guard of honour by the Prince. This was composed of a hundred members of the Lancing College contingent of the O.T.C. and was under Captain Neale. It was formed up in front of the Headmaster's residence. In the uniform of a Captain of the 10th Hussars, His Royal Highness was accompanied by his Equerry (Captain Howard Kerr), the Lord Lieutenant of the County (Lord Leconfield), and the High Sheriff of Sussex (Lieutenant-Colonel Roland V. Gwynne, D.S.O., D.L., J.P.). He was conducted to the Chapel by the Provost, the Right Rev. the Bishop H. K. Southwell. Here he was met by the procession, and they passed down the crypt to the eastern door of the Memorial Cloister.

In front came the cross-bearer, then came the choir, with the banners of St. Mary and St. Nicolas and of the Blessed Sacrament. Behind followed Clergy, Fellows of Lancing College, the Headmaster (Mr. C. H. Blakiston), and the principals in the central event of the day. The Bishop of Chichester was in full canonicals, and the other Clergy present were the Revs. W. H. Howitt, H. Lucas, W. F. Bond, F. A. Woodard (grandson of the founder of Lancing College) and J. R. Missen, all of Lancing College, Canon Bowlby (for a long term of years the Headmaster of Lancing), Archdeacon of Chichester, the Bishop in Corea (the Right Rev. Dr. Trollope) and Canon R. J. Lea, R.D.

Among the Fellows of the College present were the Hon. Henry G. G. Pelham, Mr. Justice Sankey, Colonel C. W. Whittaker, Canon R. J. Lea, Mr. H. M. Gibbs, Mr. F. Witherington and Mr. E. G. P. Wyatt.

On either side of the Cloister entrance were Provost's mace and the mace of the Headmaster. Massed in the immediate front were the main body of pupils of the College with Mr. G. M. T. Smythe, the Second Master, who has an association with the College extending back perhaps over thirty years, and is an old Brighton College boy, and the other Masters. The choir was ranged on the east side of the entrance, within the Cloister were relatives of the Fallen. The ceremony was brief, but it was marked by dignity and solemnity. When the Prince arrived at the Cloister door the hymn, "O God, Our Help in Ages Past," was sung. The dedicating prayers were rendered by Canon Bowlby.

Then the Headmaster said:—

"Your Royal Highness, in the name of the School, I ask you to unveil this Memorial Cloister as a thank-offering to Almighty God, and as a Memorial to Old Boys of this School who fell in the Great War."

The silence was broken by the piercing note of the bugles. Prince Henry drew aside the veil which symbolised the opening of the Cloister, when the "Last Post" rang out. Then followed one minute's silence. Then there was a clarion call, the "Réveillé," to signify the passing over, the Resurrection.

The Provost, the Right Rev. Bishop Southwell, spoke the dedicatory sentences, the hymn, "Blest are the Pure in Heart," was sung, and the Bishop of Chichester brought the ceremonial to an end with prayer and the pronouncement of the Blessing.

The address which Prince Henry gave was notable for terseness of expression, coupled with clarity of thought. His Royal Highness said :—

"Right Rev. Provost, Mr. Headmaster, Boys of Lancing College, and Ladies and Gentlemen. It is with great pleasure that I have come here to-day to open this War Memorial Cloister erected to the glorious memory of those Boys of Lancing College who gave their lives for King and Country in the Great War. You have reason to be proud of their war service which this magnificent Cloister commemorates, set up in undying love and gratitude by their relations and friends. The decorations gained and honours received are indeed very numerous, but to-day we are here to pay our tribute of honour to your Dead, whose fine record is in every sense worthy of this great School. I have read the Lancing "Roll of Honour," and note that of the Eight Hundred Boys who fought in the Great War, One Hundred and Fifty Six made the supreme sacrifice. From every part of the world old Lancing Boys came to England's call and willingly laid down their lives for King and Empire.

"The spirit of unselfishness is that which we understand by the Public School tradition, and it is taught from the very beginning of our school days in the classroom and on the playing fields.

"To play for your side and not for yourself, this is the spirit so drilled into you that when you leave school to go out into the world it has become part of your very self. Keep before you that Lancing tradition of team play, which spells unselfishness. Keep that tradition ever before you. Make this spirit your very own; it will enable you to conquer manhood, as in your school days, when you excel in the sports field, where your prowess is well known, not only in cricket and football, but also in athletics, swimming and rifle shooting.

"In doing this, you will honour not only the School, but also the memory of those whose services we commemorate to-day. This Memorial Cloister which I have just opened commemorates your Dead in the Great War, and it does more than this. It stands as an inspiration for the future generations of boys who will pass this building every day and have before their eyes the example of those who gave their lives for King and Country and Empire.

" For over seventy years your School, together with the other great Public Schools of England, has been sending men to the remotest parts of the world, trained in character and leadership to the infinite good and glory of the Empire. It is by the way in which English Public Schoolboys are trained that our best traditions at home and abroad are always upheld.

" I now thank you for the reception you have given me to-day, and I should like to say how honoured I feel that I have been asked to perform this act at Lancing."

LANCING COLLEGE MEMORIAL

# MONMOUTH GRAMMAR SCHOOL

*" Serve and obey."*

HE Memorial Cross and the laying out of the Close was designed by Mr. Thomas Ridgway-Bridson, of Wrington, Somerset. The sculpture and masonry was carried out by Mr. Alfred William Ursell, of Ross, whose brilliant son, a Baliol scholar, is among those honoured in the Roll of Seventy Five Old Boys.

The Cross is of Cornish granite—a small cross on a pillar and base, the whole standing upon a plinth which is mounted on three steps. The names are inscribed on the plinth, and the dedicatory inscription on the base of the pillar is: *" In memory of the Old Boys of Monmouth Grammar School who gave their lives in the Great War,* 1914-1919."

The Memorial was unveiled by Captain Angus Buchanan, V.C., M.C., who was blinded in the War, on Saturday, October 1st, 1921. The dedicatory prayer was said by the Lecturer, and the service was in

the following order: Hymn, "God of our fathers, known of old" placing of wreath; address by Captain Buchanan; three opening prayers; lesson (Rev. vii, 9-17); hymn, "Their grief is turned to pleasure"; reading of the Roll; three remembrance prayers; dedication of the Cross; hymn, "For all the Saints who from their labours rest"; the Benediction; the "Last Post"; the "Reveille"; the National Anthem. The great beauty of this service is in the choice of hymns and general simplicity.

The Memorial Fund will also provide for additional Playing Fields and Pavilion, an open-air Swimming Bath, and Scholarships.

MONMOUTH GRAMMAR SCHOOL MEMORIAL

# KING WILLIAM'S COLLEGE, ISLE OF MAN

*" Assiduitate non desida."*

THE Memorial Cross, of grey Cornish granite and Celtic design, is situated in front of the east wing of the School Buildings. The architect was Mr. Ronald F. Dodd, a former student, late of Castletown. The execution of the work is by Mr. W. H. Oxtell, of Oxford.

The Memorial Cross stands 20 feet high upon a base of three steps. On four sides of the plinth, inscribed upon brass tablets, appear the names of the One Hundred and Twenty Seven Old Boys and Masters who fell in the War. The following words appear on the Cross: *" In memory of those from this College who, on land and sea and in the air, gave their lives in the War, 1914-1919."*

On the face of the Cross is a bronze sword, the replica of the Sword of State of the Isle of Man, which was carried before the Governors and the Bishop of Barrow, who was the founder of the College.

Prior to the unveiling of the Memorial by Sir George Beatson, M.D., K.C.B., of King William's College, at a service held on Friday, July 28th, 1922, Sir William Fry, Lieutenant-Governor of the Island, inspected the College O.T.C. and the Guard of Honour. The service was conducted by Bishop Denton Thompson, and Bishop Kempson, of Warrington, a former Principal of the College, dedicated the stained Glass Light in the East Nave of the Chapel. The Archdeacon of Man and Canon Kermode assisted in the service. The window, designed by Mr. C. G. Gray, of Cambridge, consists of two panels, one containing a figure of St. George and the other one of King Arthur. Beneath the window are the words: *" Ad majorem dei gloriam et in piam memoriam alumnorum qui pro patria et fide mortem occubuerunt. MDCCCCXIV— MDCCCCXIX."*

Sir G. Beatson, at the unveiling of the Cross, said: " This Cross is now the emblem of all that is noble, self-sacrificing and good." The Head Boy of the College, H. C. Easton, laid a laurel wreath on the Memorial.

KING WILLIAM'S COLLEGE, THE MEMORIAL CROSS

KING WILLIAM'S COLLEGE, THE MEMORIAL WINDOWS

# CITY OF LONDON SCHOOL

*" Domine dirge nos."*

IN the early days of the War Mr. F. A. Lindsay Smith, an Old Boy of the School, expressed a wish to erect a Memorial Tablet to the boys who gave their lives. He was a member of the Court of Common Council and had occupied the chair of the Committee of his old School. He died on June 19th, 1915, and the work which he had proposed was executed by his son. The architect was Sir Banister Fletcher, F.R.I.B.A. The marble panels contain the names of Three Hundred and Fifty Old Boys, with two beautiful figures of youthful soldiers, one on each side. Below is the inscription: *" In fulfilment of the wish of the late F. A. Lindsay-Smith, J.P., C.C., Chairman of the City of London School Committee 1913. This Monument was erected by his son to the memory of the Old Boys of the City of London School who gave their lives for their Country in the Great War, 1914-1919. Their glory shall not be blotted out. Their name liveth for evermore."*

It stands on the grand staircase leading to the Hall and harmonises beautifully with its marble surroundings.

The School was fortunate in having this record of the names of the fallen provided by a private donor, and the Committee of the School War Memorial was free to entertain other schemes. The result of this Committee's labour is summed up in an inscription on a stone tablet erected in the entrance lobby of the School, and unveiled on May 13th, 1927, by Lord Marshall, of Chipstead, the President of the War Memorial Committee. The inscription is as follows: *" In memory of Old Citizens who fell in the Great War, 1914-1918, Playing Fields were acquired and a Pavilion was built at Grove Park, a War Memorial Scholarship was endowed and this Tablet was erected by the Corporation of London, the John Carpenter Club and Pupils and Friends of the City of London School."*

The School War Memorial thus consists of the Playing Fields at Grove Park, with the Pavilion, a Scholarship tenable by boys of the School at a place of higher education and called the War Memorial Scholarship, and this Tablet in the Entrance Hall.

THE MEMORIAL PAVILION

THE MEMORIAL PAVILION

The playing fields are of more than 20 acres in extent. The handsome pavilion was designed by Mr. Ralph Knott, the designer of the County Hall, and his partner, Mr. E. Stone Collins, both of whom are Old Citizens. The tea-room is decorated by a series of war pictures, symbolising Self-Sacrifice, painted by Mr. Steven Spurrier, another Old Citizen. The foundation stone was laid on November 3rd, 1924, by the Lord Mayor, Sir Louis Newton, and the ground and pavilion were opened by the next Lord Mayor, Sir Alfred Bower, on July 10th, 1925.

Across the front of the pavilion runs the inscription: "*MCMXIV. Liberatis vindicibus vitam pro patria largitis condiscipuli. MCMXVIII.*"

CITY OF LONDON SCHOOL, THE MEMORIAL TABLET

# THE STATIONERS' COMPANY'S SCHOOL
## HORNSEY

*" Verbum Domini manet in æternum."*

THE Memorial Service was held at Christ Church, Newgate Street, on Tuesday, June 3rd, 1919. The procession through the dark city alleys from the Stationers' Hall to the Church was headed by the present scholars, followed by the Staff of the School, the Governors, and the Master, Wardens, Court and Livery of the Stationers' Company. The service was conducted by the Rector of Christ Church, the Rev. T. R. Hine-Haycock, and the Chaplain to the Company, the Rev. Joseph Miles. After the National Anthem, the hymn, " O God our help in ages past," and the Psalm xxiii were sung. The Headmaster, Major J. Huck, read the lesson from Wisdom iii. Then followed the hymns, " Let Saints on earth in concert sing " and " They whose course on earth is o'er," with prayers said by the priest. The address was given by the Rev. Prebendary E. Hobson, M.A., from the text, " Not one of them is forgotten." Then was sung the hymn, " On the resurrection morning," and after the Blessing the " Dead March " in " Saul " was played. The " Last Post " was sounded by a bugler of the School Cadet Corps.

The War Memorial is an Organ, erected in the School Hall. The instrument was built by Messrs. Hunter & Son, of Clapham, and when complete will compare favourably with any other organ of its size. The tone is well graded and of excellent quality. The following is a specification of the completed organ :—

Two Manuals and Pedals.

Great Organ: Compass CC to A, 58 notes.—Open Diapason, 8 ft.; Clarabella, 8 ft.; Dulciana, 8 ft.; Principal, 4 ft. Two Composition Pedals.

Swell Organ: Compass CC to A, 58 notes.—Geigen, 8 ft.; Lieblich Gedeckt, 8 ft.; Salicional, 8 ft.; Voix Celeste, 8 ft.; Harmonic Flute, 4 ft.; Oboe, 8 ft.; Tremulant, Balanced Swell Pedal, Two Composition Pedals.

Pedal Organ: Compass CCC to G, 32 notes.—Bourdon, 16 ft.; Bass Flute, 8 ft.

Couplers.—Swell to Pedal, Great to Pedal, Swell to Great.

The Organ is placed on a gallery erected above the east entrance to the Hall. Round the gallery are eleven oak panels recording the names of the One Hundred and Fifty Four Old Boys who fell. The design for the panels was by Mr. H. G. Crothall, F.R.I.B.A., and the work was executed by Messrs. Cottrell.

The Memorial was dedicated on Saturday, March 4th, 1922, in the presence of the Master, Court and Wardens of the Stationers' Company, the Governors, and relatives and friends of the Fallen. After a short service, the Master of the Company unveiled the Organ, which was dedicated by the Bishop of London " to the honour and glory of Almighty God, in memory of those Old Boys of this School who, at the call of duty, left all that was dear to them, endured hardness, faced danger on land and sea and in the air, and finally passed out of the sight of men by the path of duty and self-sacrifice, giving up their own lives that others might live in freedom."

The President of the Old Boys' Association (Mr. T. H. Nicholson) presented the Memorial to the School, after which the Bishop addressed the assembly. The hymn, " O Valiant Hearts," was sung, and the impressive service closed with the Benediction and the National Anthem.

---

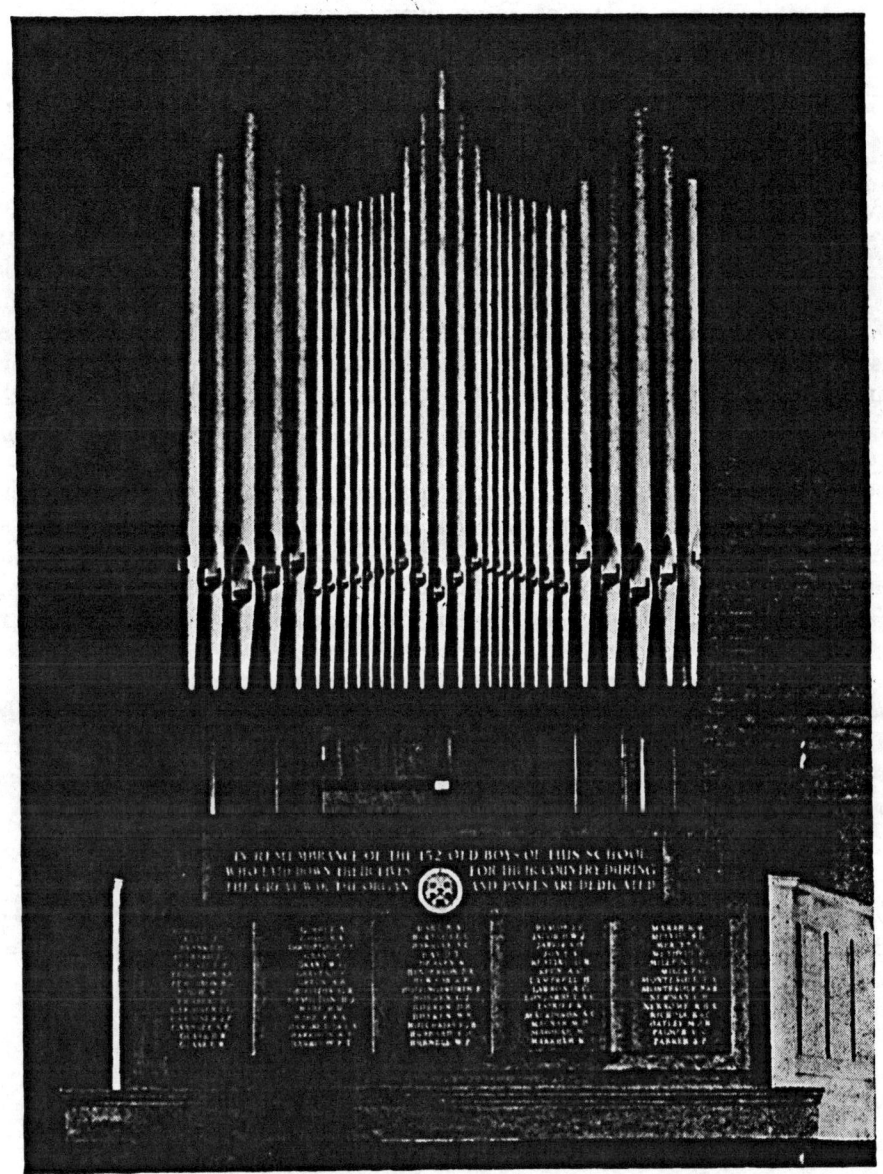

THE STATIONERS' COMPANY'S SCHOOL MEMORIAL ORGAN

# WESTMINSTER SCHOOL

*"Dat Deus incrementum."*

THE Memorial is a beautifully carved Screen in British oak, covering the entire south wall of the "School" and surmounted by windows containing the Arms of Westminster School, Christ Church, Oxford, and Trinity College, Cambridge. The Screen is in the Renaissance style with modern ornaments, and was designed by Sir Robert Lorimer, A.R.A. Inscribed on panels set in the Screen are the names of the Two Hundred and Twenty Six who fell in the War. The Screen itself has in the centre, above the dedicatory panel, a large coloured carving of St. George and the Dragon cut out of solid oak. On either side of the central panel are two Corinthian columns, and similar columns are on either side of the oak entrance doors to the "Big School." At the top of these columns are the Coats of Arms of the five Field-Marshals who were Old Boys of the School. In the design above the doorways and running the whole length of the Screen are reproduced various implements of war, including Trench Mortars, Bombs, Lewis Guns, Gas Masks, Steel Helmets and other paraphernalia. The inscription is:

*" Westmonasteriensibus qui in bello omnium maximo periculum in auditum a patria populisque liberis depellentes mortalii immortalem mutaverunt vitam Victoria repositata monumentum. Dedicavimus suorum fortitudeni acceptem referentes quacumque ipsi ceterique finimur felicitate as MCMXX."*

The Memorial was unveiled by H.R.H. the Duke of Connaught on October 29th, 1921. The chief speeches were made by His Royal Highness, Lord Phillimore and the Headmaster (Rev. H. Costley-White, M.A.).

---

WESTMINSTER SCHOOL MEMORIAL

MILL HILL MEMORIAL GATEWAY

# MILL HILL

*" Et Virtutem et Musas."*

THE Memorial Gateway is erected in a central position in front of the main School buildings. The columns are of Grecian design, with capital in the Corinthian. It takes the form of a loggia with enclosing walls on three sides. The opening on to the road is fitted with wrought iron gates. The whole structure is of Portland Stone. Carved on the panel walls are the names of the Two Hundred Fallen. The inner ceiling is in cedar wood enriched in colours. The terrace extends on either side and is paved in stone.

Mr. Stanley Hamp, of Messrs. Colcutt & Hamp, of Wigmore Street, W.1, was responsible for the design; the modelling and carving was executed by Mr. P. G. Bentham, and Mr. G. Murray carried out the colour decoration on the ceiling. The general contractors were Messrs. G. E. Wallis & Sons, of Maidstone and London.

The inscription on the frieze facing the road and the main entrance of the School is *" Pius patriæ servatoribus servati memores D.D.D."*

The opening ceremony of the Gate of Honour took place on Saturday, October 30th, 1920, commencing with the National Anthem. Sir Albert Spicer congratulated the architect, and said: " It is intended that on special occasions the Gate shall be opened and the School pass through it, so that the gallantry and sacrifice of those who had fallen may be kept in mind by the future generations."

Sir John McClure, the Headmaster, then said: " The Nobler life that is in store for us is part of the crown of life that is theirs for evermore. This Gate has been erected as a symbol of our thanksgiving, as a warning lest we should forget, but chiefly to keep in mind those who preferred duty to life."

The Gate was dedicated by the Rev. H. Arnold Thomas, D.D., with these words: " In grateful and imperishable memory of those whose names are inscribed. Here may it stand when we are gone to bear witness of the valour and fidelity of those who fell. . . ."

General Lord Horne opened the Gate, and the whole School passed through it in procession. Lord Horne then said: " Round all our Public Schools there is already woven the web of great traditions." Then, turning to the Gate, he said: "They responded to the call of Duty to their God, to the Country, to their King and themselves. It was not the players that mattered, but the game; it was not the crew, but the ship."

After the salute had been taken, trumpeters of the Middlesex Regiment sounded the "Last Post," a fitting end to so impressive a ceremony.

A fund has been established for the education of the sons of the Fallen, and a building is to be erected for the teaching of science.

---

## OWEN'S SCHOOL, ISLINGTON

*" In God is all our trust."*

HE Memorial consists of a plain tablet, 6 feet 4 inches by 4 feet 5 inches, of Delabole dark blue slate, engraved and gilded with the Roll of One Hundred and Seventy Two names of the Fallen, in five columns. Above the Roll appears the following inscription: " 1914-1919. *Scholæ Owenianæ Alumnos Alumni Salutant.*"

This Memorial was unveiled by Major-General G. Jeffreys, C.B., C.M.G., G.O.C., London Command, on November 8th, 1921.

The Architect was Mr. Alfred Buxton.

The Memorial Fund is chiefly devoted to assisting Old Boys and their families who may be in need as a consequence of the War.

# DULWICH SCHOOL

*" Detur gloria soli Deo."*

THE Memorial Cross rests upon an octagonal pedestal, in which are set eight bronze panels containing the names of the Five Hundred and Eighteen Boys and Four Masters who fell in the War.

Below these panels are three steps, on which wreaths can be placed. The entire Memorial is situated in the School grounds with a picturesque background of trees. The architect was Mr. W. H. Atkin-Berry, F.R.I.B.A., an Old Alleynian. The unveiling was performed by another Old Alleynian, Major-General Sir Webb Gillman, K.C.M.G., C.B., D.S.O., on Founders' Day, June 17th, 1921.

DULWICH SCHOOL MEMORIAL

In addition to the Memorial Cross, the Memorial Fund provides for the dependants of Old Alleynians who fell, including the education of the sons of Old Alleynians who served in the forces.

A book known as the "Dulwich War Record" was published, and in it are portraits and biographies of all who fell, a list of Honours and Distinctions, and a Roll of over 3,000 who served in the forces.

---

## ST. OLAVE'S AND ST. SAVIOUR'S SCHOOL

ON July 21st, 1922, Major-General Sir Frederick B. Maurice unveiled the Memorial, which was designed by W. Reynolds-Stephens, President of Royal British Sculptors' Society. It consists of a handsome bronze figure of a Roman soldier, overlaid upon a marble wall slab. This is in the form of a Cross, on which is inscribed the following: "*Olaf bear along, Olaf to right the wrong, Till all our Fight be fought.*" Below the tablet on which the statue rests is the following inscription:—

> "*True love by death*
> *True love by life is tried*
> *Live thou for England,*
> 1914 *We for England died.* 1919."

The Roll of Honour contains One Hundred and Ninety One names, and these names were read after the unveiling ceremony.

OLAF·TO·BEAR·ALONG OLAF·TO·RIGHT·THE·WRONG

TILL·ALL·OUR BE·FOUGHT

1914

TRUE·LOVE·BY·DEATH
TRUE·LOVE·BY·LIFE·IS·TRIED
LIVE·THOU·FOR·ENGLAND
WE·FOR·ENGLAND·DIED

1919

ST. OLAVE'S AND ST. SAVIOUR'S SCHOOL,
THE MEMORIAL.

# KING'S COLLEGE SCHOOL, WIMBLEDON

*" Sancte et sapienter."*

IR Cecil Hertslet, an Old Boy of the School, unveiled the Memorial Monument on Friday, October 14th, 1921. During the ceremony he gave an address, in which he said there must be a note of sadness in unveiling a War Memorial. Their thoughts went forth that day to family circles, now for ever deprived of one of their best-loved members, and their hearts turned to the relatives of the Fallen and to the mothers who were mourning the loss of their sons—perhaps their only son. England had been saved by the self-sacrifice of her sons, and it was to honour their sacrifice, and to show their gratitude for it, that they were unveiling that Memorial that afternoon. There were some people in his country who thought there was some danger that the War and all its suffering might be forgotten. They looked round at our crowded racecourses and at the professional football matches and they wondered if we were really forgetting. But the mourners might be reassured; they knew that the heart of England really beat as true to-day as it has always beaten truly in the past.

After the unveiling, the O.T.C., still presenting arms, the buglers sounded the "Last Post."

Speech Day has been postponed from the Summer Term so that it might coincide with the unveiling of the Memorial. The Guard of Honour was supplied by the O.T.C. There was a large gathering of relatives and friends, and after the ceremony wreaths were laid on the Memorial.

The Memorial takes the form of a stone pedestal surmounted by a bronze statue of a Greek Athlete holding aloft a wreath of Victory. The shape of the pedestal is circular and there are five panels on which are inscribed the names of One Hundred and Sixty One Old Boys who fell in the War. The monument is situated among the trees on the side of the Old Field opposite the Science Laboratory, and on the face of the pedestal are inscribed the Greek characters meaning " Theirs is the prize of fair-garlanded death."

The statue itself is the work of Mr. Charles Hartwell, A.R.A., while Mr. Arthur Stratton, F.R.I.B.A., designed the rest of the Memorial.

A Memorial Library was also opened, and before it a Lobby, on the walls of which are the names and many photographs of the Fallen. Mr. Arthur Stratton also designed the decorations for the Library; the lettering was the work of the Art Master of the School, Mr. G. F. Rhead.

The painting in the Library is signed " Herbert Finn, 1920." It represents Sunset on the Thames.

Part of the Memorial Fund has been put aside to provide for the education of the sons of the Fallen.

KING'S COLLEGE SCHOOL, WIMBLEDON, THE MEMORIAL

# UNIVERSITY COLLEGE SCHOOL, HAMPSTEAD

## "*Paulatim.*"

ON Friday, March 3rd, 1922, a War Memorial Tablet, designed by Sir Edwyn Lutyens, A.R.A., was unveiled by Major-General Sir Theodore Fraser, K.C.B., who stated that 1,600 Masters and Boys went to the Front. Of these, 300 were wounded, and the Roll of Honour contains the names of Three Masters and Two Hundred and Fifty One Old Boys who died. Dr. Spencer read the names, which are inscribed on the Tablet situated in the Great Hall.

After a short speech by Sir Gerald du Maurier, the Captain of the School lit the lamp which is to burn perpetually before the Memorial Tablet.

Sir Theodore Fraser then said the Memorial embodied the words: "*Not self but service; service to my country, service to my fellow-men and service to my God.*"

---

# ST. PAUL'S SCHOOL

## "*Fide et Literis.*"

THE Memorial takes the form of a Chapel designed by Mr. MacDonald Gill; it was designed in keeping with the surrounding School Buildings. There is a Greek inscription over the altar, meaning "To-day, Yesterday and Forever."

A Mural Tablet, containing the names of the Five Hundred and One Old Boys who fell in the War, was unveiled by the Bishop of London on May 11th, 1926. There was a large gathering of present Scholars and Masters, relatives and parents of the Fallen.

A Cupola drinking-fountain in the Playing Field recalls the South African War (1899-1902).

ST. PAUL'S SCHOOL MEMORIAL CHAPEL—THE ALTAR

# HABERDASHERS' ASKE'S HATCHAM SCHOOL

*" Serve and Obey."*

THIS is one of the Haberdashers' Company Aske Foundation Schools in London, the other being at Hampstead.

On February 16th, 1924, General Sir George Milne, G.C.M.G., K.C.B., D.S.O. (G.O.C. Eastern Command), unveiled the stained oak tablet erected in the School Hall, to the memory of One Hundred and Thirty Old Askeans killed.

Mr. E. B. Falkner (Headmaster) said : " All must have come with mixed feelings—sorrow for the loss of our sons, and pride in that they elected to put love of Empire before love of self." Sir G. Milne said

THE MEMORIAL PAVILION

that 350 Old Askeans volunteered for active service in France, Gallipoli, Jutland, Palestine and East Africa. Among the fallen were Gabriel Dadd, that promising sculptor, and the naval veteran Admiral Lister.

Later the assembly proceeded to the Pavilion, which was opened with the key Sir G. Milne received from Sir Robert Blair (who, thirty years ago, was Second Master of this School).

The idea of the Memorial originated with Mr. John Lees. Mr. Stanley Ramsay (O.A.) was architect for the Pavilion.

The inscription at the Hatcham School is: " 1914. *Inscribed on this Roll are the names of Old Askeans who gave their lives in the Great War,* 1918."

---

## HABERDASHERS' ASKE'S SCHOOL, HAMPSTEAD

N Saturday, November 11th, 1922, a short service was held in the Assembly Hall conducted by Rev. Prebendary Prosser (Chairman of the Governors), Rev. E. Corns Davies (Minister, Brondesbury Baptist Church), Rev. A. A. Green (Minister, West Hampstead Synagogue) and Rev. W. H. Braine (School Chaplain).

The Form of Service was: Hymn, " Lord of our life "; Collect, For All Saints Day; Two prayers and the Lord's Prayer; Collect, For Easter Day; the Blessing; Unveiling of the Tablet; the " Last Post " and " Reveille " sounded by the bugles.

The Tablet was unveiled by Henry Allan, Esq., Worshipful Master of the Haberdashers' Company, who said: " This Memorial will serve to perpetuate the memory of their sacrifice and inspire future generations to rise to the same height of devotion if the occasion should unhappily arise. The Masters and Boys of our Public Schools were the first to volunteer for the Front. With such a sacrifice we deserved a better Peace." Mr. A. H. Mann expressed gratitude on behalf of all the parents. The ceremony ended with " God Save the King."

The Inscription on the Tablet, which bears Ninety Eight names, is: " *To the glorious memory of the boys of this School who obeyed the call of freedom and honour and served unto death.*"

MERCERS' SCHOOL MEMORIAL

# MERCERS' SCHOOL, HOLBORN

*" Honor Deo."*

HE War Memorial is an Organ erected in the School Hall, and used every morning for prayers. The Organ case was designed by Mr. H. C. Constantine, F.R.I.B.A., an Old Mercer, and constructed by the Headmaster, Mr. C. H. Bicknell, M.A., in the School workshop, entirely of English oak. The panel in front records the names of the Eighty Three Old Boys and Masters who fell in the War. Over the manual is carved, *" Ne frustra fratres mortui sint."*

There was no formal opening, but the Organ was presented to the Governors at the Prize Distribution in July, 1921. The cost of the Memorial was covered by subscriptions from parents and past and present boys.

---

# MERCHANT TAYLORS' SCHOOL, LONDON

*" Homo plantat, homo irrigat, sed Deus dat incrementum."*

HE Memorial consists of three large panels, the centre one containing the following inscription : " 1914-1918. *These members of Merchant Taylors' School served and died.*

*Soe have I thought good to sett downe*
*A remembraunce of them for myne*
*Own good that whoe so list to overlooke*
*Them may followe after with more*
*Ease and happely finde a fayrer waye than*
*They which have gone before."*

Above this inscription is a School Coat of Arms. On either side are panels containing the names of Three Hundred and Nine Old Boys who gave their lives in the Great War.

At the top of the right-hand panel is the inscription : "*Faire branch of honor, flower of chevalrie, Joy have thou of thy noble victorie,*" whilst above the left-hand panel is written : "*Nought is more honourable to a knight, Than to defend the feeble in their right.*"

The names of the five Masters who died are inscribed on a separate panel placed below the large central one.

The inscriptions quoted are respectively from "View of the Present State of Ireland," "Prothalamion" and "Færie Queen" (Book 5, canto II)—all the work of Edmund Spenser, an Old Merchant Taylors' Boy.

The panels were unveiled by Mr. Walter L. Thomas, Master of the Merchant Taylors' Company, on Speech Day, June 11th, 1923. They are the work of Messrs. C. Westcott-Reeves and S. P. Schooling, architects and Old Taylorians; the work was executed by Messrs. W. Aumonier & Son. Brown teak wood was used for the panels, and the lettering is in gold.

The War Memorial Pavilion also was designed by Messrs. Reeves & Schooling. It was opened at Teddington on Saturday, November 25th, 1922, by Viscount Cave, who declared the playing ground open and unveiled the Memorial Tablet, which is situated over the fireplace in the Pavilion.

In the private pavilion at Bellingham a Memorial Tablet is to be erected bearing the names of the Fallen. The names will be carved by relatives as an everlasting memorial, and will not be exhibited publicly.

A fund for providing for the education of the sons of the Fallen has been established.

---

# HIGHGATE SCHOOL

*" Altoria in votis."*

THE Memorial Cross, designed by Sir Reginald Blomfield, is in the same style as the Battlefield Memorial Crosses—an unsheathed sword upon a cross. The Memorial was unveiled by Sir Michael Rimmington, K.C.B. (O.H.S.), in January, 1921. There are Two Hundred and Twenty Five names upon the Roll of Honour, and there is on the base of the cross the following inscription : "*In the Great War for us and our Country they died, remember.*"

HIGHGATE SCHOOL, THE MEMORIAL CROSS

# CHRIST COLLEGE, BRECON

*" Possunt quia posse videntur."*

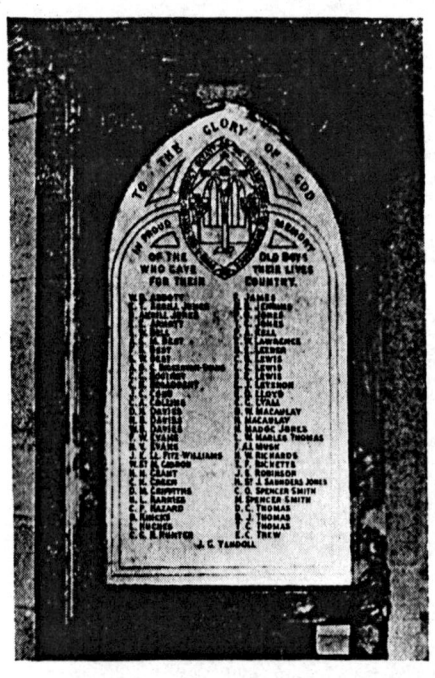

HE War Memorial is in three parts: (1) a Memorial Cross erected in the Chapel Yard; (2) an elaborate alabaster Tablet containing the names of the Fifty Seven Breconian dead; (3) a new Cricket Pavilion.

The Cross and Tablet were unveiled by Lord Glanusk, Lord Lieutenant of County Brecknock, and dedicated by the Bishop of St. David on July 28th, 1922. The ceremonials were both of a military and ecclesiastical character.

The cross bears the inscription: " 1914-1918 " and " *To the glorious memory of those Old Breconians whose names are recorded on the Tablet in the Chapel.*"

The Tablet is erected in the Ante-Chapel of the School. It is surmounted with the College Crest and bears these words: " *To the Glory of God, and in proud memory of the Old Boys who gave their lives for their Country,* 1914-1918." The designer of the Cross and Tablet was Mr. W. M. Best, an Old Boy.

The Cross is a typical Latin, or Crusader's Cross, placed upon an octagonal base with three steps.

The Pavilion which was formerly in use was demolished and a new one, of much larger dimensions, erected opposite the Hostel. The new Pavilion was opened by Mr. W. M. Llewellyn, an Old Breconian. The match between the Old Boys and the School had to be abandoned owing to the bad weather.

CHRIST COLLEGE, THE MEMORIAL CROSS

# LLANDOVERY COLLEGE

*" Gloell dysg na golud."*

THE Memorial Fund has not yet been closed, and it is hoped that part of the War Memorial will be additional Playing Fields.

The number on the Roll to be commemorated is between Eighty and Ninety.

---

# RYDAL SCHOOL, COLWYN BAY

*" Prodesse quam conspici."*

SPEECH Day, June 10th, 1921, was a memorable one, for on that day the War Memorial was dedicated. At 10 a.m. a service was held at St. John's, and the sermon preached by Dr. Barratt.

A memorial service was afterwards held in the Hall, when Mrs. T. G. Osborn, mother of one of the Old Rydalians who was killed in the Great War, unveiled the Memorial Window.

The Headmaster, Rev. J. Costain, gave a short address, and the following hymns were rendered: " O Valiant Hearts," Blake's " Jerusalem " (setting by Parry), " Lord of the brave Who call'st Thine Own " as an anthem. Beethoven's " March Heroique " as a voluntary was played at the termination of the Service.

The Roll of Honour contains Fifty Five names.

The Memorial Window is situated in the " Great Hall " and consists of Four Lights in three tiers. The upper one contains the arms of the Colonies, while the centre one has figures of Christ crucified and Christ as a shepherd. On either side are the Crests of the Principality and Bishopric. On the lower lights on either side are the names of the Fallen, while in the centre are figures of St. George and Sir Galahad, with dedicatory inscriptions underneath.

240

RYDAL SCHOOL MEMORIAL WINDOW

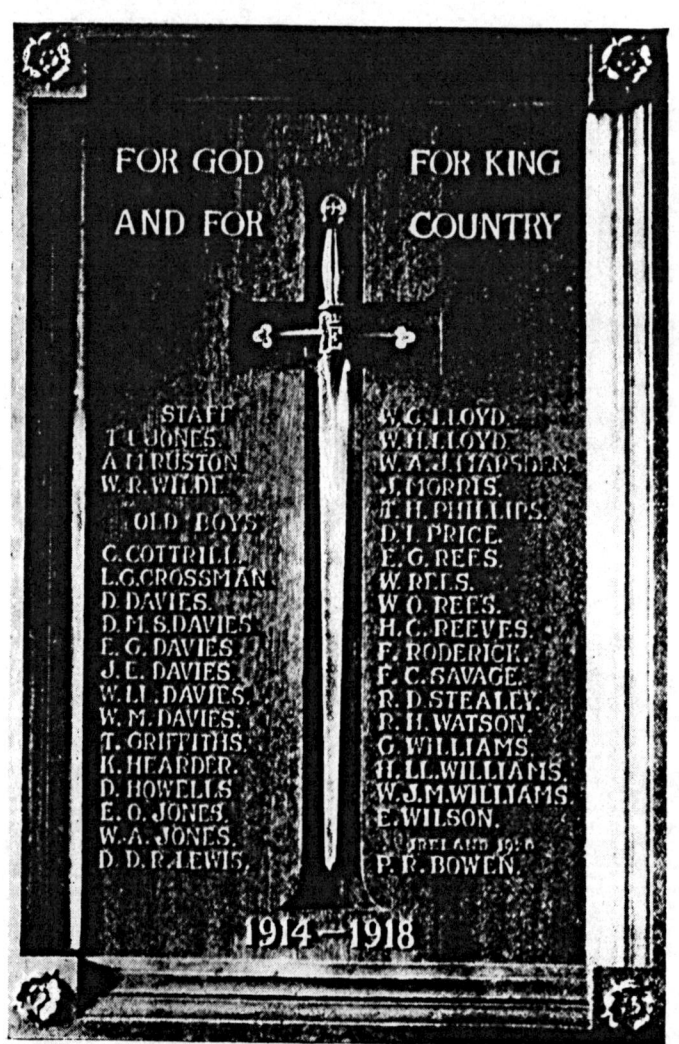

FOR GOD AND FOR

FOR KING COUNTRY

STAFF
T. C. JONES.
A. H. RUSTON
W. R. WILDE.

OLD BOYS
C. COTTRILL.
L. G. CROSSMAN.
D. DAVIES.
D. M. S. DAVIES.
E. G. DAVIES.
J. E. DAVIES.
W. LL. DAVIES.
W. M. DAVIES.
T. GRIFFITHS.
K. HEARDER.
D. HOWELLS.
E. O. JONES.
W. A. JONES.
D. D. R. LEWIS.

W. G. LLOYD.
W. H. LLOYD.
W. A. J. MARSDEN.
J. MORRIS.
T. H. PHILLIPS.
D. I. PRICE.
E. G. REES.
W. REES.
W. O. REES.
H. C. REEVES.
F. RODERICK.
F. C. SAVAGE.
R. D. STEALEY.
R. H. WATSON.
G. WILLIAMS.
H. LL. WILLIAMS.
W. J. M. WILLIAMS.
E. WILSON.
IRELAND 1920
F. R. BOWEN.

1914—1918

QUEEN ELIZABETH GRAMMAR SCHOOL MEMORIAL

# QUEEN ELIZABETH GRAMMAR SCHOOL, CARMARTHEN

A BRONZE Memorial Wall-Tablet, measuring 3 ft. 4 ins. by 2 ft. 3 ins., is mounted on the west (Dehu) wall of the " Big School " immediately under a bust of Queen Elizabeth.

The Memorial was unveiled on Thursday, September 22nd, 1921, by the Headmaster and dedicated by the Venerable Archdeacon of Cardigan. The order of service was as follows: Hymn, " O God our help in ages past "; reading of Ecclesiastes xliv by Major George Thomas, and reading of Revelation vii, 9 to end by the Venerable Archdeacon of Cardigan; hymn, " O frynian Cæsalem " (" Oh, Mountains of Jerusalem! "); prayers, Welsh by the Venerable Archdeacon of Cardigan, and English by Major George Thomas; " The Lord's Prayer "; Address by the Headmaster; the Venerable Archdeacon of Cardigan dedicated the Memorial; " The Last Post "; hymn, " Dan dy fendith wrth ymadæl " (" Under thy Blessing before leaving "), tune Ronda; Benediction; " God Save the King."

There arc on the Tablet the names of Thirty Three Old Boys who fell, and Three of the Staff. The following inscription appears on the Tablet: " *For God for King and for Country*," and the dates, " 1914-1918." In the centre of the Tablet is a battlefield sword and at each corner a national emblem.

## "O Valiant Hearts."

## "The Supreme Sacrifice."

*Words by John S. Arkwright.*      *Music by Rev. C. Harris, D.D.*

O valiant hearts, who to your glory came
Through dust of conflict and through battle-flame;
Tranquil you lie, your knightly virtue proved,
Your memory hallowed in the Land you loved.

Proudly you gathered, rank on rank to war,
As who had heard God's message from afar;
All you had hoped for, all you had, you gave
To save Mankind—yourselves you scorned to save.

Splendid you passed, the great surrender made,
Into the light that nevermore shall fade;
Deep your contentment in that blest abode,
Who wait the last clear trumpet-call of God.

Long years ago, as earth lay dark and still,
Rose a loud cry upon a lonely hill,
While in the frailty of our human clay
Christ, our Redeemer, passed the self-same way.

Still stands His Cross from that dreaded hour to this
Like some bright star above the dark abyss;
Still, through the veil, the Victor's pitying eyes
Look down to bless our lesser Calvaries.

These were His servants, in His steps they trod
Following through death the martyr'd Son of God;
Victor He rose; victorious too shall rise
They who have drunk His cup of Sacrifice.

O risen Lord, O Shepherd of our Dead,
Whose Cross has bought them and whose Staff has led,
In glorious hope their proud and sorrowing Land
Commits her Children to Thy gracious hand.

*by kind permission of Skeffington & Son, Ltd.*

## "Recessional"

### From Rudyard Kipling's "The Five Nations."

God of our fathers, known of old,
Lord of our far-flung battle-line;
Beneath whose awful Hand we hold
Dominion over palm and pine—
Lord God of Hosts, be with us yet,
Lest we forget—lest we forget!

The tumult and the shouting dies;
The captains and the kings depart:
Still stands Thine ancient sacrifice,
An humble and a contrite heart.
Lord God of Hosts, be with us yet,
Lest we forget—lest we forget!

Far-called, our navies melt away;
On dune and headland sinks the fire:
Lo, all our pomp of yesterday
Is one with Nineveh and Tyre!
Judge of the Nations, spare us yet,
Lest we forget—lest we forget!

If, drunk with sight of power, we loose
Wild tongues that have not Thee in awe,
Such boastings as the Gentiles use,
Or lesser breeds without the Law—
Lord God of Hosts, be with us yet,
Lest we forget—lest we forget!

For heathen heart that puts her trust
In reeking tube and iron shard,
All valiant dust that builds on dust,
And guarding, calls not Thee to guard,
For frantic boast and foolish word—
Thy Mercy on Thy People, Lord!

*By kind permission of the Author and Messrs. Methuen & Co., Ltd.*

# ELIZABETH COLLEGE, GUERNSEY

*" Semper eadem."*

THE Memorial, a Cast Metal Bronze Plate upon a marble slab 5 feet by 3 feet, is placed on the north-western wall of the Hall—the side nearest England. It is surmounted by a coat of arms with the superscription: *" Pro mortali condicione vitæ immortalitas."* At the pediment are two small tablets bearing the words *" War," " Peace."* One Hundred and Eight names are inscribed on the Memorial in raised letters. The architect was Mr. W. Marsden, M.C., A.R.C.A.

ELIZABETH COLLEGE—THE MEMORIAL PAVILION

The Memorial Service was held on July 30th, 1922. His Excellency the Lieutenant-Governor, Major-General Sir J. E. Capper, K.C.B., K.C.V.O., unveiled the Memorial, upon which Lady Ozanne placed a floral cross. The service was conducted by the Rev. J. A. F. Ozanne, late Captain R.G.A., and the Principal of the College performed the dedication, saying: " In proud and loving remembrance of the members of this College who gave their lives for God, King and Country in the Great War." The Benediction was pronounced by Rev. W. Campbell-Penney. Six members of the O.T.C. stood on either side of the Memorial with arms reversed during the whole ceremony.

The Service Roll contains Six Hundred and Sixty Two Elizabethans, of whom 234 were mentioned in despatches and 180 gained distinctions.

The Memorial Fund will also provide for a Pavilion and Cricket Field, and Scholarships for sons of the Fallen, and, where needful, daughters.

---

# VICTORIA COLLEGE, JERSEY

*" Amat victoria curam."*

THE Memorial consists of a life-sized statue in bronze of Sir Galahad, and is the work of Mr. Alfred Turner, A.R.A. The figure stands on a pedestal of Jersey granite about 8 feet high on which are inscribed the words: " *The figure of Sir Galahad commemorates the Victorians who gave their lives in the Great War, 1914-1918,*" and the following quotation: " *And come thou too, for thou shalt see the vision when I go.*" The names of the One Hundred and Twenty Seven of the Fallen in letters of gold cover three sides of the pedestal.

His Excellency the Lieutenant Governor unveiled the Memorial on Thursday, September 25th, 1924, and it was dedicated by the Rector of St. Saviour's. His Excellency stated that among the list of names appeared those of Captain Bruce and Captain McReady Diarmid, who were awarded the Victoria Cross posthumously. The name of Major Edmund Talbot Stanley, who died in hospital at Rouen on February 27th, 1919, had to be added to the roll.

VICTORIA COLLEGE JERSEY - THE MEMORIAL

# TRINITY COLLEGE, GLENALMOND

*" Soirbheachadh le Gleann Amuinn."*

THE Memorial Fund was used for the education of the sons of Old Glenalmond Boys who fell in the War, and to erect a Reredos and Panelling in the Chapel.

Sir Francis Davies, K.C.B., K.C.M.G., K.C.V.O., A.D.C., G.O.C., the Scottish Command, unveiled the Memorial on Wednesday, July 26th, 1922. It was dedicated by the Right Rev. W. J. F. Robberds (O.G.), Chairman of the School Council, Bishop of Brechin and Primus of all Scotland.

The architect was Mr. J. N. Comper (O.G.) and the work was executed by Mr. Gough, of Kennington. The following is a brief description of the Memorial in the Chapel. The old panelling has been removed and replaced by six oak panels, three to the north and three to the south of the Altar on the east wall. On these panels are the names of the One Hundred and Fifty Seven who fell. On either side of the Altar and the whole breadth of the east window there is a carved canopy, under which are two medallions. On one side is St. George, the type of Christian chivalry, and on the other, St. Andrew of Scotland and St. Denys of France, signifying comradeship in arms.

Between the medallions, which are surrounded with a laurel wreath design, is the Reredos. This contains the twelve figures of the Scottish saints, representing the kingdoms of Scotland. They are: St. Ninan, representing Galloway; St. Kentigern, representing Clydesdale; St. Columba, representing Argyll and the Isles; St. Maelrubha, representing Ross and the North; St. Magnus, representing Orkney; St. Machar, representing Aberdeen; St. Fillan and St. Serf, representing Perthshire and the Middle East: St. Cuthbert and St. Aidan, representing Lothians and Tweeddale; St. David and St. Margaret stand for the Capital.

The inscription on the Memorial is: *" This Memorial erected as an abiding witness of the love for freedom, truth, justice and mercy which moved the heart of this Country to enter into War, and also in proud and grateful memory of those sons of Glenalmond who died for God and the right."*

Of the 576 who served in the Forces, 164 gained English distinctions, including 2 A.F.C., 88 M.C., 31 D.S.O., and 24 Foreign Orders, including 4 Legion of Honour, 6 French Croix de Guerre, 2 Belgian Croix de Guerre, and 3 Italian decorations. 76 were wounded, and 10 reported missing.

TRINITY COLLEGE MEMORIAL—REREDOS AND PANELLING

# MERCHISTON CASTLE SCHOOL, EDINBURGH

*" Ready, ay ready."*

THE Memorial will take the form of a School Hall, from designs by Mr. Norman A. Dick, of Messrs. Sir John Burnet & Dick, of Glasgow. The Hall has not yet been built as the site of the School is to be moved to Coliston.

The Roll of Honour contains One Hundred and Seventy-Six names. Eight Hundred and Eighty Old Boys served in the Forces.

---

# GLASGOW ACADEMY

THE Committee had three objects in view for the School War Memorial—to record the names of the Fallen in a suitable position in the School, to endow the School itself, and to record the endowment and erect a memorial outside the School.

The endowment of the School meant the purchase of all the shares of the Glasgow Academy Co., winding up the concern and founding the Glasgow Academicals' War Memorial Trust. Thus the School is now owned by the Trust.

Inside the School the names of the Three Hundred and Twenty Seven who fell are inscribed in letters of gold on carved oak panels. This Memorial is situated in the gallery by the first floor of the School, over-looking the Main Hall (known as the Writing Room). Above the panels are the words: " *Say not that the brave die,*" and below: " *These former members of this School left all that was dear to them, endured hardship, faced danger and finally passed out of the sight of man by the path of Duty and Self-Sacrifice, giving up their own lives that others might live in freedom. Let those who come after see to it that their names be not forgotten.*"

At a ceremony held on June 22nd, 1921, Mr. Rintoul, the Chairman, gave a short outline of the Memorial scheme, and introduced General Sir Ian Hamilton, G.C.B., G.C.M.G., D.S.O., who unveiled the Memorial. Sir George Adam Smith, the Principal of Aberdeen University, then dedicated the panels, on which the names of two of his sons appear.

On Armistice Day, November 11th, 1924, the Governors and assembly met in the Rector's Room and proceeded to the south gallery. The Rector explained the object of the gathering and introduced Sir Robert Mackenzie, who made a brief speech. The School was drawn up in Colebrook Street, and the audience made their way to the Memorial, which is placed at the corner of Colebrook Street and Great Western Road. Sir Robert Mackenzie unveiled the Tablet, revealing the following inscription: "*The Glasgow Academy, founded in 1845, reconstructed in 1923 by the Glasgow Academicals' War Memorial Trust as a living and enduring Memorial of those former Members of the School who served in the War of 1914-1918, and in the confident hope that the memory of their Sacrifice will be an inspiration to all who come after.*"

A prayer was said by the Rev. A. M. Stevenson, M.C. Sergeant MacMurray sounded the "Last Post" and the "Reveille," and Sergeant Piper H. A. Brown played a lament.

The following distinctions were gained by Old Boys: 2 V.C., 1 G.B.E., 2 K.B.E., 2 C.B., 12 D.S.O., 99 M.C., 2 D.F.C., 2 D.S.C., 3 D.C.M., 5 M.M., and 12 Foreign Orders.

GLASGOW ACADEMY MEMORIAL

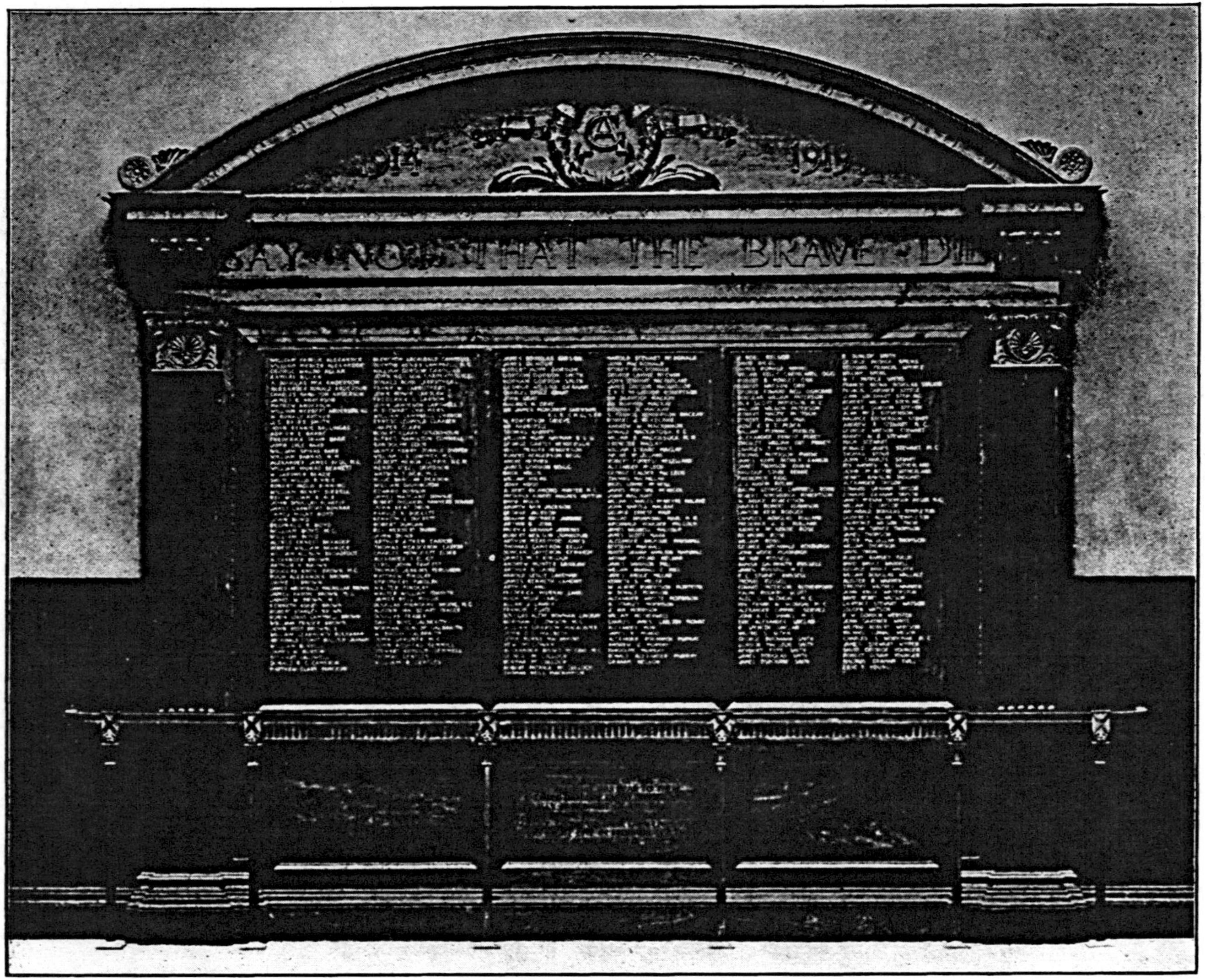

GLASGOW ACADEMY MEMORIAL TABLET

LORETTO SCHOOL MEMORIAL PANELS

LORETTO SCHOOL MEMORIAL ALTAR

# LORETTO SCHOOL

*" Spartam nactus es hanc exorna."*

THE War Memorial at Loretto consists of (1) the Playing Fields of two Rugby pitches and a Cricket pitch between them, and (2) an Organ Screen and Memorial Altar designed by Sir Robert Lorimer and erected in the School Chapel.

The Screen is of carved oak surmounting a series of fourteen oak panels, on which are inscribed the names of the One Hundred and Forty Three Old Boys who died and the year in which they fell. The centre and dedicatory panel is larger than the others, with figures of angels on either side. The following is the inscription: *" To the glory of God and in proud memory of the sons of Loretto who, in the greatest of all wars, by land and sea and air, faced death for freedom and passed out of the sight of men."* Under this inscription is

LORETTO SCHOOL MEMORIAL ALTAR

257

a scroll, supported by angels, on which is written: "*All that they had they gave.*" The arms of France, Belgium, Italy and America are on the left of the central panel; those of Canada, Australia, New Zealand and South Africa are on the right. The carving was done by Messrs. Clow Bros. and Mr. Nathaniel Greive.

The severe design of the stone altar bears in centre face a Cross surrounded by laurels. The inscription below this is: "*He gave His only begotten Son.*"

The service was held on February 3rd, 1922, in Loretto Chapel and was conducted by Rev. E. W. Clarke. Mr. H. B. Tristram read the lesson (Wisdom ii, 23, and iii, 9) and the Headmaster read the Roll of Honour, calling each boy by his Christian names. The panel was unveiled by Mrs. Almond, and Mr. C. J. G. Paterson gave the address.

Over 500 boys answered the call to arms.

---

# EDINBURGH ACADEMY

THE dedication of the War Memorial Building took place on Sunday, June 24th, 1923. The Rev. W. B. Stevenson performed the ceremony, and the Building was opened by Lieutenant-General Sir Aylmer Haldane.

The edifice is in the Doric style, with two floors. The upper contains a Gymnasium, the lower a Workshop, the Armoury and Instruction Rooms. Near the flight of the broad main staircase is a panel on which are inscribed the words "*Pro patria.*" A recess in the panel is flanked by columns carrying bronze panels bearing the names of the Two Hundred and Ninety Eight Old Boys who fell in the War. Over each panel is the dedicatory inscription: "*In piam memoriam*, 1914-1918," and the School Crest.

The architect was Mr. R. S. Reid, an Old Boy, of the firm of Messrs. Leadbetter, Fairley & Reid, of Edinburgh. The bronze work is by Mr. H. S. Gamley, R.S.A.

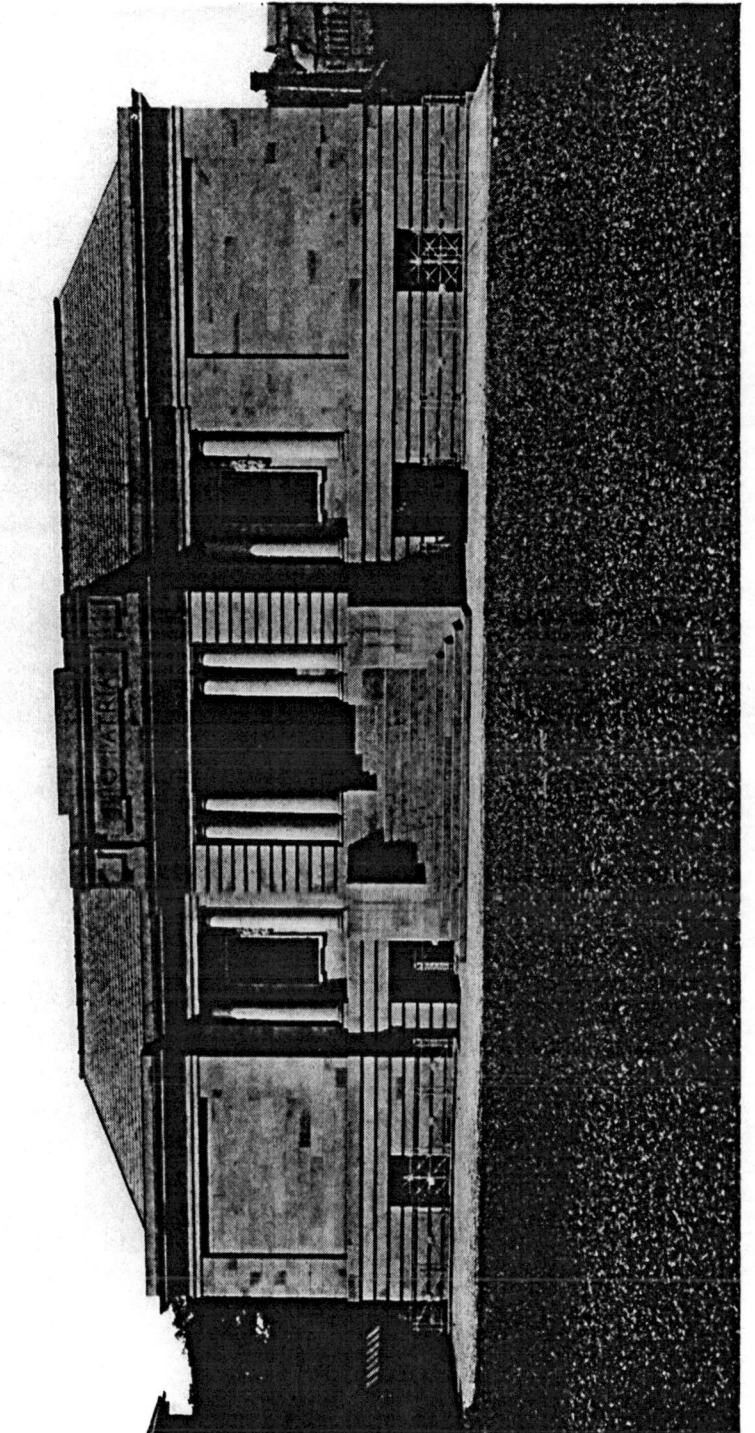

EDINBURGH ACADEMY MEMORIAL BUILDING

# IN · PIAM · MEMORIAM

MCMXIV – MCMXVIII

EDINBURGH ACADEMY MEMORIAL PANEL

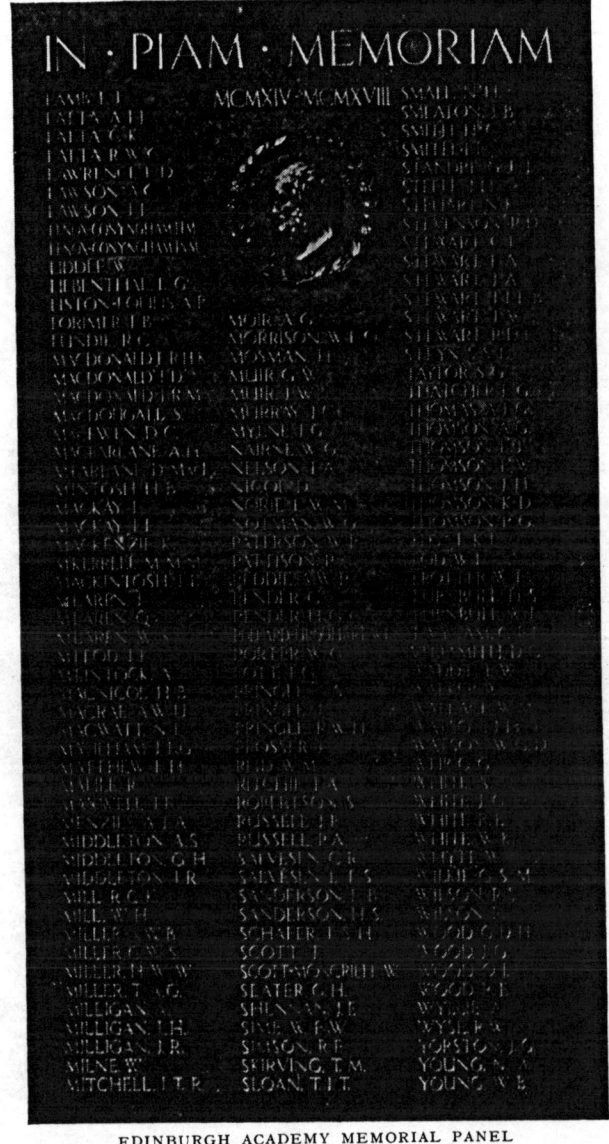

EDINBURGH ACADEMY MEMORIAL PANEL

261

FETTES SCHOOL MEMORIAL

262

# FETTES SCHOOL

## " *Industria.*"

THE Dedication of the Memorial took place on October 15th, 1921. A service in the Chapel was conducted by the Headmaster; Lieutenant-Colonel N. Macleod, C.M.G., D.S.O., read the lesson, and the Rev. Dr. Wallace Williamson, of St. Giles' Cathedral, Edinburgh, preached a sermon on the text " We are compassed about by so great a cloud of witnesses."

The congregation then passed to the Memorial (situated between the College and the head of East Avenue), which was dedicated by Dr. Wallace Williamson and unveiled by Major-General Sir William Macpherson, K.C.M.G.

The sculptor of the Memorial was Mr. Birnie Rhind, R.S.A., of Edinburgh. The design is a beautiful bronze figure of an Officer of a Highland Regiment. He is lying, resting upon his left hand—struck down while fighting. His right hand is held up aloft in a beckoning action, as if to signify to his men " Carry on."

The figure rests upon a stone plinth with two steps around it. On the front panel of the plinth are the figures of two angels bearing a shield, on which is inscribed: " *To the Old Boys. In memory of Fetesians who gave their lives for King and Country in the Great War,* 1914-1918." On the side panels are the names of those who fell. Surrounding the plinth is an ornamental border in the form of oak leaves, whilst on the front of the pediment appears the words " *Carry on* " in bold characters.

Sir George Paul accepted the Memorial on behalf of the Governors, and the O.T.C. marched past at Slow Time.

The hand of the statue points ever onwards and heavenwards—one recalls to mind the words of Rupert Brooke (son of a Fettes Master):—
> " And those who would have been
>   Their sons, they gave their immortality."

The names of those who fell in the War numbered Two Hundred and Forty Six.

The number of Old Boys who served was 1,094, of whom two gained the Victoria Cross, 59 D.S.O., 135 M.C. and 424 were mentioned in despatches.

# ROYAL BELFAST ACADEMICAL INSTITUTION

I*N memory of those Instonians who gave their lives in the Great War*, 1914-1918, *and in honour of those who served and returned.*"

These simple and eloquent words and the names of the Dead are emblazoned on the Memorial Tablet which adorns the south wall of the Common Hall.

The Service Roll contains 703 names; 132 were killed and 121 wounded.

The following distinctions were gained: 1 V.C. (Major J. A. Sinton, in Mesopotamia), 16 D.S.O. (2 with bar), 46 M.C. (3 with bar), and 24 Foreign Decorations.

At the unveiling ceremony on November 1st, 1922, Mr. J. H. Stirling, Chairman of the Governors, said: "Our joys and triumphs we may share, our sorrows we cannot." He then introduced Mr. Justice Wilson, an Old Boy of the School, who said: "There are things of 'Good' beyond calculation of worldly goods and earthly uses; such things are love, honour and the soul of man—which cannot be bought with a price, and which do not die with death. 'Qui procul hinc'—the legend's writ; the grave in France is far away. 'Qui ante diem periit sed miles sed pro patria'—such were the words (by Sir Henry Newbolt) inscribed on the Brass at Clifton."

Mr. Justice Wright, who unveiled the Memorial, said: "Education consists far more in the foundation of character inspired by highest ideals."

The Headmaster, Mr. Jones, said: "This ought not to be a day of sadness, but rather of pride and even exultation. We learn much of what the humblest hearts were capable of in heroism, fortitude and cheerful sacrifice."

The ceremony ended with the sounding of the "Last Post."

ROYAL
BELFAST ACADEMICAL
INSTITUTION.

TO THE MEMORY OF THOSE INSTONIANS
WHO GAVE THEIR LIVES IN THE GREAT WAR 1914-1918.

| | | | |
|---|---|---|---|
| ADRAIN, W. K. | ELLIOTT, G. K. | LEGATE, CHARLES | McMULLEN, E. H. |
| ASHMORE, R. H. | ELLIOTT, T. B. J. | LEGATE, GEORGE | NEILL, J. D. |
| AUSTIN, JAMES | ERSKINE, W. R. | LEGG, CHARLES | O'FLAHERTY, D. H. |
| BAILLIE, H. M. | FISHER, H. B. | LEGG, W. N. | OSBORNE, H. C. |
| BANNISTER, H. S. | FORBES, J. D. | LEONARD, F. P. M. | OSBORNE, W. J. |
| BARLOWE, J. A. B. | FORBES, W. F. | LETTS, B. C. | PETTIGREW, R. MacC. |
| BENNET, T. M. | FRANKLIN, F. R. | LYNESS, HAROLD | POLLOCK, PAUL |
| BILL, J. A. P. | GALWAY, J. C. | MacCOLL, G. E. | RAMSEY, JOHN |
| BOAS, E. G. | GALWAY, J. L. | MacCORMAC, J. S. D. | REA, H. F. |
| BOSTON, THOMAS | GORDON, A. W. | MACILWAINE, JULIAN | READ, S. T. |
| BOYD, BRIAN | GRAHAM, W. R. | MACKAY, JAMES | REILLY, A. M. |
| BOYD, W. G. | GREEN, A. V. | MACREADY, O. H. | RIGGS, J. S. |
| BROWN, HUGH | GUNNING, B. T. | MARKS, J. G. | ROSS, W. S. B. |
| BROWN, JOHN B. | GUNNING, J. ST C. | MILLER, H. T. | SEYMOUR, W. M. |
| BROWN, THOMAS. F. | HAMILTON, R. V. | MILLIKEN, JAMES | SINCLAIR, G. S. |
| BROWNE, M. H. | HANNA, F. L. | MITCHELL, A. G. | SMYTH, G. D. L. |
| BUCHANAN, T. G. | HEWITT, ERNEST | MOORE, D. S. | STANLEY, R. O. |
| BURNSIDE, E. E. | HEWITT, HOLT | MORRIS, W. O. E. | STEVENSON, H. G. |
| CAMBRIDGE, ROBERT | HEWITT, WILLIAM | MORROW, H. G. | STEWART, A. L. |
| CAPPER, A. C. | HOLLYWOOD, ARTHUR | MYDDLETON, H. W. | STORY, L. P. ST J. |
| CHAMBERLAIN, H. N. | HOLLYWOOD, JAMES | McBURNEY, J. W. | TAYLOR, A. S. |
| CLARKE, JOHN | HOUSTON, W. W. | McCANN, W. R. A. | TAYLOR, NATHANIEL |
| CRYMBLE, C. R. | HUGHES, J. I. | McCLINTON, J. S. | THOMSON, A. M. |
| CRYMBLE, J. C. | IRELAND, JAMES | McCONNELL, R. B. | TODD, E. V. |
| CURRAN, HERBERT | IRELAND, RALPH | McCULLAGH, E. S. | TURNBULL, A. M. |
| CURRY, W. G. | IRWIN, W. J. | McCULLOUGH, JOHN | TYRRELL, J. M. |
| DAVIDSON, J. S. | JACKSON, BALFOUR | McCULLOUGH, F. J. | TYRRELL, W. A. |
| DEANE, ARTHUR. D. | JACKSON, GEORGE | McCURRY, W. T. | VANCE, EZEKIEL |
| DESPARD, C. B. | JOHNSTON, SIDNEY | McDOWELL, JOHN. B. | WALKER, C. A. L. |
| DICKSON, J. H. | KENNEDY, JAMES | McFARLAND, GEORGE | WARWICK, W. N. |
| DUNLOP, CHARLES | KENNEDY, WILLIAM | McINTYRE, R. W. | WHITE, THOMAS |
| DUNWOODY, T. C. | KERTLAND, E. B. | McKINNEY, T. G. | WILSON, R. H. |
| EKIN, F. W. | LEES, J. L. | McKINSTRY, J. McN. | WRIGHT, ROBERT |

AND IN HONOUR OF THOSE
WHO SERVED & RETURNED.

ROYAL BELFAST ACADEMICAL INSTITUTION MEMORIAL TABLET

CAMPBELL COLLEGE MEMORIAL

# CAMPBELL COLLEGE, BELFAST

*" Ne obliviscaris."*

THE Memorial was unveiled on April 7th, 1923, by General Godley, in the place of Field-Marshal Sir Henry Wilson, on account of whose lamented death the ceremony had been postponed. It was dedicated by the Rev. Dr. Simms.

Captain James R. Young, an Old Campbellian who had served in the War, designed this Memorial. The names of the One Hundred and Twenty Five of the heroic band who served in the Forces and fell are inscribed in everlasting bronze, framed in carved stonework and surmounted by the words: *" These sons of the School passed out of the sight of men by the path of duty and self-sacrifice."* The names of the Six Hundred and Ten Old Boys who served are inscribed on four bronze tablets, two on either side of the Roll of Honour Tablet. Over each panel is an appropriate inscription.

Among the decorations won by Old Boys was one Victoria Cross and one Distinguished Flying Cross—the latter the first won by an Irishman. In all, 154 decorations were won—a record of which the School might well be proud.

---

# PORTORA ROYAL SCHOOL, ENNISKILLEN

*" Beati Pacifice."*

THE Memorial consists of a Tablet and a new School Sanatorium. The unveiling ceremony was conducted by the Lord Primate of All Ireland on October 26th, 1921.

The Memorial Tablet is cast in solid bronze, the work of William Morris & Co., and is placed in the School Dining Hall. There are Seventy names upon it.

The Sanatorium is situated on the slope of a hill to the south-east of the main buildings. It is of a bungalow type and comprises every modern requirement. It thus forms a most perfect Memorial, by the utility of which the School will greatly benefit in health. On the Memorial Tablet are the following: "*Portora Royal School, Enniskillen*"; then the Royal Coat of Arms, and underneath: "*Erected by the School in proud and loving memory of Portora's Gallant Sons who, obeying the call of duty, went forth and gloriously died for their King and Country in the Great War, 1914-1918.*"

Three hundred and forty-seven Old Boys served in the War, and the following distinctions were won: 1 V.C., 9 D.S.O., 35 M.C., 1 D.C.M, 1 Legion of Honour, 3 Croix de Guerre, 1 Serbian Order of the White Eagle, and 1 Greek Order of the Redeemer.

PORTORA ROYAL SCHOOL, ENNISKILLEN—THE SANATORIUM.

# COLLEGE OF ST. COLUMBA, DUBLIN

*" Prudentes sicut serpentes et simplices sicut Columbæ."*

O N St. Columba's Day, June 9th, 1921, the War Memorial was dedicated by the Bishop of Derry. The three-panel tablet is placed on the south wall of the Ante-Chapel. The centre panel bears the inscription, under a cross : " *To the glorious memory of the members of this College who gave their lives on active service in the Great War, begun on the 4th day of August, 1914, and terminated on the 11th day of November, 1918. 'Hi procul hinc animam spreta dulcedine vitæ, servata patria deposuere suam.'* " The names of Five Masters follow. The two side panels, under the emblem of the Dove, bear the names of Sixty Seven Old Boys. The names are cut on white marble, with carved rich canopy in stone, flat bands of Cork marble flanking the panels, and the surround being in green Connemara Marble. The Latin inscription is by the Warden (Rev. C. B. Armstrong, D.D.).

The Memorial Cross stands outside the Chapel on the south side of the Cloister Square. It is of Celtic design executed in Dublin Granite, with the College Emblem, the Dove, placed centrally on the Cross. All

the carved work and the panel at the foot of the Cross are in limestone. The inscription reads thus: " *This Cross, with the terrace on which it stands and the Mural Tablet in the Chapel, were erected as a Memorial to those members of the College who gave their lives on active service between the 4th day of Agust, 1914, and the 11th day of November, 1918. 'Quasi morientes et ecce vivimus.'* "

The architect for the Cross and Tablets was R. C. Orpen, R.H.A.

There are also two Memorials of a special nature, namely, the Blackburn (Warden) Reredos, in the Chapel, and restoration of Benefactor Windows in the Hall, and the Masterman Library, in memory of Sec.-Lieutenant F. M. Masterman, 3rd Bat. Royal Irish Rifles, who was killed at the Somme (France).

The Service Roll contains Three Hundred and Eighty Five names out of 880 who entered the College since 1870. Thus, 43 per cent. served in the War, and of these 71 Old Boys were wounded.

# THE MENIN GATE AT YPRES

HIS Memorial Arch was designed by Sir Reginald Blomfield, R.A., and was unveiled by Field-Marshal Lord Plumer, the leader of the Second Army of the Ypres salient, on Sunday, July 24th, 1927. The great Gate, in stone, was erected by the Governments of all the nations within the British Commonwealth, with the co-operation of the Imperial War Graves Commission.

The inscription over the Arch reads: "*To the Armies of the British Empire who stood here from 1914 to 1918, and to those of their Dead who have no known grave.*" Their names are inscribed on the walls grouped under their regiments. Fifty Six Thousand British soldiers are thus commemorated. The sculptor was Mr. W. Reid Dick.

The decorative carving took four years to complete: it is the work of Mr. W. Aumonier, President of the London Master Stone Carvers' Association.

The Music rendered at the Dedicatory Service included Schubert's "Unfinished Symphony," Handel's "Largo," and "The Flowers of the Forest" Lament, by Pipers of the 1st Battalion of the Scots Guards, standing on the Ramparts of Ypres.

The King Albert of the Belgians said, "There is certainly no ground in the world more sacred than that of the Ypres Salient. It was to avenge the unjustifiable attack on Belgium that the British Empire took up arms to the remotest parts of its possessions. It was to hoist and hold high the drooping flag of Justice and Civilisation that legions of proud warriors came to Flanders. At once Ypres became one of the vital points in the World War. It was Hill 60 which for two years was the theatre of ceaseless mine warfare. It was from this historic Menin Gate that at dawn on September 28th, 1918, divisions of the Second Army marched out with the Belgian Army and conquered the famous Flanders Ridge to press on to the final victory. For fifty months Ypres marked the threshold of the Empire, symbol of British courage and endurance. Ypres was to the British Army what Verdun was to the French Army. I come to render profound and sincere homage in the name of my country to the memory of 90,000 Soldiers of the British Empire who died a hero's death for the ideal of Justice and Liberty."

LOOKING FROM YPRES, DOWN THE "MENIN ROAD"

THE MENIN GATE LOOKING TOWARDS THE GRANDE PLACE

Sir Laming Worthington Evans, Minister of War, said, "It is a permanent Memorial to the heroism with which they and their comrades stood through four years an immovable and unconquered rampart against the bitterest onslaughts that the history of war has ever recorded."

Field-Marshal Lord Plumer said, " Now it can be said of each one in whose honour we are assembled ' He is not missing, he is here! ' This ground for all time known as the Ypres salient is a historical record of the friendship and comradeship which will always exist between the two armies—British and Belgian—who fought here side by side."

The inscription over the first stairway from the entrance, is : —

" Here are recorded Names of Officers and Men who fell in Ypres Salient but to whom the fortune of war denied the known and honoured burial given to their comrades in death."

The foundation stones of the English Church, and Ypres Memorial School (designed by Sir R. Blomfield) were laid by Lord Plumer on July 24th, 1927. The School is being erected by Etonians in memory of Etonians who lost their lives in the Ypres salient. In the Town Cemetery at Ypres are the graves of Prince Maurice of Battenberg, Lord Charles Mercer-Nairne and Major Hon. W. Cadogan.

# A VISIT TO THE BATTLEFIELDS

THE journey to Ypres by motor from Ostend is made via Forest of Houthulst, St. Pierre Capelle, Poelcappelle (for St. Jean), St. Julien—(the *Canadian Memorial*)—Hill 60 and Sanctuary Wood; at Ypres the *Menin Gate* is visited. The return journey is past Essex Farm Cemetery—(the *West Riding Yorkshire Monument* is here)—Bixschoote, Couckclaere (" Big Gun Long Max " is here) and the Mole at Zeebrugge.

The Somme and Champagne (Arras and Artois) Battlefields may be visited from Amiens. In the Somme area can be visited Villers Bretonneux Chuignolles (" Big Bertha " Gun was here), Bray-sur-Somme, Albert—(*Newfoundland Memorial Park*)—Beaumont Hamel—(*Highland Memorial*),—Thiepval—(*Ulster Memorial Tower*),—Poziers—(*Tank Corps and Australian Monument*),—High Wood—(*New Zealand Memorial*),—Delville Wood—(*South African Memorial*),—Mametz Wood, Contalmaison—(*King's Royal Rifles Memorial*),—La Boiselle —(Mine Craters).

On the way from Amiens to Arras the following may be visited:— St. Catherine's Vimy Ridge and Notre Dame de Lorette—(the Sacred Hill in the war), for which plans of a memorial Basilica have been prepared by M. Louis Cordonnier, of Lille. This point overlooks Souchez, Vimy, Loos, Lens and Mount St. Elroy. Continuing the journey from Lille to Ypres, Roubaix, Tourcoing, Dickebusch, Mount Kemmel, Bailleul and Armentiers are passed.

On the journey from Amiens to Etaples the " Empire Cemetery " can be visited; there are 11,000 graves here, and 1,984 are those of men from overseas. During the War the Base Hospitals were here; eleven General Hospitals, including one stationary base, four Red Cross, and one convalescent depot.

Continuing by rail to Wimereux a drive can be taken to Meerut, where the *Indian Cemetery Memorial*—opened by Lord Birkenhead on October 7th, 1927—is situated.

The journey may end at Boulogne, where, near Napoleon's Column, is situated the Cemetery of Terlincthun.

" *We cannot but believe that the existence of these visible Memorials will eventually serve to draw all peoples together in sanity and self-control, even as it has already set the relations between our Empire and our Allies on the deep-rooted basis of a common Heroism and a common Agony. We remember and must charge our children to remember that, as our Dead were equal in sacrifice, so are they equal in honour. For sacrifice and honour are no vain things, but truths by which the world lives, and I fervently pray that, both as nations and individuals, we may so order our lives after the ideals for which our brethren died that we may be able to meet their gallant souls once more humbly but unashamed.*"

—From a speech by His Majesty the King at the Terlincthun Cemetery, May, 1922.

# "British Colonial Schools"

# ST. ANDREW'S COLLEGE, GRAHAMSTOWN
# CAPE PROVINCE, SOUTH AFRICA

*" Sancti Andræ Collegii Apua Græmvillenses Sigil."*

HE open ground to the east of the Chapel was selected as the site for the St. Andrew's Memorial Tower. The Tower itself conforms to the round-arched Gothic style of the existing Chapel.

The plan provides a square porch with a massive diagonal buttress at each corner, with porch being ceiled with concrete groin. On each side there is a wide-open arch. At an angle across each corner of the porch is a marble slab inscribed with the names of the One Hundred and Twenty Five who fell. Over the main entrance (facing Somerset Street) a tablet records the purpose of the Memorial. The Tower has a clock with a dial on each side, and bells which chime the quarters. A feature of the design is the large tower light or opening which adorns each face. the upper part is open, the lower portion filled with wood louvres. A battlemented parapet is crowned with a small pointed tile roof and weather vane. The garden adjacent to the Tower has been laid out as a part of the Memorial.

Messrs. Baker, Kendall & Morris, of Capetown, were the architects, and Messrs. Carr & Co., the contractors.

The foundation stone was laid by Vice-Admiral Sir W. E. Goodenough, K.C.B., M.V.O. (who took part in the Battle of Jutland), at 5.30 p.m. on November 29th, 1921, in the presence of the Bishop of Grahamstown and the Mayor, Mr. L. L. Giddy (Chairman of College Council). The stone, which was laid with a silver trowel, the gift of the architects, bears the inscription: " *A.D.G.M. This stone was laid by Vice-Admiral Sir William E. Goodenough, K.C.B., M.V.O., 29th November, 1921.*"

In his address, the Admiral said: " But were each memorial as fine as Westminster Abbey, or as beautiful as the Taj-Mahal, there would yet be something wanting if it were not imbued with the personal spirit of each one of us. Nothing really suffices, but I would refer to Stonewall Jackson: ' Press forward, not to obtain the prize, but to overcome the obstacle.' Let me counsel two things: one, purpose, the other unselfishness, and don't forget your comrades. However late the " Last Post " may sound, the " Reveille " will sound in the morning.

The service began with Kipling's Recessional, " God of our fathers known of old "; prayer followed, led by the Rev. W. G. Dowsley, Chaplain; the Roll of Honour was read by the Headmaster, and the Dedicatory Prayer said by the Bishop of Grahamstown—" laying the stone both truly and well." Then was sung the hymn, " Now all men thank we God," and the ceremony concluded with the Benediction, the " Last Post " and " God Save the King."

ST. ANDREW'S MEMORIAL TOWER

The Cadet Corps of St. Andrew's, Kingswood College, and Victoria High School attended.

On St. Andrew's Day, 1923, the Bishop of Grahamstown, the Dean and other Clergy, met the Headmaster, Council and Staff of the College at the Tower, and after dedicatory prayers had been said by the Bishop, General Sir Henry Lukin, K.C.B., unveiled the Memorial Tablet, which bears the inscription: "*MCMXIV—MCMXVIII. Mementote hujus collegii alumnorum qui ubique terrarum marium cælorum fortiter et patienter militantes libertatem nobis sibi pacem moriestes consciverunt.*"

The Headmaster, in welcoming Sir Henry Lukin, referred to his journey of 800 miles to perform the unveiling, and mentioned that he had commanded the South African Brigade in Egypt, France and Flanders. General Lukin said, in the course of an impressive address: "On Christmas Day, 1916, when the Ninth Division held the line east of Arras, facing Vimy Ridge, on turning to a sentry in the trenches, I said, 'Well, my lad, I hope that you will live to see many more Christmases.' He returned my greetings and blurted out: 'I remember so well, sir, the first time I saw you.' I said: 'Where was that?' and he answered: 'I was in the Cadet Corps at St. Andrew's College, Grahamstown, when you came down there to inspect us.' Tradition is the life-blood of a School or a regiment, and I make a suggestion that, on the anniversary of this day, the Boys should be assembled at this arch and told the story of the devotion to duty of those whose names are inscribed on it."

Mr. E. W. Douglass (the Attorney-General), President of the O.A.C., presented the Memorial to the Chairman of the Council, Mr. L. L. Giddy. The Rev. R. G. Mullins read the Roll of Honour.

The Service numbers were over One Thousand, although, in South Africa, there was no Conscription Act. There were One Hundred and Twenty Five killed on Service. Distinctions gained included 1 V.C., 13 D.S.O., 1 D.S.C., 4 D.F.C., 6 D.C.M., 36 M.C. (4 with bar), 2 M.M., 2 C.M.G., and 25 Foreign Orders.

---

# DIOCESAN COLLEGE, RONDEBOSCH, CAPE TOWN, SOUTH AFRICA

## " *Pro fide et patria.*"

THE War Memorial Chapel was dedicated on October 31st, 1926, by the Archbishop of Cape Town, in the presence of the Governor-General and the late Vice-Admiral Sir Maurice Fitzmaurice. The architect was Mr. C. P. Walgate, A.R.C.A., A.S.I.B.A., who is at present engaged on the new University of Cape Town at Groste Selzoor. The plan and the internal treatment of the Chapel has been based on early Christian tradition. Its prototype is the ninth-century Church of the Theotokos at Constantinople; the intersection of a basilica by transepts, creating a Nave, crossing and Sanctuary. The date of the origin of the baldachino or criborium over the Altar is not later than A.D. 500. The stately columns of the Bishop's Chapel bear the symbols of Africa's Saints, St. Augustine's shell, St. Catherine's wheel, St. Athanasius' broken chalice, St. Cyprian's gleaming book and sword, calling us of the South to be as true to the faith, as fearless for the way, as our Northern comrades.

On the day of the Unveiling Ceremony there was torrential rain. The Ceremony opened with the singing of the first verse of " God save the King," on the arrival of the Governor-General. In the collonade were waiting the College Council and the Architect, with the Head Prefect, P. Van de Byl, and the Second Prefect, R. J. Milligan.

According to custom, the Archbishop knocked thrice on the closed door and claimed admittance. On entering, Judge Gardiner, in the Council's name, prayed them to proceed to dedicate. The procession formed by a Cross-bearer, Choir, Clergy of the College Staff and the preacher, the Rev. J. C. H. Brooke, M.A. (O.D.), Rector of St. Aidan's, Johannesburg, the Principal of the College, Rev. R. H. Birt, Rev. J. O. Nash, Co-adjutor Bishop of Capetown, and the Primatial Cross, followed by the Archbishop of Capetown and attendant chaplains, passed from the Old Chapel to the Sanctuary of the New Chapel.

T

The following is the order of the service: The two Prefects opened the doors for the entry of the Archbishop. The Processional Hymn, "All things are Thine, no gift have we" (Public School Hymn Book, 253), was sung to the tune of "The Old Hundredth." Dedicatory sentences were said at the Altar, the Choir Stalls, the Lectern, the Place where the preacher shall stand, the Place for the "Laying on of hands in Confirmation," and the Sanctuary. The hymn, "Faith of our fathers taught of old" (English Hymnal, 544), was sung as the Archbishop proceeded to the Founder's Chapel. The Recessional Hymn was "Praise my soul the King of Heaven" (A. & M., 298). The Bidding Prayer was read and a sermon was preached by the Rev. J. C. H. Brooke, M.A., a son of a former Headmaster and brother of one of the Fallen. The commemoration of the Founder and of those killed in the War followed, and the Archbishop pronounced the Blessing. The hymn, "O Valiant Hearts, who to your glory came," was then sung, and the "Last Post" and "Reveille" were sounded by buglers. The Doxology (A. & M., 379, last verse only) ended the service.

THE MEMORIAL CHAPEL

The first Holy Communion in the new Chapel was celebrated at 7.45 a.m. on November 1st, 1926, the architect serving at the altar.

Thus were commemorated the brave and true who " have died the death of honour and departed in the hope of Resurrection to Eternal Life."

A Bronze Tablet will record the One Hundred and Eight names of the Fallen. It will be placed over the main entrance to the Chapel. The illuminated book containing the Roll of Honour is at present in the War Memorial Chapel, but is to be transferred to the Library in the Old Chapel.

The following is the College War Record: On Active Service, 800: Killed or Died, 108; Wounded, 160; Honours and Awards, 170; Commissions (from Second Lieutenant to General), 500.

THE ALTAR

The following is an extract from the sermon preached by the Rev. J. C. H. Brooke: "We meet this morning with feelings of thanksgiving mingled with sorrow . . . thanksgiving to see this Chapel an accomplished fact; for the spirit of generous giving which the War Memorial has aroused. Proud thanksgiving for what they did in 1914: God called with a voice of thunder 'Come out'; they scarcely knew it: perhaps they had another name for 'God'—'Duty calls, or Self-respect, or Shame.' In obedience to that inner call they gave up all. For what?— the freedom of the peoples, honour among nations, the peace of the world. It was a triumph of the spiritual over the material. There are times and crises when men feel that 'Man cannot live by bread alone' and all considerations of personal gain and safety are nothing to the urgency of the higher call to give. So it was in those dark days of 1914 to 1918. They died like Christ to save the world, they live to work with Him. Take Him as your leader; follow Him."

Some notes about the Chapel. The old geometric figure of two circles cutting each other was used for the design. The central part common to both circles is known as the "Vesica picis." Since the fourth century all seals of Abbeys, Colleges and ecclesiastical personages have been of this eliptical shape—the halo of the saints depicted by mediæval artists. This Vesica is placed in a rectangle, and the large rectangle divided into three smaller rectangles of equal size. The general rectangular shape of the whole interior circumscribes one vesica, and its sub-divisions are the basis of every dimension of the building. The diagonals of the smaller and greater rectangles are used for setting out the vaulting and tracery window patterns. The other factor was the canonical relationship of the Narthex, Choros and Bema. The numerical significance of the words is 228, 1,040, 51, and these numbers in inches were given to the Ante-Chapel, Chapel and Altar respectively. "Bema" was the Greek orators' stone for outdoor speeches—later, the Roman rostrum within the Basilica. In early Churches the Last Supper was celebrated on this stone, which thus became the Altar.

The oldest measurement is the British Inch, which is one twenty-fifth of the Egyptian Sacred Cubit. The Cathedrals of Chartres, Rheims, and Beauvais are built on the principle of the "Vesica picis," this sacred emblem typifying "Regeneration or New Birth."

In many of the Great War cemeteries a Stone of Remembrance has been placed. The origin of this custom is the "Bema."

## DALE COLLEGE, KING WILLIAM'S TOWN, CAPE TOWN

*"Per ardua."*

IN front of the School Building is erected a beautiful stone Cenotaph, on top of which is a bronze figure of a Cadet, with head bowed and arms reversed. The Memorial commemorates the Ninety Three who were killed—a noble record for so young a School.

The unveiling ceremony took place in June, 1922. A short service was held, conducted by the Rev. J. G. Sutton, M.A., assisted by his son, the Rev. F. Y. Sutton. The monument was unveiled by Sir Frederic de Waal.

---

## CHURCH OF ENGLAND GRAMMAR SCHOOL, GEELONG, VICTORIA

*" Christus nobis factus sapientia."*

ON Friday, June 24th, 1927, the dedication of the Memorial Cloister and Bronze Group was performed by Rev. Harrington C. Lees, D.D., Archbishop of Melbourne, after being unveiled by His Excellency Lord Stonehaven, Governor-General. The following was the Order of Service: Hymn, "Let Saints on earth in concert sing"; Request for Dedication by President of the Old Boys' Association, Dr. E. R. White; Acceptance of the Memorial by the Archbishop; Hymn, "O Valiant Hearts"; Lesson, Hebrew xi, 13-16, by the Headmaster, Dr. F. E. Brown; Sentences and Prayers of Remembrance, followed by the Benediction, which was said by the Archbishop.

Unveiling of the Memorial by Lord Stonehaven, who, in his speech, said : " Such memorials not merely enrich the School site, but they enrich the Nation. What place is more fitting than the headquarters of one of Australia's great educational centres? Lord Milner had said: ' It is not the soil of England, dear though it is to me, that is fashioning my patriotism. It is the language, the inspiration, the spiritual inheritance and traditions of the British race; and if they are transplanted overseas they do not cease to be mine. My horizon is widened.' You will see statues erected to great men—this statue is erected to a team—the Australian Team—whose members' names are engraved on the tablets,

Eighty Eight Boys are not available for service to the State. For that reason you are required to give Greater Service."

Dr. Lees said that the figure of the soldier was emblematic, that there was a power which could come to their aid in keeping the beast within submission.

The National Anthem was followed by the "Last Post." The Senior Prefect, F. E. T. Jelfcott, placed a laurel wreath on the Memorial.

The following War Distinctions were gained: 42 M.C. (6 with bar), 2 C.M.G., 4 D.S.O., 7 M.M., 3 Air Force, and 4 other distinctions, while 23 were mentioned in despatches, and 5 Foreign Orders were gained.

The Bronze Group was designed and sculptured by Mr. G. W. Lambert, A.R.A., of Sydney, and it is symbolic of the triumph of Youthful Heroism over Evil. Two war-weary Australian soldiers, one in equipment of the French trenches and the other representative of the Light Horse of Palestine, support the immense bird—symbolic of the Germanic purpose of war, and also of all evil destroying the virtue and beauty of civilisation. The figure of Youth is naked except for a close-fitting headpiece and loin armour. It represents the spirit of heroism, the young warrior of all ages to fight a noble cause, while in his hand is a long two-handed sword.

The founders of the Bronze Group and of the tablets containing the names were the Alloy Castings Co., of South Melbourne. The builders of the masonry were Albert Howarth, of South Yarra. The makers of the doors of the Chapel and School were John Paget, of Elsternwick.

The Memorial Cloister forms a background for the Bronze Group. It is built on a gentle curve between the doors opening into the nave of the Chapel and the main quadrangle, designed by Mr. H. Desbrowe-Annear, of Melbourne, in the English Perpendicular Style of the Gothic period. It is carried out in chiselled and rubbed Freestone from Ross, Tasmania, and roughed spalled Barrabool Freestone from Geelong.

The paving is of granite and bluestone. The four mural tablets have on them Eighty Eight names and that of one Master.

At the head of the first tablet is : " *Dulce et decorum est pro patria mori.*"

At the head of the second tablet is: "*Their name liveth for evermore.*"

At the head of the third tablet is: "*Greater love hath no man than this that a man lay down his life for his friends.*"

At the head of the fourth tablet is: "*Esto fidelis usque ad mortem, et dabo tibi coronam vitæ.*"

These tablets are placed on the walls of the Cloister, at the base of the pedestal, of which is the Bronze Group is the inscription: "*Faithful unto death. 1914-1918.*"

The foundation of the Chapel was laid by the mother of Mr. Norman Falkiner, and he himself offered to complete the original design at his own expense (some £10,000). Seventy years ago the School was founded by Bishop Charles Perry, the first Anglican Bishop of Melbourne, and June 24th will be known hereafter as "Founder's Day."

CHURCH OF ENGLAND GRAMMAR SCHOOL MEMORIAL

# SCOTCH COLLEGE, MELBOURNE

*'Deo patriæ litteris."*

OLD BOYS of this College contributed £50,000 to provide new School Buildings and a School Hall as a War Memorial.

The foundation stone of the Hall was laid by Sir John Monash, G.C.M.G., who was Dux of the School in 1881. Brasses showing the names of the Two Hundred and Seven of the Fallen are placed in the apse of the Hall. The distinctions gained were: 22 D.S.O. (6 with bar), 2 D.F.C., 2 D.S.C. (2 with bar), 64 M.C. (6 with bar), 3 D.C.M., 29 M.M. (2 with bar), 20 other British Orders, 17 Foreign Orders, 2 Legion d'Honneur (French), 8 Belgian Croix de Guerre, 3 French Croix de Guerre, 1 American D.S.M., and 1 Russian Cross of St. Anne. The inscription on the foundation stone is: "*Scotch College New Buildings. Deo patriæ litteris. This Foundation Stone of the Memorial Hall, erected by the Old Boys in honour of those who served in the War, 1914-1918, was laid by Lieutenant-General Sir John Monash, G.C.M.G., K.C.B., V.D., M.C.E., Dux of the College in 1881, 5th March, 1920. Their name liveth for evermore.*"

The Hall at Hawthorn was opened on the seventh anniversary of Anzac Day, April 25th, 1922, when the proceedings were as follows:—

Twelve hundred youthful voices sang the "Old Hundredth," Mr. W. H. Melville, M.A., LL.M., read the lesson (Psalm xix); J. D. Burn's hymn, "The Bugles of England," was sung, followed by the recital of the names of the Fallen by the Principal, Mr. W. S. Littlejohn, M.A., who then quoted the stanza:

> " And you our brothers who, for all our praying,
>     To this dear School of ours come back no more,
> Who lie, our Country's debt of honour paying,
>     And not in vain—upon a foreign shore
> Till that great Day when at the Throne in Heaven
>     The Books are opened and the Judgment set.
> Your lives for Honour and for England given:
>     The School will not forget."

Then the " Last Post " was sounded.

The Hon. Arthur Robinson, C.M.G., said: " It is more than thirty years since I left the College. I have felt a love for her, a pride in her. In the War a test of manhood was offered, not of physical courage merely, but of moral courage : —

" ' O! England, I heard the voice of those that died for thee
Sounding like an organ voice across the winter sea;
They lived, and died for England and gladly went their way
England, O! England—how could I stay? '

" Quoting Pericles, he said : ' The whole earth is the sepulchre of brave men, whose story is not only engraven in stone, but lives on, far into the future, woven into the stuff of other men's lives.'

" The history of that effort is part of each boy's individual history. He has the power to enlarge the history and tradition, to beautify it and to strengthen it."

The Moderator of the Presbyterian Church of Victoria (Rev. D. A. Cameron, M.A.) offered the dedicatory prayer, after which was sung " For all the Saints."

Sir John Monash, who commanded the whole Australian Army, said : " I should like to think that for all time to come this Hall will be associated with Anzac Day, to render homage to the men who played their part so nobly in the Great War—it was the day on which Australia and New Zealand stormed the beetling cliffs of Gallipoli. As a military feat it was sublime; it established the tradition of the A.I.F. ' Remember Gallipoli ' became their watchword. On the third anniversary of Anzac Day, Villers-Bretonneux was recaptured; it was the terminating point of the War. We should look for leaders in the future, first in the boys of the great Public Schools. You should be proud to be the inheritors of such a record."

Maxwell's grand hymn was then sung : —

" O God, beneath Whose hand we hold
The battle standard, and the sword
Upon Whose never-changing word
Our fathers set their trust of old.
Because Thy love is full and free
Our darkness lifts its voice to Thee."

The service closed with the Benediction and the singing of the
National Anthem. A service was held on Tuesday, November 11th, 1926,
Remembrance Day—in the School Hall. The order of service was as
follows: Lawrence Binyon's hymn, " They went with songs to the
battle, they were young "; the hymn, " The Saints of God, their conflict
past "; the Lesson, from Revelation vii, 9-17; the recital of the names of
the Fallen; John Oxenham's hymn, " Peace after strife, and after labour,
rest," and prayers. At 11 a.m., two minutes' silence, then the " Last
Post," the hymn, " Peace, perfect peace in this dark world of sin," and
the Benediction, followed by " God save the King."

SCOTCH COLLEGE, THE MEMORIAL

# BRISBANE GRAMMAR SCHOOL

*" Nil sine labore."*

NE Hundred and Seventy Five of the 1,025 Old Boys of this School who served fell in action, 72 were mentioned in despatches, and 160 gained military honours, including 52 M.C., 5 M.S.M., 28 M.M., 22 D.S.O., 3 D.C.M., 4 C.B., 12 C.M.G., 14 Croix de Guerre and 11 other Foreign Orders. Over half the volunteers won commissions, and five reached the rank of Brigadier-General in the A.I.F.

There are various forms of Memorials, dedicated with appropriate ceremonies. On August 14th, 1916, H.E. the Right Hon. Ronald Munro-Ferguson, P.C. (now Viscount Novar), unveiled an Honour Board in the Assembly Hall. The Board was designed by Mr. T. R. Hall, and bears the inscription at the head: " *Lecti juvenes—fortissima corda.*" At the foot was added: " 1914—*Enlisted in the Great War—* 1919."

In the centre of the main drive stands a captured field gun, presented to the School by the Commonwealth Government. The gun was captured by Brigadier-General L. C. Wilson (3rd L.H. Brigade) at Jenin, in Palestine, on September 20th, 1918. On August 11th, 1921, this Memorial was unveiled by the Right Hon. Lord Forster, P.C., Governor-General, who said: " This stands as an emblem of victory to remind you of the spirit in which Australia answered the call of the Mother Country." The short service commenced with the National Anthem, followed by Prayer by the Chaplain, Major J. E. N. Osborn, M.C., M.A., the hymn, " O God our Help in ages past," and introductory remarks by J. L. Woolcock, B.A. (Chairman of Trustees). After the unveiling by the Governor-General, the story of the gun was told by Brigadier-General L. C. Wilson, C.B. Q.M.S. J. E. England, M.S.M., sang " Land of Hope and Glory," and the Headmaster (F. S. N. Bousfield. M.A.) gave an address. The ceremony concluded with the " Last Post " and the Doxology.

The next ceremony was on the occasion of the laying of the foundation stone of the Memorial Library, on April 25th, 1923. H.E. the Governor of Queensland, the Right Hon. Sir Matthew Nathan, P.C., performed this duty. The stone was the gift of Mr. A. M. Midson

(O.B.G.), who also carried out the work of preparation for the stone-laying ceremony. £600 was laid on the stone towards the Library Fund.

The Library itself was built by Mr. P. Frew from the plans of Messrs. J. Barr and A. E. Brooks. The building is of Gothic design. Over the entrance is inscribed: "*Nobis neminisse relictum.*" Inside are placed two tablets recording the names of the Fallen. The Memorial Windows, twelve in number, were designed and executed by Mr. C. E. Tute. They represent:—

1. Victoria (presented by the Trustees).
2. Pax (presented by the Old Boys' Association).
3. Aequitas (in memory of Captain R. W. L. Chambers).
4. Magnanimitas (the gift of the present School).
5. Fides (in memory of Captain J. V. Atkinson).
6. Humanitas (the gift of Mr. J. L. Woolcock).
7. Honestas (in memory of Lieutenant F. G. Haymen).
8. Fortitudo (in memory of Sergt. C. A. Bell and Pte. A. G. Fox).
9. Reverentia (in memory of Lieutenant Hugh Dalrymple).
10. Officium (in memory of Captain F. H. H. Plant, M.B.).
11. Pietas (in memory of Lance-Corporal E. H. Paten).
12. Veritas (in memory of Fifteen Fallen).

The service at the opening of the Memorial Library on Armistice Day, November 11th, 1924, was in the following order: The National Anthem; Prayer, "We shall remember them," by the Chaplain (Major J. E. N. Osborn, M.A., M.C.); Two Minutes' Silence; the Hymn, "O God our Help in ages past"; an Address by the Headmaster; Introductory Invitation by J. L. Woolcock, B.A.; the Dedication and an Address by H.E. Sir Matthew Nathan, P.C.; Addresses by Lieutenant-Colonel D. C. Cameron, M.H.R., D.S.O., and Lieutenant Stuart W. Cameron, R.A.N.; Song, "There's a land, a dear land," by Q.M.S. J. E. England, M.S.M.; Address by Brigadier-General C. H. Foott, C.B., D.S.O., and Lieutenant P. L. Hart (President of the Old Boys' Association); a Statement by S. Stephenson, M.A., the Hon. Secretary for the Memorial Fund and Second Master, concluding with the Doxology.

In a crystal cabinet in the Library is kept a Golden Book, skilfully produced by Mr. C. B. Fox, with illuminated borders by Miss Madge Roe, daughter of R. H. Roe, M.A., formerly Headmaster. This Record is in four volumes and took two years to complete. The title page bears an inscription written by the Headmaster, Mr. Bousfield: "*Sors alia est alii data-letum vulnera honores non animo fuerint ingeniove pares. Omnibus est eadem laus est· hæc summa dedisse omnia non parca quæ potuere, manu."*

The Fallen are remembered by other gifts. A complete German Field Telephone was presented by Lieutenant N. C. Nevitt, a carved Table by Mr. A. T. Fraser, and various Tablets erected by relations and friends, including a Gallipoli Tablet erected by old comrades. Stuart Stephenson, M.A., has edited the B. G. S. Annals from 1869-1922.

<blockquote>
" Salut.

Comrades!  This fane of living thought records
    Your valiant service in a cause divine.
Supreme o'er fateful years and clashing swords
    Your names for ever shrine."
</blockquote>

*E. W. H. Fowles.*

BRISBANE GRAMMAR SCHOOL MEMORIAL

# UNIVERSITY SCHOOL, VICTORIA, BRITISH COLUMBIA

THE Seven Captains of the School Cadet Corps, between the foundation of the School in 1906 and August, 1914, all served, and Four died on the battlefields.

The illuminated Memorial Roll contains 293 names, and 65 were killed.

The following distinctions were gained: 1 D.S.O., 17 M.C. (2 with bars), 1 D.F.C., 2 M.M., 1 Croix de Guerre.

Of the Bell-Irving family, five brothers and one cousin passed through the School; all served, and two were killed, and the following distinctions were won by them: 3 M.C. (1 with bar), 1 D.S.O., 1 Croix de Guerre, 1 mentioned in despatches.

---

# UPPER CANADA COLLEGE, TORONTO

*" Palmam qui meruit ferat."*

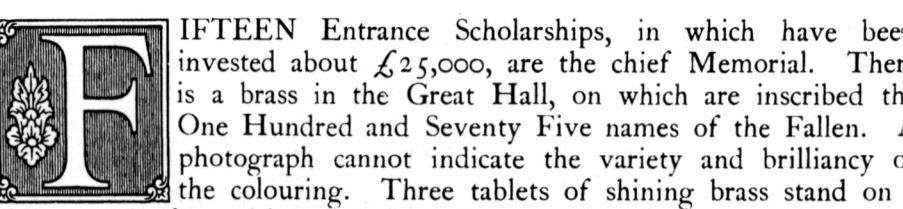

FIFTEEN Entrance Scholarships, in which have been invested about £25,000, are the chief Memorial. There is a brass in the Great Hall, on which are inscribed the One Hundred and Seventy Five names of the Fallen. A photograph cannot indicate the variety and brilliancy of the colouring. Three tablets of shining brass stand on a background of greyish-green, framed and united by a broad border of gold. Three sides of the border contain the inscription: " *This Tablet was erected to the memory of the Old Boys of this College who died on Active Service, 1914-1919.*" Across the bottom are the words: " *Their name liveth for evermore.*"

The following is the Order of Service, held on May 1st, 1921, the fourth anniversary of Canada Day: Invocation, The Provost of Trinity College; the Lord's Prayer, The Provost of Trinity College; hymn, " For all the Saints "; First Lesson, Ecclesiastes xliv, 1-4, 7-15, Mr.

J. H. Crake; hymn, "O God our Help in ages past"; Second Lesson, Revelations vii, 9-17, Mr. J. H. Crake; Nunc Dimittis; Statement about the Memorial, The Principal; Unveiling of the Memorial, Colonel G. T. Dennison; Reading of the Roll, Mr. C. F. Mills; Memorial Prayers, The Provost of Trinity College; Address, The Principal; hymn, "The Recessional"; Prayers and Benediction, The Provost of Trinity College, The Rev. Dr. Macklem.

The Principal, W. L. Grant, M.A., said that the Memorial was erected by Mrs. Sweeny at the wish of the late Colonel George Augustus Sweeny, late of the Royal Fusiliers and for many years a member of the Board of Governors of the College.

A Memorial Record has been designed by P. R. Wilson (one of the Boys), and after the Armistice in 1918, Mr. Robert Holmes, a Master, wrought a Tablet bearing the names, which hangs in the front entrance of the Great Hall.

Colonel Dennison, who was an Old Boy, a Governor, an author and a soldier, then spoke of the Foundation of the College by Lord Seaton, of his long friendship with Colonel Sweeny, who had urged the necessity of preparedness, and referred to the two former V.C.s of this College, namely, Colonel Arthur Dunn, V.C., who was in the Charge of the Light Brigade, and Major Churchill Cockburn, who won the V.C. in the South African War.

The Principal said: "Too many memorials typify the sadness of death. Ours tells the deeper truth that

"'To the saner mind
We rather seem the dead who stayed behind.'
Let us set the same stout hearts to the task of Peace.
"'Say to the world with brows down-bent,
That in the Britain thus endowed,
Imperial means beneficent,
And strength is service vowed.'"

Distinctions gained were: 115 M.C. (7 with bar), 5 D.S.C., 7 D.F.C., 5 A.F.C., 4 M.M., 21 other British Orders, 11 French, 4 Legion d'Honneur, and 22 other Foreign Orders.

# TRINITY COLLEGE SCHOOL, PORT HOPE, ONTARIO

*" Beati mundo corde."*

N an imposing position in front of the School, and facing Lake Ontario, there is a Cross 20 feet high, recording on the base the names of One Hundred and Twenty One Boys who were killed in the War. The plan was supervised by Mr. Frank Darling, F.R.I.B.A., the Cross being designed and made by the Mackintosh Granite Co., of Toronto.

It was dedicated at a service held on Trinity Sunday, June 11th, 1922. Choral Celebration was at 11 o'clock, concluding with the Psalm xxiii, sung by the Choir. The assembly then proceeded from the Chapel to the Cross, where there was a Guard of Honour formed by sixteen Old Boys, Cadets at the Royal Military College. To the east of the Cross stood the Headmaster, with Dr. Bethune (a former Headmaster) and Major-General Sir A. C. Macdonell. After the hymn, " How bright those glorious spirits shine," General Macdonell unveiled the Cross, and in his speech, said: " The doctors, gallant and skilled, full of initiative, were leaders of every reform tending towards the welfare of the men on the Western Front . . . the Padres, as I have known personally, gave consolation to the wounded; they gave Christian burial to the Fallen of other denominations than their own . . . against evil circumstances men, real men, are always merry. When asked the type of man usually found in the Honours List, I reply, ' Show me a boy with a good, God-fearing mother, and I will show you a boy who will have his name on the list.' For years Canadians did not sing when going into battle: their thoughts were with you at home. That is the reason why a Canadian mother said to people who sympathised with her in the loss of her two sons, ' It was my privilege.' "

Mrs. Lawrence Baldwin then said: " We, the members of the Ladies' Guild, present this Cross to the School of our brothers and sons in memory of those whose greater love constrained them to lay down their lives for their friends." The Headmaster, Dr. Orchard, acknowledging the gift, said: " It shall be our constant care to keep in hallowed seclusion this garden of loving memories."

Dr. Bethune, former Headmaster, dedicated the Cross with the words: " Grant rest and illumination to the souls of Thy servants, whose memory we here perpetuate. May their example be ever followed in this our Dominion; and may there be men who will not count their lives dear for the cause of Righteousness and Honour. Requiem æternum dona eis, Domine, et lux perpetua luceat eis."

The service ended with the Sevenfold Amen and the stanza, " Lord our wounds Thy healing give." The " Last Post " was sounded and the School Hymn, " Blest are the pure in heart," sung as a Recessional.

As a further Memorial, there was built a Junior School Building, to house Eighty Boys from eight to fourteen years of age. The building is constructed from stone and steel, and cost $250,000. It was designed by Mr. Henry Sproat, F.R.I.B.A.

The ceremonies of dedication commenced on November 9th, 1924, with a service conducted by Dr. Orchard. The Archbishop of Algoma preached from Psalm ciii, 1. He spoke of the foundations and building up of buildings, and of character, closing with a few words on the joy of the Christian life—a joy more than pleasure, and could not be taken away.

On Monday, November 10th, the Building was dedicated by the Archbishop of Algoma, assisted by the Bishop of Toronto, and a Tablet unveiled bearing the inscription: " *To the undying memory of the Fallen Old Boys, to whose honour the new School was built.*" The service commenced with the School Hymn, " Blest are the pure in heart "; then followed Psalm xxiii and the hymn, " And did those feet in ancient time." After the special lesson, Wisdom iii, 1-9, and the Creed, the Honour Roll was read by the Headmaster, and the Building dedicated.

---

TRINITY COLLEGE SCHOOL, PORT HOPE

# RIDLEY COLLEGE, ST. CATHERINE'S, ONTARIO

HE School was founded in September, 1889, was destroyed by fire in 1903, and rebuilt a few years later.

A Memorial Chapel, dedicated in June, 1923, was the gift of the Old Boys' Association. A new Dormitory was the gift of President G. H. Gooderman and Major Ross Gooderman, and Playing Fields were also added as part of the Memorial.

The Service Roll contains Two Hundred and Seventy Nine names, of whom Sixty were killed; Fifty Three died from wounds.

The following distinctions were gained: 25 M.C., 2 A.F.C., 5 Foreign Orders, and 20 other British Orders.

---

# ST. ANDREW'S COLLEGE, AUORA, TORONTO

HE Memorial Service was held on February 2nd, 1919. On the outbreak of war, the School was thirteen years' old, and 98 per cent. of the Old Boys volunteered for service. 60 gained the M.C., 9 the D.S.O., 8 the Croix de Guerre, 7 the M.M., 1 the D.F.C., 2 the D.S.C., and 5 other Orders.

In the Hall is placed a Memorial Tablet, designed and erected by Mr. Alfred Howell and presented to the School as a Mother's Thank-offering. The Tablet records the names of the Fallen, incised on the white marble in two columns, and the words: "*To the Glory of God and in honoured memory of the One Hundred and Four Andreans.*" On each side of the names are beautifully carved figures of angels, and in the centre is represented an angel with a sword. The inscriptions are: "*Andreani, qui pro nobis et pro patria ante diem perierunt,*" the dates "1914-1918," and "*Corpora ipsorum in pace sepulta sunt et nomen eorum vivit in generationem et generationem.*" On either side of the Tablet are the two Union Jacks which flew over the School during the War, and were lowered to half-mast in memory of each Old Boy who was killed.

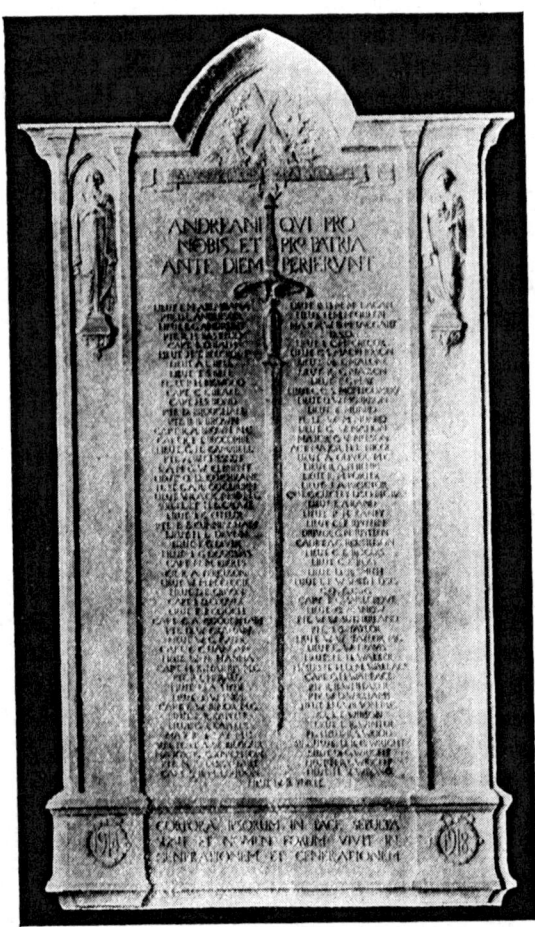

ST. ANDREW'S COLLEGE MEMORIAL TABLET

The unveiling ceremony, on Prize Day, November 30th, 1921, began with the School Hymn, " Fight the good fight "; Psalm CXXII (the Schoolmasters' Psalm) was read by the Rev. Provost Seager, and prayer said by the Rev. James Little. The Headmaster, the Rev. D. Bruce Macdonald, M.A., LL.D., made a statement, and the Senior Master read the Roll of the Fallen Andreans. The Tablet was unveiled by His Excellency Baron Byng of Vimy, and after a Lament, "Flowers of the Forest," by pipers and the sounding of the "Last Post," was dedicated by the Headmaster in the following words: "To the sacred memory of Andreans who gave their lives in the Great War, in the certain expectation of the Resurrection, and with the fervent hope that for generations to come it will serve to remind the Boys of this School of the readiness of their forerunners to respond to the call of duty even to the giving of their lives; and that thus it may play its part in maintaining in the life of the School a high tradition of service to the King, to Country and to Humanity." After a pray by the Headmaster, the Old Boys' Song was sung:—

"Played St. Andrews, Old St. Andrews,

At the trumpet call of duty

To rise up and fight the wrong;

In the prime of manhood's beauty

And with simple faith and strong

Fought St. Andrews, fell St. Andrews

Fighting furiously and long."

The prizes were presented by Baron and Lady Byng, and the procedings closed with the singing of the National Anthem.

By the efforts of the Old Boys, a Memorial House has been built. It includes a Library, in which are preserved a photograph and record of each of the Fallen; a Common Room, in which are recorded the Eight Hundred names of those who served, and a Corridor, stating the names of those Old Boys who made the building possible. The House also provides a place of residence for all boys, who, prior to leaving, come under the direct attention of the Headmaster. His Excellency Viscount Willingdon opened this Memorial on November 18th, 1926.

# BISHOP'S COLLEGE SCHOOL, LENNOXVILLE, QUEBEC

*" Recti cultus pectora roborant."*

HE Memorial is a Bronze Tablet, which records the names of Sixty One Old Boys and Three Masters who fell in the War. Since it was erected the names of Three more boys have been added to the list. The Tablet, which is in the School Entrance Hall, is of bronze, measuring 5 feet by 2½ feet. It was designed and executed by Henry Birks & Sons, of Montreal, and was unveiled by Colonel E. B. Worthington, C.M.G. (an Old Boy of the School) in June, 1921, in the presence of the School Cadet Corps and Visitors. The Bronze Tablet bears the dates " 1914," " 1918," with the School Crest and Motto. Below the names is the inscription: *" Pulchrum mori in armis."*

In 1925 a Memorial Skating Rink was built at a cost of $29,000. The walls are brick and the steel roof is carried on steel stanchions. The ice surface measures 175 feet by 75 feet and is surrounded by a running track, 6 feet wide, which, during the hockey season, affords accommodation for spectators. Above the entrance there is the inscription: *" Erected 1925 in memory of the boys of this School who fell in the Great War, 1914-18."*

The building was designed by the Headmaster, Mr. S. P. Smith, M.A. (Oxon), formerly a Professional Associate of the Surveyors' Institute of London.

There was no opening ceremony.

Of the Old Boys of Lennoxville who took part in the Great War, there were Seven Generals and One Admiral, namely, Lieutenant-General Henry Burstall, K.C.B., K.C.M.G.; Major-General Louis Bols, K.C.B.; Brigadier-Generals C. M. Cory, W. C. G. Heneker, K.C.B., W. C. Joly de Lothiniere, C.B., C.S.I., R. G. E. Leckie, C.B., C.M.G., A. G. L. McNaughton, and Admiral Sir Dudley Le Chair.

Honours won by the School were: 7 D.S.O., 11 M.C., 2 D.C.M., 1 Legion of Honour, 1 Order of Leopold, 2 Order of St. Stanislaus, 1 Order of St. Anne.

THE MEMORIAL TABLET

BISHOP'S COLLEGE SCHOOL—THE SKATING RINK

# HIGH SCHOOL, QUEBEC

*" Per ardua tendimus alte."*

THE School was founded as a Royal Grammar School in 1804 by the Rev. Daniel Wilkie, and continued until 1839, when it was suspended by Lord Sydenham, the Governor-General. In 1843 it was revived as the High School.

On St. Patrick's Day in 1845 it was incorporated by Act of Parliament. In 1846 Orders in Council were given. The Rectors are still known as Masters of the Royal Grammar School.

The School has been modelled on the High School, Edinburgh.

Two Hundred and Sixty Four served in the Forces, 38 made the Supreme Sacrifice, and the following honours and distinctions were gained: 3 V.C., 3 K.B., 8 D.S.O., 17 M.C., 1 A.F.M., and 1 Chev. d'Honneur. Of the Old Boys who served, 1 reached the rank of Lieutenant-General, 4 of Major-General, 1 Brigadier-General, 2 Colonels, 2 Lieutenant-Colonels, and 10 Majors.

There is no visible War Memorial, although the War Record has been kept.

---

# ASHBURY COLLEGE, OTTAWA

THIS School originated as a Day School in 1891, and moved to Wellington Street in 1894 under the present Headmaster, the Rev. G. O. Wollcombe, LL.D. In 1900 it was incorporated as a Company and a residence was purchased in Argyle Avenue. In 1909 some ten acres of ground was purchased at Rockcliffe Park. It is now a Trust Foundation. The Cadet Corps, to which every boy belongs, was established in 1905.

The War Memorial Wing consists of classrooms and offices with a completely fitted gymnasium.

During the four War years practically every senior boy leaving enlisted for Active Service. Three hundred in all served, the great majority entering as privates; 201 were later granted commissions.

The following is the War Record: Prisoners of War, 9; wounded, 69; killed in action, 40.

The distinctions gained were: 2 C.M.G., 4 D.S.O., 19 M.C., 1 D.F.C., 1 Mons Star, 9 Foreign Orders, 2 French Croix de Guerre; 2 Belgian, 1 Merite Agnicole, 1 Chev. of King Leopold (Belgian), 1 French Legion D'Honneur, 2 Russian, 26 mentioned in despatches.

---

# CHRIST'S COLLEGE, CHRISTCHURCH, NEW ZEALAND

*" Artes quas doceat quivis eques atque senator semet prognatos."*

ARLY in 1917 it was decided that a Memorial Hall be erected, and in July, 1918, a general appeal was made. Mr. C. W. Wood, A.R.I.B.A., was appointed architect in May, 1919, and on May 16th, 1920, H.R.H. the Prince of Wales visited the School and signed the plans for the Hall. The site selected was that formerly occupied by the Old Library in Rolleston Avenue. The tender of Messrs. P. Graham & Son was accepted and the foundation stone laid by Lord Jellicoe on November 30th, 1922.

The external walls of the Hall are of Hoon Hay stone faced with Oamaru and Redcliffs red stone. It is 106 feet long and 36 feet wide, and will seat 350 boys for meals. At the north end is a dais, and at the south end a gallery. All external and internal carving was done by Mr. F. G. Gurnsey, of Christchurch. The stone fireplace was a Memorial to Dr. A. C. Barker; the furniture, tables, chairs and benches on the dais are the gift of Mr. Wood, the architect. The heating arrangements were by Messrs. H. Vale & Co., the electric lighting by Mr. J. P. Smail, and the electric light fittings, "Armour Bright," by Oslers, of London.

The Active Service Roll bears the names of 550, of whom One Hundred and Forty Nine were killed. The names of the Fallen are recorded in beaten brass on an oak tablet in the Chapel, with the inscription: "*To the Glory of God in memory of the Old Boys and Masters of this School who died on Service in the Great War, 1914-1918.*"

The Service of Dedication was held on April 23rd, 1925. On the dais were His Grace Julius, Archbishop of New Zealand, Mr. G. T. Weston, President of the Old Boys' Association, and the Rev. E. C. Crosse, D.S.O., M.C., M.A., the Headmaster. Mr. Weston said: "In 1916 this project was formed and a committee was set up to devise ways and means of securing a War Memorial. Immediately after the Battle of the Somme there was a desire to commemorate in some way those who served. . . . The Hall stood for two great things—the duty of every grown man to serve his Country; the duty every boy owed to his School." He then read the Deed Gift of the Hall as follows:—

"To the Most Reverend Churchill Julius, D.D., LL.D., by Divine permission, Bishop of Christchurch, Warden of Christ's College, Canterbury, and Primate and Archbishop of New Zealand and to the Fellows of Christ's College.

"Whereas a Commemorative Hall, together with other buildings has lately been erected by the Old Boys of Christ's College and Friends of the School upon a portion of the premises belonging to the said College, to commemorate the services of the Old Boys and Masters of Christ's College who took an active part in the Great War, 1914-18 And Whereas it is the desire of the subscribers to the said Hall that the same shall be handed over as a permanent gift to Christ's College. Now these presents witness that Christ's College Old Boys' Association (Incorporated) doth hereby transfer and assure to the Warden and Fellows of Christ's College, Canterbury, as a permanent gift from the Old Boys of Christ's College, the said Hall, the buildings appurtenant thereto to the intent that the same shall be held as a permanent Record and Memorial of the personal services of each and every Old Boy or Master of the School who took an active part in the Great War, and to serve as an inspiration to future generations of Boys of the School towards like-minded devotion to the cause of King and Country. The purpose of this Commemorative Hall is to provide a Common Dining Hall for the School and for Commemoration Meetings and for such other objects as may be for the use and benefit of the School.

" The Common Seal of Christ's College Old Boys' Association (Incorporated) was hereto affixed this sixteenth day of April, 1925, under the authority of a resolution passed by the Committee of the said Association on the fourth day of February, 1925, in the presence of :

Common Seal

G. A. U. TAPPER,     N. L. MACBETH,
E. R. WEBB,          A. E. FLOWER,
MEMBERS OF THE COMMITTEE."

His Grace the Archbishop referred to the fact that during the past thirty-five years the School had become so vigorous and had maintained so high a tone. It had revived by the spirit within it, and to the boys he would say, " Keep your end up." Dr. W. Irving mentioned the three great principles, " Loyalty," " Faith " and " Service," and stated that it was proposed to fill the bays between the windows with portraits of Wardens and Fellows. A portrait of His Grace the Archbishop was presented to the School, and the ceremony ended with the School Song.

THE MEMORIAL HALL

THE MEMORIAL HALL—INTERIOR

# AUCKLAND GRAMMAR SCHOOL

*" Per angusta ad augusta."*

A VERY beautiful Memorial Column has been erected in the grounds. It was unveiled by H.E. the Governor-General Viscount Jellicoe, of Scapa, on Tuesday, December 19th, 1922.

The Mayor and Mayoress (Mr. and Mrs. Gunson) and Colonel H. R. Potter (Officer Commanding the District), Lord and Lady Jellicoe and A.D.C. Captain P. R. M. Mundy inspected the Guard of Honour of the School Cadet Corps under Lieutenant C. R. Jones. The order of the ceremony was as follows: Psalm xlvi, prayers read by the Headmaster, welcome by Professor A. P. W. Thomas, introductory address by Mr. T. Stanton, address and unveiling by Viscount Jellicoe, "Last Post" and hymn, "O Valiant Hearts," address by Professor A. P. W. Thomas, an acknowledgment on behalf of the parents by Mr. J. W. Tibbs, Headmaster and father of one of the boys commemorated, hymn, "O God our help in ages past," and the National Anthem.

Mr. J. Stanton, President of the Old Boys' Association, explained the symbolic significance of the Monument. The bronze figure of a boy, standing on tiptoe, on the top of the tapering column is "The soul uplifted," the human soul reaching ever upwards in its aspirations towards the ideal. The octagonal shape suggests the Eight Cardinal Virtues; the Roman Fasces stand for the Right of State over the individual; the mediæval Cross suggests the idea of "Sacrifice," and the Sword pointing downwards denotes "Peace."

In his speech, Lord Jellicoe said that the Monument was a record of Loyalty to the Empire—a beacon to light the future boys in the path of Duty and Self-Sacrifice; an everlasting reminder to the Nation's boys of great traditions and an example which those gallant souls had made on their behalf.

A wreath was laid by Mrs. G. Gribbin on behalf of the mothers of the Fallen.

Mr. Tibbs said that the uplifted hand of the statue appeared to him to be protecting the world against that arrogant militarism which was the undoing of Rome centuries ago.

The architects for the Memorial were Messrs. Prouse & Gummer, of Auckland. New South Wales sandstone is used for the column.

Inscriptions on the bronze plates around the base are in raised letters. Within a laurel wreath on the centre panel are the words: " *To the Glory of God and in grateful remembrance of the Old Boys of the School who gave their lives in the service of the King and Empire and in the cause of Righteousness in the Great War, 1914-1918. This Column was raised by their Schoolfellows. A.D. 1922.*" And the School Crest—a lion rampant.

The following distinctions were gained : 1 V.C., 7 D.S.O., 53 M.C., 11 D.C.M., 23 M.M., 2 M.S.M., 7 other British Orders, 38 mentioned in despatches, 1 Croix de Guerre, and 1 Medaille d'Honneur.

The Active Service List contains over One Thousand names, while the Roll of Honour contains Two Hundred and Sixty Eight.

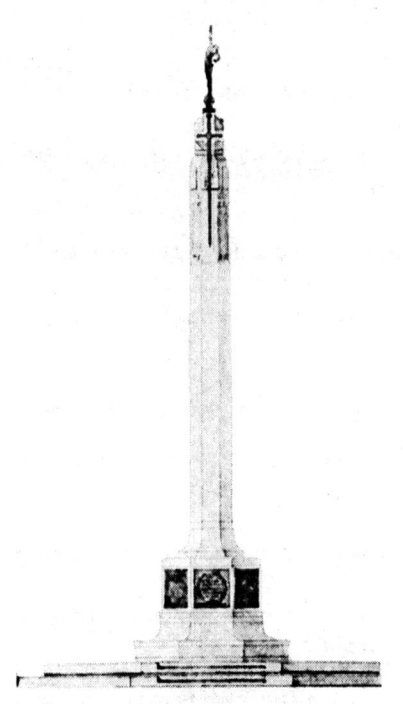

THE MEMORIAL COLUMN

# WAITAKI BOYS' HIGH SCHOOL, OAMARU

*" Quanti est sapere."*

THE Memorial takes the form of a " Hall of Memories." It is situated at the east of the School Quadrangle and was erected by the Old Boys at the cost of £16,000. The style of architecture is Perpendicular Gothic. The facade is flanked by two towers, in which stone stairways lead to the balcony. The interior of the Hall is panelled in oak. The Great Eastern Memorial Window symbolises " The spiritual unity of the Empire, by War Sacrifice." The central panel depicts an Anzac warrior flanked by the figure of King Alfred, typifying spiritual and moral virtues of the soldier, and Richard Cœur de Lion, typifying the fighting virtues. The external panels represent the Royal Arms and the Arms of New Zealand. Below are five vignettes of Palestine, Gallipoli, Britannia, France, Germany, in that order from left to right. In the vignette of Germany is represented Cologne Cathedral.

Grouped near the Window are Commemorative Brasses recording the Seven names, and a tablet with the inscription: " *To the Glory of God and in sacred memory of the Old Boys of this School who gave their lives in the Great War, 1914-1918. In the high cause of Empire this Window is dedicated.*"

" Nothing is here for tears, nothing to wail, or knock the breast, no weakness, no contempt, dispraise or blame, nothing but well and fair and what may quiet us in a death so noble."—*Milton, " Samson Agonestes."*

The following quotations appear under the vignettes:—

Palestine.—" *Their bodies are buried in peace but their name liveth for evermore.*"

Gallipoli.—" *Because I live ye shall live also.*"

Britannia.—" *Truer love hath no man than this, that a man layeth down his life for his friends.*"

France.—" *Lovely and peaceful in their lives, and in their death they were not divided.*"

Germany.—"*All these were honoured in their generation and were the glory of their times.*"

In the vestibule is a large dedicatory brass, on which are the words: "*In memory of the Old Boys of this School who served in the Great War* (1914-1918) *this Hall is erected by their comrades and friends in the sure hope that their example will inspire all future generations of Waitakians with the same loyalty to the Empire.*" Then follows the well-known quotation from "Pericles": "'*So they gave . . . into the stuff of other men's lives.*'"

The following distinctions were won: 1 V.C., 6 D.S.O., 42 M.C., and 20 M.M.

The Service Roll contains Seven hundred names.

The foundation stone of the "Hall of Memories," for which Mr. J. M. Forrester, Esq., of Oamaru, was the architect, was laid by Admiral Earl Jellicoe in 1919. The Hall was opened by His Royal Highness the Duke of York on March 16th, 1927.

The following is the programme of the Opening Ceremony:—

1. Hymn, "Song of the Children" (Rudyard Kipling):
   "Land of our birth, we pledge to thee
   Our love and toil in years to be,
   When we are grown and take our place
   As men and women with our race."
2. Welcome by Mr. E. P. Lee, M.P., Chairman of the Governors.
3. Prayer of Dedication, Rev. Walter Maclean, M.C.
4. Unveiling of the Memorial Window and Declaration of Opening by His Royal Highness the Duke of York.
5. Hymn, "For all the Saints."
6. Expression of thanks by the Rector, Mr. F. Milner, C.M.G.
7. National Anthem.

After the ceremony the Duke of York planted a Memorial Yew in the Quadrangle to commemorate the occasion. In the evening, at 8 p.m., a Commemoration Service was held in the Hall. The following was the form of procedure:—

1. The National Anthem.
2. Address by E. P. Lee, Esq.
3. Address by the Rector.
4. Voluntary Coronach by Mr. G. E. Wilkinson.
5. Scripture Sentences: Wisdom iii, 1-13, 14.
6. Prayer of Invocation by Rev. W. Maclean, M.C.
7. Hymn (St. Anne), "O God our Help in ages past."
8. Scripture Lesson, Ecclesiastes xliv, 1-17, 14, and John xiv, 1-4, by Rev. Adam Clark.
9. Prayer of Commemoration by Venerable Archdeacon Russell: "In the night of such love, ever strive for a cleaner earth, and a cleaner Heaven."
10. Hymn, "With heart and soul and voice" (Darwell).
11. Address by Rev. W. Maclean, M.C.
12. Hymn, "O Valiant Hearts" (Tune "Eventide").
13. Benediction, "Last Post" and "Reveille."

The Duke of York made a speech singularly beautiful in its phrasing and dignified reserve. After thanks for his welcome, he recalled the Prince of Wales' visit in 1920, and then said: "A Hall of Memories requires very few words. Its associations and all it stands for call rather for silence than for a speech. But I do ask you not to let those words, 'Hall of Memories,' become merely an empty name to you. Remember that this Hall stands for all that was best and noblest in those who gave their lives for the Empire to which you and I belong. Remember the loyalty and self-sacrifice of those Old Boys, and see to it that the generations which come after you shall learn the lesson which they taught. For as they served their Country in war, so must you serve her in peace, and if you cherish those ideals of truth and right for which they fought, you will be completing the task they began, and these lives will not have been given in vain. I have now much pleasure in declaring this Hall open."

---

WAITAKI BOYS' HIGH SCHOOL MEMORIAL WINDOW

H.R.H. THE DUKE OF YORK, PLANTING A MEMORIAL YEW
OUTSIDE THE "HALL OF MEMORIES"

# Some War Statistics

*Losses in the War per head of Population.*

France, 1 in 28; Germany, 1 in 35; Austria, 1 in 50; Great Britain, 1 in 66; Italy, 1 in 79; the United States of America, 1 in 2,000.

| August, 1914. | | November, 1918. |
|---|---|---|
| 24,896 (Officers) | ... ... ... | 193,102 |
| 706,618 (Other Ranks) | ... ... | 4,755,242 |

These figures exclude 400,000 Indian Troops and 43,000 Officers and 825,000 men who were killed.

*The Mobilised Armies of 1914-1918.*

| | *Men.* |
|---|---|
| France ... ... ... ... ... | 7,000,000 |
| Great Britain ... ... ... ... | 5,704,000 |
| Italy ... ... ... ... ... | 5,600,000 |
| United States of America ... ... | 3,707,000 |

The Ordnance issue of 1918 states that during the War forty million pairs of boots, twenty-seven million pairs of trousers, forty and three-quarter millions of blankets and thirty-four thousand eight hundred and sixty-five motor bicycles were issued.

The Ministry of Food bought and sold 85 per cent. of all food in Great Britain in 1918, and its staff consisted of some thirty-three thousand persons, while the printing bill of this Ministry was one and a half million pounds sterling annually.

The administrative staff of the Ministry of Munitions consisted of about twenty-five thousand people, while at the Gretna Green factory, which cost eight million pounds sterling, was produced as much acid as the whole of Great Britain produced during a pre-war year.

*Cost of Artillery Bombardment* before infantry attacks at the following battles was :—

| *Battle.* | *Cost in £.* | *Tons of Ammunition fired.* |
|---|---|---|
| Messines ... | 17,500,000 ... | ... 85,000 |
| Third Battle of Ypres ... | 22,000,000 ... | ... 480,000 |

On September 29th, 1918, the British Army in France fired just under one million rounds of ammunition, at a cost of more than three and three-quarter million pounds. During the third quarter of 1918 six hundred and forty-one thousand tons of shells were used and five and a quarter million rifles were produced, together with fifty-four thousand aeroplanes, sixteen thousand field-guns and nine thousand million rounds of small ammunition. To produce these requirements three million people were employed.

---

## Acknowledgment

EDITOR'S NOTE.—I have tried to make the following list complete, and tender my sincere apologies for any omissions. Reference is made in the Index to those Schools which loaned blocks. I would express my thanks also to Schools and the following gentlemen and firms for the use of photographs:—

The Proprietors of the " Daily Mail " (Menin Gate); the " Southern Daily Echo " (King Edward VI, Southampton); " Sussex Daily News " (Lancing and Ardingly); " The Kent Messenger " (Sutton Valence); Mr. Stewart Bale (Merchant Taylors, Crosby); Messrs. P. A. Buchanan & Co , Ltd. (Rossall); Messrs. Collcutt & Hamp (Mill Hill); Mr. J. R. Edis (Durham); Mr. F. W. Foulsham (Reading); Messrs. Hills & Saunders (Eton and Harrow); Mr. T. Lonnergan (Wakefield Grammar); Messrs. G. Maile & Son (King's, Ely and Silcoates); Messrs. George Over, Ltd. (Rugby); Mr. Charles H. Price (Whitgift); Messrs. J. Russell & Sons of Southsea (Portsmouth); Messrs. Russell & Sons of Windsor (Beaumont); Mr. N. Melville Richards (Warwick); Mr. J. Swales and the Rev. E. H. Stenning (King William's, I.O.M.).

# EVENTS IN THE GREAT WAR

**1914.**

Aug. 4.—GREAT BRITAIN DECLARES WAR on Germany.

7.—Germans enter LIEGE.

13.—British bombard DAR-ES-SALAAM.

23.—BATTLE OF MONS.

25-31.—BATTLE OF TANNENBERG.

26.—FIRST BATTLE OF LE CATEAU.

28.—BATTLE OF HELIGOLAND BIGHT.

31.—Dominion Forces capture SAMOA.

Sept. 6-10.—FIRST BATTLE OF THE MARNE.

12-20.—FIRST BATTLE OF THE AISNE.

22.—Cruisers, " Aboukir," " Hogue " and " Cressy " torpedoed.

Oct. 20.—FIRST BATTLE OF YPRES.

Nov. 1.—BATTLE OF CORONEL.

3.—Germans bombard YARMOUTH.

9.—German raider " EMDEN " destroyed.

14.—Earl Roberts dies.

Dec. 8.—BATTLE OF THE FALKLANDS.

16.—Germans bombard SCARBOROUGH, WHITBY and HARTLEPOOL.

24.—FIRST AIR RAID of War on Dover.

25.—Air Raid on Kent.

---

**1915.**

Jan. 24.—BATTLE OFF DOGGER BANK.

Feb. 19.—Naval Attack on DARDANELLES FORTS.

21.—Air Raid on Essex.

April 22.—SECOND BATTLE OF YPRES.

25.—LANDING IN GALLIPOLI.

May 7.—"LUSITANIA" torpedoed.

23.—ITALY DECLARES WAR on Austria.

31-June 1.—FIRST ZEPPELIN RAID on East London.

July 9.—German South-West Africa surrenders.

Sept. 7-8.—Zeppelins over East Suffolk and London.

26-28.—First Battle of Kut.

Oct. 3-8.—ALLIES LAND AT SALONICA.

12.—BULGARIA JOINS GERMANY. Nurse Cavell shot in Brussels.

Dec. 20.—EVACUATION OF GALLIPOLI.

---

1916.

Jan. 31-Feb. 1.—Zeppelin Raid over Midlands and West Suffolk.

Feb. 19.—General Smuts in command in German East Africa.

Mar. 19.—Air Raid over Dover, Ramsgate, Margate and Deal.

24.—S.s. "Sussex" torpedoed.

April 17.—GERMAN ATTACK ON VERDUN.

24.—IRISH REBELLION IN DUBLIN.

25.—Germans bombard LOWESTOFT.

29.—SURRENDER OF KUT to Turks.

May 15.—Austrians attack in the Trentino.

31.—BATTLE OF JUTLAND. Brusiloff begins offensive against Austrians.

June 5.—Lord Kitchener drowned off Scotland.

July 1.—BATTLE OF THE SOMME begins.

7.—British occupy German East Africa.

27.—Captain Fryatt shot.

Aug.  9.—Italians capture Gorizia.

17.—RUMANIA JOINS THE ALLIES.

Sept.  3.—First Zeppelin brought down in England at Cuffley.

15.—Tanks first in action in Battle of Somme.

Oct. 24.—French recapture Douaumont.

Nov. 13-18.—BATTLE OF ANCRE.

21.—British Hospital Ship "Britannic" torpedoed.

27-28.—Zeppelin Raid on Durham, Yorkshire and London.

Dec. 13.—SECOND BATTLE OF KUT.

16.—Fall of Bukarest.

---

1917.

Feb.  1.—Germany begins "Unrestricted Submarine Warfare."

23.—British recapture Kut.

Mar. 11.—British capture Bagdad.

15.—Tsar of Russia abdicates.

17.—RUSSIAN REVOLUTION.

20.—British Hospital Ship "Asturias" torpedoed.

26-27.—FIRST BATTLE OF GAZA.

April 6.—UNITED STATES DECLARE WAR on Germany.

9.—VIMY RIDGE captured.

16-20.—FRENCH ATTACK ON THE AISNE.

20.—SECOND BATTLE OF GAZA.

June 7.—British storm MESSINES RIDGE.

July 31.—THIRD BATTLE OF YPRES.

Sept. 4-30.—Series of Air Raids on London.

Oct. 19-20.—Zeppelin Raids on Midlands and Eastern Counties.

24.—Austrians break through at Caporetto.

Nov. 20.—FIRST BATTLE OF CAMBRAI.

Dec. 9.—CAPTURE OF JERUSALEM.

18.—Air Raid on Kent, Essex and London.

---

1918.

Jan. 28-29.—Air Raid on London, Kent and Essex.

Feb. 16-19.—Air Raids.

Mar. 13-14.—Zeppelin Raid on East Yorkshire and Durham.

21.—German offensive on the Somme.

30.—Big Bertha shells Paris.

April 9.—FOURTH BATTLE OF YPRES.

22-23.—NAVAL ATTACK ON ZEEBRUGGE.

May 10.—Naval attack on Ostend.

19-20.—Air Raid on Kent, Essex and London.

27-June 18.—THIRD BATTLE OF THE AISNE.

July 15-17.—SECOND BATTLE OF THE MARNE.

18.—Allied counter-attack in France.

Aug. 2.—Allied Forces land at Archangel.

8-12.—Allied attack before Amiens.

Sept. 2.—Canadian Troops storm Wotan Line.

12.—Americans attack St. Mihiel.

13.—Austria issues Peace Note.

19.—Great British attack in Palestine.

29.—SURRENDER OF BULGARIA.

Oct. 1.—British occupy Damascus.

4.—GERMAN PEACE NOTE to President Wilson.

6-12.—SECOND BATTLE OF LE CATEAU.

12.—Germany accepts President Wilson's Terms.

14.—Allies' Victory in Belgium.

18.—Zeebrugge and Bruges occupied.

31.—SURRENDER OF TURKEY.

Nov. 3.—SURRENDER OF AUSTRIA.

8.—Abdication of the Kaiser.

10.—British reach Mons.

11.—ARMISTICE WITH GERMANY.

14.—Von Lettow's Forces in German East Africa Surrender.

21.—German Fleet Surrenders.

22.—King Albert re-enters Brussels.

Dec. 6.—British occupy Cologne and Rhineland.

---

1919.

June 28.—PEACE TREATY SIGNED AT VERSAILLES.

---

1926 (Post War).

The Seventh Assembly of the League of Nations met at Geneva in September. Forty-seven States were represented.

Sept. 8.—Germany elected to a Permanent Seat. Spain withdraws.

14.—Treaty of Locarno ratified.

Oct. 10.—Delville Wood S. African Memorial unveiled by Mrs. Botha.

1927.

June 19.—Memorial at Tyne Cot (Paschendaele) unveiled by Capt. G. J. C Dyett (President of Australian Returned Soldiers' Association)

Memorial at Ploegsteert to London Rifle Brigade unveiled by Lieut.-Gen. Sir H. F. M. Wilson.

July 24.—Menin Gate Ceremony by Lord Plumer.

Foundation of " Etonian " Memorial School, Ypres, by Lord Plumer.

Oct. 7.—Indian Memorial at Neuve Chapelle unveiled by Lord Birkenhead.

---

## Roll of Honour.

Britain's total Roll of Honour, as stated in the House of Commons, was :—

| The United Kingdom and Ireland | ... | 743,702 |
|---|---|---|
| India ... ... ... ... | ... | 61,398 |
| The Colonies ... ... ... | ... | 140,923 |
| Total | ... | 946,023 |

---

" So they gave their bodies to the commonwealth and received each for his memory praise that will never die and with it the grandest of all sepulchres, not that in which their mortal bones are laid, but a home in the minds of men, where their glory remains fresh to stir to speech or action as the occasion comes by. For the whole earth is a sepulchre of famous men; and their story is not graven only on stone over their native earth, but lives on far away without visible symbol woven into the stuff of other men's lives."—*Pericles.*

Lightning Source UK Ltd.
Milton Keynes UK
UKOW02f0421280614

234177UK00004B/28/P

# BRITISH PUBLIC SCHOOLS
# WAR MEMORIALS

FIRST EDITION
NOVEMBER, 1927

DISTINGUISHED
SERVICE ORDER

VICTORIA CROSS

DISTINGUISHED
SERVICE CROSS

DISTINGUISHED
FLYING CROSS

MILITARY CROSS

# British Public Schools
# War Memorials

## By

C. F. KERNOT, B.A. (Cantab:)

**1927**

ROBERTS & NEWTON LIMITED

TOTTENHAM LANE, HORNSEY, LONDON, N.8